Economic and Monetary Union:
Implications for National Policy-Makers

European Institute of Public Administration

Economic and Monetary Union:
Implications for National Policy-Makers

Edited by
Klaus Gretschmann

MARTINUS NIJHOFF PUBLISHERS
DORDRECHT / BOSTON / LONDON

Library of Congress Cataloging-in-Publication Data

Economic and monetary union : implications for national policy-makers
 / edited by Klaus Gretschmann.
    p.   cm.
  ISBN 0-7923-2062-X (alk. paper)
  1. Monetary policy--European Economic Community countries.
 2. Monetary unions--European Economic Community countries.
 3. European Monetary System (Organization) 4. Europe--Economic
 integration.   I. Gretschmann, Klaus.
 HG930.5.E232 1993
 332.4'566'094--dc20   92-37942

ISBN 0-7923-2062-X

Published by Martinus Nijhoff Publishers,
P.O. Box 163, 3300 AD Dordrecht, The Netherlands.

Sold and distributed in the U.S.A. and Canada
by Kluwer Academic Publishers,
101 Philip Drive, Norwell, MA 02061, U.S.A.

In all other countries, sold and distributed
by Kluwer Academic Publishers Group,
P.O. Box 322, 3300 AH Dordrecht, The Netherlands.

Printed on acid-free paper

Printed in the Netherlands

TABLE OF CONTENTS

Acknowledgements   *vii*
List of Contributors   *ix*
List of Abbreviations   *xi*

Preface   *xiii*

INTRODUCTION

Klaus Gretschmann
EMU: Thoughtful Wish or Wishful Thinking?   3

SECTION 1:

FROM EMS TO EMU: THE WINDS OF CHANGE ARE BLOWING HARD

Klaus Gretschmann, Hans-Helmut Kotz, Olaf Sleijpen
The European Monetary System: The Geography of
Economics versus the Politics of Money?   27

Alexander Italianer
Mastering Maastricht: EMU Issues and
How They Were Settled   51

Alexander Dörfel, Barbara Eggl, Aurel Schubert
Insider or Outsider? The Case of Austria   115

SECTION 2:

CENTRAL BANK POLICY IN A NEW INSTITUTIONAL FRAMEWORK

Ian Harden
The European Central Bank and the Role of National
Central Banks in Economic and Monetary Union   149

Sylvester Eijffinger
Convergence of Monetary Policies in Europe –
Concepts, Targets and Instruments   169

Reimut Jochimsen
Economic and Monetary Union: A German Central
Banker's Perspective   195

SECTION 3:

SPILL-OVERS RESULTING FROM EMU

Willem Molle, Olaf Sleijpen, Marc Vanheukelen
The Impact of an Economic and Monetary Union on Social and
Economic Cohesion: Analysis and Ensuing Policy Implications   217

Paul van den Bempt
The Impact of Economic and Monetary Union on
Member States' Fiscal Policies   245

CONCLUSION

Klaus Gretschmann
By Way of Conclusion: Will Policy-Makers be EMUsed?   265

ACKNOWLEDGEMENTS

Economic and Monetary Union is like a ship in troubled waters, it follows the rolling of the waves and the turning of the tide. In a way, editing a book on EMU involves similar problems and imponderables, similar ups and downs. To embark upon such a risky voyage and to make it to the final destination requires the support of a good team.

This comparison gives me reason to express my gratitude and appreciation to those who joined the skipper in mastering the vagaries of the sea. First, I would like to thank the helmsman of the ship, my assistant Olaf Sleijpen, who did a great job in sticking to the captain's course, despite the many cliffs and shallows we had to circumvent. But, of course, the ship would not have left the port without the contribution of the entire crew, so special thanks go to Daniela Bankier for reading the manuscript and for making many useful comments; to Pat Arpino and Chris Dart, who turned the English into a readable standard; for the work of type-setting and lay-out, I thank Denise Grew; and without the patience and tactful pressure of Veerle Deckmyn, who was responsible for the contacts with our publisher, the ship would have stranded. Thanks also to Jan Peeters and Rudi van Lent for redoing the graphs and figures in this book. And of course thanks to all the authors, who made quite a few sacrifices to comply with the editor's guidelines and deadlines – without them the ship would have never been launched. Appreciation finally goes to the Dutch Ministry for Economic Affairs, which provided the endowment and the funds for the shipyard where the ship was built.

Last but not least, I would like to thank the admiral-in-chief, EIPA's Director-General, Spyros A. Pappas, for his support and help in setting the course.

Maastricht, January 1993

Klaus Gretschmann

LIST OF CONTRIBUTORS

Paul van den Bempt   Honorary Director-General, Commission of the
European Communities; Senior Research Fellow,
TEPSA, Brussels (B)

Alexander Dörfel   Chief, International Organization Division, Austrian
National Bank, Vienna (A)

Barbara Eggl   Economist, International Organization Division,
Austrian National Bank, Vienna (A)

Sylvester Eijffinger   Associate Professor of Monetary Economics, Tilburg
University, Tilburg (NL)

Klaus Gretschmann   Professor of Public Economics and International
Economics, Head of Community Policies Unit,
European Institute of Public Administration,
Maastricht (NL)

Ian Harden   Senior Lecturer, Department of Law, University of
Sheffield, Sheffield (UK)

Alexander Italianer   Head of Unit, Directorate-General II, Commission of the
European Communities, Brussels (B)

Hans-Helmut Kotz   Chief Economist and Head of Department, Deutsche
Girozentrale, Frankfurt am Main (D)

Reimut Jochimsen   President of the Landeszentralbank North Rhine-
Westphalia, Dusseldorf; Member of the Central Bank
Council of the Deutsche Bundesbank, Frankfurt (D)

Willem Molle   Director, Netherlands Economic Institute; Professor of
Economics of European Integration, Erasmus
University, Rotterdam (NL)

Aurel Schubert   Economist, International Organization Division, Austrian National Bank, Vienna (A)

Olaf Sleijpen   Economist, International Affairs Department, Nederlandsche Bank, Amsterdam (NL)

Marc Vanheukelen   Administrator, Directorate-General II, Commission of the European Communities, Brussels (B)

LIST OF ABBREVIATIONS

ANB	Austrian National Bank
CD	Certificate of Deposit
CEC	Commission of the European Communities
CPI	Consumer Price Index
DI	Direct Investments
EBRD	European Bank for Reconstruction and Development
ECB	European Central Bank
ECOFIN-Council	Council of Ministers in the Composition of Economic and Finance Ministers
ECU	European Currency Unit
EFRD	European Fund for Regional Development
EFTA	European Free Trade Association
EMCF	European Monetary Cooperation Fund
EMI	European Monetary Institute
EMU	Economic and Monetary Union
EMS	European Monetary System
ERM	Exchange Rate Mechanism
ESCB	European System of Central Banks
FRS	Federal Reserve System
GDP	Gross Domestic Product
IMF	International Monetary Fund
M0	Monetary Aggregate 0
M2	Monetary Aggregate 2
M3	Monetary Aggregate 3
M4	Monetary Aggregate 4
OCA	Optimal Currency Area
OECD	Organisation for Economic Cooperation and Development
OPCVMs	*Organismes de Placement Collectif en Valeurs Mobilières*
PEP	*Plan d'épargne populaire*
PPS	Purchasing Power Standards
PSBR	Public Sector Borrowing Requirement
PSL	Private Sector Liquidity
ZBG	*Zentralbankgeldmenge* (Central Bank Money Supply)

PREFACE

In December 1991, when the Heads of States and Governments of the European Community decided on the political and legal framework laying down *European Political Union* and *Economic and Monetary Union* in the Maastricht Treaty, Maastricht seemed to be the centre of Europe for a few days.

Since those days, Maastricht, which has been the site of the headquarters of the European Institute of Public Administration for more than 10 years, has joined the exclusive club of those famous small towns in the world which have become well-known for a single outstanding event. One of these is Waterloo, but this is not exactly a name with much connotation with *European integration*. However, in the preparation for and in the aftermath of the Maastricht Summit, much banter was heard comparing Maastricht with Waterloo. The claim was that Maastricht might end up being another Waterloo.

Some time has elapsed since then and we certainly have gone through some turbulent times. It may suffice to mention the stormy days of the Danish and French referenda on the Treaty or the typhoon which has recently hit the *European Monetary System*. Nonetheless, the Maastricht ship has succeeded in holding water up till now and the outlook is not too bad so we should be able to bring it back on course. This difficult task can only be accomplished if Europe proves her political will and her political capacity to set her sails and cross against the wind. This looks like being a Herculean task for both supranational and national policy-makers.

Due to the fact that EIPA was aware, already at an early stage, of the special efforts that would be needed to make the Maastricht Treaty 'tick', it prepared and organized a Round Table on the subject exactly two weeks after the Summit, with the generous financial support of the *Dutch Ministry for Economic Affairs*. For two days, experts from both academia and politics, with different national backgrounds, were invited to discuss the approach and the provisions of EMU as well as the implications and the requirements for national policy-makers in the stimulating ambience of EIPA.

The picture that was painted with broad brush-strokes during the Round Table was that of a long and difficult journey. The Round Table succeeded in giving some orientation to help determine the course. However, we cannot claim to have provided the compass setting.

The (updated) results of the considerations and observations expressed are presented in this volume. In a sense, it may serve as a log-book for those interested in and involved with EMU. In conjunction with the already published EIPA book on Political Union, the European Institute of Public Administration hopes to contribute to both the monitoring of and the learning from the process of European integration on its way to the 3rd millennium.

It has become apparent, that the bull on which 'Europa' is riding has increased his pace and, consequently, riding him has become more difficult. However, Europeanists should strive to make sure that 'Europa' is not thrown from the saddle, turning the young beauty into a crippled old lady.

Finally, it should not go without noting that this book would never have been published without the dedication of the EIPA staff involved and the support of the Ministry for Economic Affairs in The Hague. Special thanks go to the editor, Professor Klaus Gretschmann, and to Drs Olaf Sleijpen, Researcher, who gave him a helping hand.

Maastricht, January 1993

Spyros A. Pappas
Director-General of EIPA

INTRODUCTION

EMU: THOUGHTFUL WISH OR WISHFUL THINKING

Klaus Gretschmann

Yet destiny's forces conceive
No close ties to weave

Friedrich Schiller, Song of the Bell

EMU is in the Air , or is it ...

History has – it seems – shifted into high gear. The world has been turned upside down by the downfall of the Soviet Empire, by German unification, by the end of US economic hegemony and by the re-emergence of nationalism and secessionism in Europe. Rather than reaching the 'End of History', the ultimate 'Golden Age', as some 'prophets' would have us believe, we are witnessing more social unrest, economic uncertainty, political instability and revision rather than vision. It seems as if tectonic shifts are making Europe and the world a permanent construction site.

This is the background against which the EC has set its course towards an ever closer union in the Maastricht Treaty. Indeed, this Treaty on 'Political Union' – the second substantial revision of the Rome Treaties after the Single European Act of 1987 – is the EC's response to the new historical developments. Its objective is to make Europe a core of stability in a world of risk and uncertainty by setting new targets, by opening potential options and by committing itself to promote further political and economic integration. As the received view has it, the centrepiece and driving force in the Maastricht Treaty is its section on Economic and Monetary Union (EMU). With the latter, the Member States have acknowledged – as they did repeatedly in the history of European integration – that it is the (collective and individual) economic interests of the Member States which makes Europe go round.

Therefore, in economic terms, the negotiations indeed placed considerable emphasis on EMU as a driving belt for general integration. Consequently, the Treaty of Maastricht:

 – has laid out a precise timetable for making EMU operational;

3

K. Gretschmann (ed.), Economic and Monetary Union: Implications for National Policy-Makers, 3–23.
© 1993 European Institute of Public Administration. Printed in the Netherlands.

   – has drawn up economic criteria under which individual Member States are eligible for EMU;
   – contains clauses and rules of conduct for Member States' fiscal policies;
   – outlines in detail the institutional structure and the tasks of a European Central Bank;
   – defines price stability as its primary goal to be achieved within the framework of an open market economy with free competition.

When the Maastricht Treaty was signed on 7 February 1992 it was received with much enthusiasm. However, today, more than a year later, the mood of Europhoria which held sway in 1991 has faded, ratification of the Treaty, envisaged by the end of 1993, looks gloomy, financial markets have cracked under Maastricht's uncertain fate and the political will to push integration ahead seems to be vanishing. Does this all indicate a 'Goodbye to Euro-optimism'?

As a matter of fact, on the economic front, the path towards EMU now looks less clear and the promised EMU-land does not look as bright as it did 12 months ago. Creating a common currency was meant to bring the Member States of the EC closer together, but today it seems to be driving them apart. The idea that the European Monetary System (EMS) with the Exchange Rate Mechanism (ERM) at its core may be a launching pad for EMU has been shaken to near collapse. Tensions and conflicts among the Member States on the future of the EC became obvious, right after the Heads of State and Government had signed the Maastricht Treaty on 7 February 1992. Major issues of contention have been the GATT negotiations, the EC budget, widening or deepening strategies, politics over Central and Eastern Europe, the war in Yugoslavia, the stability risks of EMU, etc. Even the completion according to plan of the Single Market, intended for the end of 1992, has not been fully achieved (Commission of the EC, 1992).

As if all these setbacks were not enough, the EMS has recently suffered a crisis without precedent and it is no daring proposition to assume that 1993 will be another year of argument about the future of monetary cooperation in Europe. The events of the past few months have not left unaffected the credibility and probability which the markets assign to the Maastricht Treaty and its centrepiece – Economic and Monetary Union (EMU).

In the past 6 months, Spain, Portugal and Ireland had to devalue their currencies and, more seriously, Italy and the UK had to take theirs out of the Exchange Rate Mechanism (see Figure 1). The French *franc* and the Danish *krone* have barely survived speculative pressure despite the heavy monetary armoury brought in to support them by the German *Bundesbank*. The European Monetary System is far from being healthy and the recent upheavals have seriously dimmed the prospects of Economic and Monetary Union.

The lessons economists and politicians draw from this experience vary: the proponents of EMU argue that the EMS crisis has clearly demonstrated the limits of ERM and the necessity to move ahead to EMU at a rapid pace, because

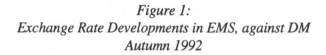

Figure 1:
Exchange Rate Developments in EMS, against DM
Autumn 1992

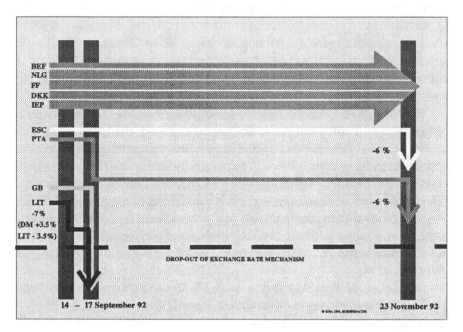

in an EMU (with a single European currency replacing the national ones) currency instability would be abolished by definition. EMU opponents advise caution and suggest that EMU's timetable (a single currency and a European Central Bank by 1999) is too ambitious. They maintain that Europe must not prematurely forego exchange-rate adjustability as long as there is a lack of convergence among the Member States and the currency markets are still too volatile in character.

To be more accurate, it is in particular the French government which wants to push ahead as quickly as possible with EMU, whereas the German *Bundesbank*, doubtful about EMU, is keen to finalize details first of a future European monetary policy before following suit. Others, like the British, plead for a more flexible, even a floating system of exchange rates in Europe.

However, from an analytical point of view, the conclusions to be drawn are neither to abandon exchange-rate management and to backtrack to floating, nor to speed up the political momentum towards EMU. Rather, what should be avoided in the future, is to defend disequilibrium exchange rates for political, ideological or any other reason (Williamson, 1993). The background to this statement is the absence of realignments since January 1987 – despite the shock waves sent through the system by German unification – which has led markets and politicians to believe that existing parities reflected sufficient convergence in economic fundamentals across EC Member States. With the French in the lead, the ERM was treated as a fixed but no longer adjustable regime. Politicians were wrong: at a certain point in time, the rigidity instilled into EMS by sticking to unrealistic parities brought markets to bet on parity changes, particularly as soon as confidence in EC governments to freeze the EMS in order to make it the launching pad for EMU had faded away. And this happened exactly when the commitment of governments to EMU was shaken by the Danish and French referenda.

Therefore, in fact, the EMS crisis was not a system failure, but rather a policy failure, since the rules had not been correctly applied: the ERM implies that economic imbalances are recognized in time and that prompt and appropriate action, i.e. realignments, is taken. The politically determined renouncement to correct fundamental disequilibria which had accumulated over time no longer convinced the markets as soon as doubts over the fate of the Maastricht Treaty arose. Markets realized that a French 'no' to Maastricht could not be ruled out, market participants sold *lira*, *pounds* and *pesetas* for *Deutsche mark*, while a weak dollar contributed to the tensions by encouraging further switching into *Deutsche mark*.

Whether or not the damage done to the EMS can be repaired and whether EMU's odds can be improved primarily depends upon

a)   the markets' belief that the EMS can be stabilized and that there is a credible and reliable political commitment either to reform the EMS fundamentally or to move towards irrevocably fixed exchange rates and a single European currency;

b)   the French choice either to go on with the '*franc fort*' and the 'policy of virtue' after the parliamentary elections in March '93 or relax the strong *Deutsche mark / French franc* link by devaluation (or choose the British solution of leaving the ERM) in order to escape the '*dictat allemand*'.

... But Resistance is Stiffening

There is no doubt, however, that the events described above have contributed to a stiffening of the scepticism and even resistance among the general public in many EC Member States against the Maastricht Treaty in general, and EMU in particular (Goldstein, 1992, p. 118). But why is it that the Treaty meets with so much aversion?

The most important reasons are the following:

–   The ratification process revealed lack of popular support and showed that Maastricht is not given a high priority in the preference orders of citizen-taxpayers.

- The EC lost its balance over the EMS and it is hard to restore confidence.
- Economic psychology has proven conclusively that, in times of crises, citizens adopt a conservative and preservative attitude so that risky experiments such as giving up national sovereignties or national currencies are rejected.

Criticism, therefore, has been expressed on different levels: *fundamental criticism*, reflecting a basic kind of anti-EC attitude, argues that the European Community compromises will lead to a stepwise destruction of the national economic, social and monetary systems. *Approach criticism* claims that the chosen approach to change monetary institutions in order to bring about greater convergence and more economic and political integration triggers a dangerous and unstable process. Institutions should follow rather than lead economic developments. *Deficiency criticism* focuses on weak spots in the Maastricht Treaty, such as the lack of Political Union, irreversibility in the integration process, democratic deficit, soft convergence criteria, the British opt-out clause, etc.

In order to understand fully these criticisms and the ongoing discussion on Maastricht and its ramifications for EMU, one has to be aware of some undercurrents in the debate.

First of all, the Maastricht Treaty must be considered primarily as a *political* undertaking and the same goes for EMU. A common currency is sought as a *symbol* of supranationalism and as a way to shift decisions on monetary and economic affairs away from the national capitals, governments and central banks.

Secondly, the President of the Commission, Jacques Delors follows a skilfully designed institutional strategy. Jean Monnet, one of the founding fathers of the EC in the fifties, expressed it as follows: 'Nothing can be achieved without men, but nothing endures without institutions'. In this tradition, the Commission is trying to create '*faits accomplis*' by changing institutional structures and establishing new Community institutions, counting on the *Eigendynamik* of the institutions to create 'institutional points of no return'.

Thirdly, it seems that the progress or stagnation in EC integration, and particular in EMU, will seriously depend on whether the political gains will outweigh the economic costs (Feldstein, 1992) although the received view holds that it is the other way round (for a closer debate cf. the concluding chapter of this volume).

Fourth, the criticism articulated does not indicate that the integration momentum is exhausted, but rather is a sign that the EC is trying to shake off false expectations and Euro-elitism. This will help create certainty and stable expectations and will do away with the volatility and doubts which have been nurtured by political division among the Member States and by national arguments about the Maastricht Treaty.

Fifth, most recently a somewhat disturbing element has been added to the debate: in Germany and France one can observe rising paranoia that the speculative attacks on the ERM are part of an American 'conspiracy' to destroy European Monetary Union and, in doing so, put the brakes on European integration. A 'Wall-Street-Mafia', so the argument goes, is trying to torpedo a Eurocurrency-to-be which might become a major competitor to the dollar in international portfolios. Although this line of argumentation is not very convincing empirically, it is certain that EMU will make a huge difference globally and it will lead to a restructuring of the financial and monetary relationship between the US and the EC.

Indeed, the dollar's dominance as a reserve currency has already faltered over the past two decades from about 80% in 1975 to 50% in 1990. Over the same period, the share of the *Deutsche mark* has risen from 7% to 15% and the share of all EC currencies including the ECU from 17% to 37%. Therefore, EMU may well encourage a further shift out of the dollar. Moreover, since a Euro-currency will eliminate intra-EC transactions in foreign exchange, reserves of about 300 billion ECU will be made redundant, a large chunk of which will be dollar reserves. It goes without saying that this will entail major shifts in economic power and influence in the global economy.

History Repeats Itself ...

Endeavours to promote monetary cooperation and integration in Europe go back a long time (Gros, Thygesen, 1992). A review in a nutshell of the most significant developments (see the following chronology) can give us some clues concerning today's chances for a monetary union.

The Rome Treaties of 1957 did not give much consideration to the issue of monetary cooperation in the EC because (a) the European Payments Union of 1950 had laid the groundwork for supporting trade in Europe on the currency side, and (b) the stable system of fixed international exchange rates (Bretton Woods) with the dollar-gold standard as the anchor currency did not call for any revision from the European side. Although Article 107 of the EC Treaty emphasized that exchange-rate policy was a matter of common interest, competences and responsibilities in the monetary, fiscal and exchange-rate areas were clearly left in the hands of the Member States.

This relatively stable constellation became somewhat shaky when it became clear that the EC's common agricultural policy (with fixed administrative prices across the Community) could conflict with intra-Community exchange-rate movements. In particular, with the appreciation of the *Deutsche mark* in 1969, the conflict between the common agricultural policy and national exchange-rate policies became evident. Together with worldwide exchange-rate problems this development prompted the EC to investigate possibilities of monetary reform.

The Summit in The Hague of 1969 decided that the Community should go for a monetary union. A blueprint for such a Union was spelled out in the famous Werner Report, the broad substance of which – a fully-fledged monetary union in 10 years time – was adopted by the Heads of State and Government in 1971. Although the Community made some preliminary steps towards a monetary union, e.g. by restricting exchange-rate movements, the project was doomed to failure and was effectively shelved at the Paris Summit of 1974. The attempt failed primarily because the Member States refused to take seriously the need to coordinate their macroeconomic policies in the face of the first oil-price crisis in 1973. Rather than joining their forces, the Member States chose national economic strategies and consequently their monetary policies also drifted apart. Moreover, the experiment unfortunately coincided with the collapse of the Bretton Woods system and the worldwide transition to floating exchange rates. With the end of the post-war golden age of growth, the project of an early EMU dropped dead.

The 'kick' for renewed endeavours to coordinate and cooperate in monetary affairs came with the increasing turbulence and irritations on the EC's financial markets resulting from dollar instability in the wake of the Vietnam War. To reduce spillovers and create a European area of relative stability were the ultimate objectives of an initiative by German Chancellor Helmut Schmidt and French President Giscard d'Estaing to set up a European Monetary System (EMS). At the 1978 Summit in Bremen, agreement was reached to make it operational. It is noteworthy that EMS was created due to *political will* and against the advice of professional economists and EC central bankers. Despite major changes over time (Hasse, 1991) the EMS has not just survived but has proved to be quite successful in bringing down inflation and interest rates in the Community and in bringing about a considerable degree of economic convergence. It was not the least the merits and the success of EMS which encouraged European policy-makers to launch another EMU initiative by the end of the eighties.

Indeed, monetary cooperation and coordination in the EC has made substantial progress in the past 35 years. However, this progress has never been a unilinear, continuous process. Rather the developments were subject to the ups and downs of European integration, there were efforts to speed up and endeavours to slow down, and there were times to step forward and periods to pull back. In this sense monetary cooperation is just a mirror of EC integration as such (see Figure 2).

A closer look reveals another interesting aspect. Apparently there is something like a ten-year cycle in promoting a monetary Community: in post-war 1950, we created a European Payments Union (EPU) in order to overcome financial and monetary restrictions to trade. In 1959 we replaced it with a Monetary Agreement involving currency convertibility, an assistance fund and rules for multilateral settlement of payments; 1969/70 saw the Werner Plan come into

CHRONOLOGY OF EUROPEAN MONETARY INTEGRATION

1950 – EPU:

The European Payments Union (EPU) comes into operation. In its capacity as a clearing house, the EPU enables payments to be settled multilaterally in post-war Europe. The participating States also grant each other short-term credit for balance of payments adjustment.

1957 – EEC Treaty:

The EEC Treaty calls for national monetary policies to coordinate. A monetary committee is set up and the exchange rates are defined as 'a matter of mutual interest'.

1958 – EIB:

The European Investment Bank (EIB) is established as an independent credit institution of the EEC with its seat in Luxembourg.

1959 – Monetary Agreement:

Having ensured complete currency convertibility in most of the European States, the EPU is dissolved and is replaced by the European Monetary Agreement, under which a fund for coping with temporary difficulties in balancing payments is set up, and rules are laid down for a multilateral settling of payments through the Bank for International Settlements (BIS).

1964 – Council of Governors of Central Banks:

The 'Committee of Governors of Central Banks of the EEC Member States' is set up on 8 May 1964. In the following years, the Committee develops into a central institution for coordinating monetary as well as credit and lending operations in Europe.

1970 – Werner Plan:

A special committee, led by the Prime Minister of Luxembourg, Pierre Werner, adopts a multi-tiered plan for achieving a fully-fledged Economic and Monetary Union by the end of the seventies. It involves the following objectives: the irrevocable convertibility of EEC currencies; complete liberalization of capital movements inside the Community; irrevocably fixed exchange rates between EC currencies; pooling of monetary reserves; monetary policy controlled by a single European institution.

1972 – Currency Snake:

In March 1972 the EEC Council of Ministers decides to restrict the margins of fluctuation of EEC currencies in respect of one another to 4.5 per cent. The central banks agree on money market interventions to ensure this objective. The 'European Currency Snake' thus comes into being. When exchange rates begin to float freely after 1973, the currency snake enforces what is known as 'block floating'.

1974 – Convergence and Stability Directive:

On 18 February 1974 the EC Ministers for Economic and Financial Affairs called for a high degree of economic convergence in the EEC (Convergence Decision) and the highest possible degree of stability, full employment and growth (Stability Directive) as a prerequisite for further monetary integration.

1975 – EUA/ECU:

The European Unit of Account (EUA) (this was later renamed ECU (European Currency Unit) in the framework of the EMS) was adopted as the accounting unit first for the European Development Fund, then for the European Investment Bank and the Community budget. The EUA/ECU is an artificial 'basket currency' composed of the individual currencies of the Member States, weighted according to the economic strength each currency represents. Although the EUA/ECU is initially only seen as a political symbol for European integration, it comes to play an important role in bond markets and as a major exchange reserve in the eighties.

1978 – D-Mark Block

Out of the initially nine members of the 'snake', only the 'D-Mark Bloc' lasts: Germany, The Netherlands, Denmark, Belgium/Luxembourg and, associated, Norway. An increasing number of countries drop out because, due to progressive inflation, they were unable to keep their currencies within the snake's margin of fluctuation.

1979 – EMS:

On an initiative of the French President, Giscard d'Estaing, and German Chancellor, Helmut Schmidt, the European Monetary System (EMS) is established. The European Council decides on 12 March 1979 to bring the EMS into effect on the following day. Fixed, yet adjustable, exchange rates between the Member States' currencies are given an overall margin of fluctuation of 4.5 per cent. The rates are set with respect to the new European Currency Unit (ECU) in a parity grid. Whereas the Member States' currencies are pegged to the ECU, the ECU itself floats freely against the dollar and other third currencies.

1981 – First ECU Bond:

The Italian telecommunications company, Stet, issues the first bonds denominated in ECU. In the following years the private use of the ECU starts to develop rapidly. Within a decade the ECU becomes the fifth largest investment currency in the world.

1979 – March 1983

Between 1979 and 1983 there are a total of seven realignments of central rates in the EMS. Most important is the realignment of March '83 (all currencies): it is established that changes would become common decisions rather than being unilateral action. Consequently, realignments become politically charged, technically difficult and, at times, even acrimonious.

1985 – White Paper:

In its White Paper, the EC Commission lays down its objective of introducing irrevocable measures towards creating a single European market by the end of 1992. Financial markets are particularly affected.

1986 – Single European Act:

The process of integration accelerates faster than expected after the signing of the Single European Act, which articulates the political will to proceed to a European Union. Regulations towards creating a future monetary union are mentioned in SEA.

1987 – First ECU Coin:

Belgium has the first legal-tender ECU coins minted on the occasion of the 30 anniversary of the inception of the EC.

1987 – Basle-Nyborg Agreement:

Ecofin, the Council of Ministers of Finance and Economics decides on 12 September to monitor monetary development in the EMS more closely, to narrow remaining inflation differentials, to improve the coordination of interest rates, and to liberalize the rules for financing 'intra-marginal' intervention.

1989 – Delors Plan:

The Delors Committee presents its final report. It calls for a three-tiered approach. First the economic and monetary policies of the individual Member States should be more closely coordinated; second, a European Central Bank is to be established; third, a single European currency is to replace the national currencies.

1991 – Maastricht:

In the Dutch town of Maastricht, the Heads of State and Government of the EC Member States agree on the well-known 'Maastricht Treaty', in which the groundwork for Economic and Monetary Union is laid.

1992 – Danish and French Referendum:

In a referendum in Denmark, the Danes reject the Maastricht Treaty. In France, there is a narrow majority in favour of the Maastricht Treaty.

1992 – EMS Holed:

Between 1987 and September 1992 no realignments take place in the EMS, giving politicians reason to think that sufficient economic convergence has been achieved to proceed to EMU. Under the influence of continuously high German interest rates and the uncertainty about the French referendum, financial markets put the EMS and particularly the 'weaker' currencies to the test. On 16 September sterling is withdrawn after extraordinary waves of selling push the British pound out of the Exchange Rate Mechanism; later Italy suspends the lira and Spain devalues the peseta by 5 per cent. The French are able to fend off similar speculation pressure on the franc a couple of days later.

---

being and a decade later, in 1978/1979, the EMS was conceived and made operational. Eventually, in 1989, the Delors Committee suggested a fully-fledged EMU, and in the Maastricht Treaty the EC committed itself to turn it from a blueprint into reality by 1999 at the latest. There seems to be some regularity behind this flow of events.

... So Why EMU?

There is more or less agreement in academic circles as well as among professional economists that Europe is far from being an optimal currency area. Neither is there sufficient factor mobility nor enough economic convergence.

However, although we know that in the traditional 'Mundell-Fleming World' (Mundell, 1961; Fleming, 1971) 'optimal' is poorly defined, the extensive literature on currency areas suggests that benefits from a monetary union will be a function of the degree of intra-union trade, the degree of labour mobility, the extent of nominal wage and price flexibility, the degree of industrial diversification and the probability of asymmetric, i.e. country-specific shocks. In the EC, labour mobility is low, intra-union trade is relatively high, wages and prices are sticky, industry clusters are distributed unevenly across Member States, and therefore the probability of asymmetric shocks is not exactly low. Although the Commission argues that the 1992 Single Market project has increased similarity of industrial patterns and that it has added to wage and price flexibility through more competition, (Commission of the EC, 1990), serious doubts remain about Europe being an Optimum Currency Area (Eichengreen, 1991).

However, if there are too few theoretically compelling arguments to move on to an EMU, what other reasons can be found?

Some proponents of EMU simply argue that a Single Market requires a single currency. This argument, nurtured by US experience, may be very popular but it is not very convincing from an economic point of view. There is consensus in professional circles that a Single Market can operate equally well in practical terms with several currencies.

Slightly more important may be the argument that a single currency presents some extra benefits like fewer exchange-rate risks, lower transaction costs, etc. Empirical calculations show that the welfare gains which can be reaped from these are not exactly high as a percentage of GDP.

To be taken more seriously is the argument that the triad of fixed but adjustable exchange rates, free capital movements and national monetary sovereignty cannot work at the same time (Padoa Schioppa, 1988). If one does not want to give up the first two achievements, strict coordination (involving limits on national sovereignty) is needed to avoid any externalities and spillovers from national monetary policy-making.

Another line of argumentation refers to the *disciplinary function* of an EMU (Fratianni, v. Hagen, 1992: 48pp.) which would limit the leeway for too lax a monetary and fiscal policy in some Member States. Experience with the EMS suggests that linking the currencies to each other involves a commitment to monetary stability, set by the most stable currency in the system. Indeed some soft currency countries have benefited greatly from the role played by the *Deutsche mark* as an 'anchor' currency in Europe. This has been due to the willingness of some Member States to follow the stability-oriented policy pursued by the *Bundesbank* in order to earn the credibility needed for the success of their own economic and monetary policy efforts. It may be assumed that a fully-fledged EMU with a strong stability commitment will even strengthen this

Figure 2:
Community Events and Economic Development

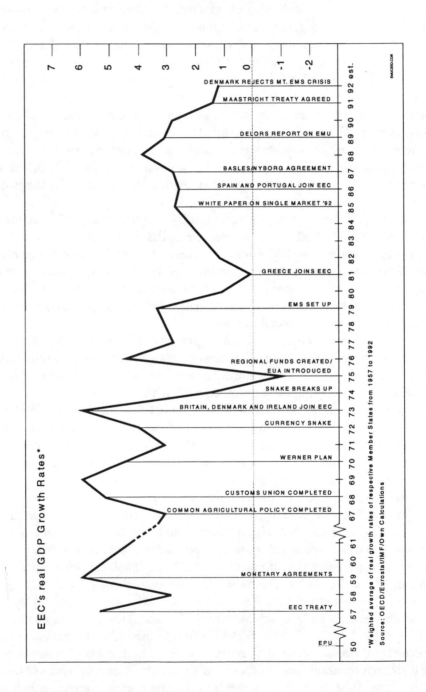

disciplinary function and increase the borrowed credibility for some national economies in Europe.

In political terms this argument can be turned around: EMU might as well contribute to getting rid of the EC's monetary master of discipline and order. It has been widely acknowledged that the very success of the EMS, built on the willingness of EC central banks to delegate voluntarily part of their sovereignty to the *Bundesbank* in order to borrow credibility, came at a political cost: the Germans had settled in the driver's seat of European Monetary Policy – and this is at odds with the idea of the EC as a *Community*. With the growing economic success of the EMS over time, the other European Member States wanted to join the driver at the steering wheel. Political acceptance of German monetary hegemony dropped sharply. Against this background, EMU represents a fine device to shake off German dominance and rebalance the asymmetric distribution of economic power and monetary influence in the EC.

Economic Benefits and Political Costs ...

Although political scientists claim that it is particularly the last one among the arguments enumerated above, which ultimately triggered EMU plans, economists ascribe primacy to large financial benefits from Economic and Monetary Union.

EMU would completely eliminate nominal exchange-rate variability. It would also eliminate uncertainty, and hence lower the risk premiums on financial and foreign exchange markets. Moreover, only a single currency completely eliminates the transaction costs of exchanging currencies. These costs are not trivial for businesses, and can be sizeable for small transactions between persons and for tourists. They add up to about 0.4% of EC GDP a year. Also, the combination of the 1992 programme and EMU may translate into not only considerable once-and-for-all gains, but also dynamic gains (a higher sustainable rate of economic growth). Reduced uncertainty would permit a reduction in the rate of return on investment demanded by shareholders, leaving more funds for reinvestment and growth of GDP. Estimates show that a moderate reduction in the risks of investment (such as exchange-rate uncertainty) could have a substantial long-term growth effect (for a critical overview, cf. Minford et al, 1992).

The European Central Bank-to-be (ECB) will most likely bring on-average inflation down in the EC, since its statutes establish price stability as a priority duty and grant it political independence to fulfil this duty. Price stability in turn is itself conducive to an efficient resource allocation. Also, the role of national budgetary policies will be substantially revised, to enhance discipline over excessive deficits and coordination to ensure an appropriate policy mix for the Community as a whole.

Gains in interest payments on the public debt and in the allocation of capital could come from the tendency to equalize real interest rates across EC Member States. Moreover, EMU will facilitate international coordination, and give more weight to the Community in encouraging developments of the world policy mix favourable to its interest. It will also facilitate the establishment of a more balanced tripolar regime.

... Or Vice Versa?

However, there are also undoubtedly financial disadvantages and costs (Goodhart, 1991) resulting from EMU such as:
  — loss of the national monetary and exchange-rate instruments;
  — budgetary constraints imposed on Member States making fiscal policy inflexible;
  — lower inflation rates implying lower inflation tax and consequently a loss of seigniorage revenues in some countries;
  — the meeting of the convergence criteria laid down in the Maastricht Treaty as the entrance ticket to EMU which may entail deflationary and contractive effects on some national economies;
  — banks losing their commission from foreign currency business;
  — substantial investment required for the creation of Euro-payment systems;
  — a Cohesion Fund to be established in order to facilitate macroeconomic adjustment in the weaker Member States;
  — adjustment costs resulting from system change, such as new computer links, payment systems, credit cards, teller machines and cheques books;
  — revision and rewriting of all contracts and records denominated in national currency;
  — unfamiliar calculations citizen-taxpayers will be compelled to make in their transactions, since the ECU will not be an exact multiple or fraction of any national currency.

Comparing the benefits and costs, Lipp and Reichert (1991) have put forward an interesting argument: they have pointed out, that the major psychological and political problems in accepting EMU mainly have to do with the fact that the expected benefits are vague and will accrue – if at all – in the distant future, whereas the costs associated with EMU are evident and can become pressing in the very short run. One may add to this observation that the degree of visibility of the disadvantages is very high but the identification of potential sizeable benefits is very hard to accomplish.

In his analysis of costs and benefits, Bean (1992) concludes that neither the financial costs nor the financial benefits are as great as opponents and proponents of EMU have made out. Therefore, the exchange of financial arguments and economic evidence appears to be no more than a storm in a teacup. The real reason for pushing for EMU and the real yardstick for judging EMU are of a political nature. The intention is to keep Europe on the integration track. Economic arguments, just put the icing on the cake.

EMU – Quo Vadis?

The main factors which will decide the future fate of EMU are not its costs and benefits. In addition, the fact that the Maastricht Treaty, EMU's foster parent, is on life support and the political will for going ahead is wavering, is troubling but not crucial for the future of monetary cooperation. Problems like potential tension between Monetary Union and Economic Union (the latter weakly defined and on shaky grounds), or technicalities like the (too soft) formulation of the convergence criteria should not be overrated.

The worst about EMU is *the fog of uncertainty*. Uncertainty over where we go from here and now, destabilizes the financial markets. When faced with a choice between a 'half-baked', 'maybe' Maastricht on the one hand and a fundamentally revised although less ambitious EMS on the other, markets may decide for the latter. As we have witnessed of late, a clash between policy-makers' ambitious EMU-plans and market forces results in serious economic turbulence.

Unfortunately, the planning horizons of politicians, markets and economists differ: politicians have a very short planning horizon and economists a very long one, whereas financial markets have a short planning horizon but a memory like an elephant. This means that they do not easily forget: on the one hand, once a monetary regime has gained credibility over time, markets will positively sanction it (even overshooting if changes in the fundamentals occur, as the German case shows). On the other hand, it is extremely difficult for governments and central banks once they have disappointed the markets, to restore confidence (an example is France, whose fundamentals are far better than the German ones, but the markets are not convinced of the sustainability and political stability). Therefore, what the European economies need most is certainty in order to enable the economic agents to form realistic and reliable expectations about the future course of events. The ups and downs after Maastricht and the ongoing arguments about EMU have definitely not done this objective any good.

But this does not lead to the conclusion that Maastricht can be easily abandoned or postponed or swapped for a better EMS. The costs of stopping EMU will not be negligible. Indeed, Maastricht has initiated a process which still has to produce many of the elements on which it is built. EMU has not taken a clear enough shape and much depends on what – in its own interpretation and as an outcome of the ongoing debate – it intends this shape to be. Taking this into account, we can be confident that monetary cooperation in the EC is still on track. There is no need for despair, because in the face of impediments, the shortest distance between two points is not a straight line but curvilinear. The same goes for monetary evolution.

From the EMU Blueprint to the Book's Design

In order to structure analytically and single out the distinctive aspects of EMU, this volume is organized in three parts. The first section deals with the developments and changes in European monetary cooperation emphasizing the transition from the current monetary arrangement in the Community, the EMS to the subsequent stages of EMU. This is analyzed not only from the perspective of the EC and its Member States, but also with reference to one country, which as a member-to-be, has already linked its currency to the EMS and is carefully preparing for EMU. The second section of the book deals with the construction of a European Central Bank and analyzes the institutional setting, the concepts and targets of monetary policies in Europe and the necessary harmonization of monetary instruments. Also the potential risks are considered: are we nourishing a viper in our bosom by embracing the idea of establishing a European Central Bank? The third and last section of this book goes into the aspects of the interplay between Monetary Union and Economic Union. It is generally accepted that a monetary union will have large spillover effects on national policy-making which have to be offset with more economic policy coordination in the areas of fiscal policy and regional economic cohesion. The book concludes with a note on how national policy-makers may be affected, i.e. either put under constraints, burdened with new tasks or relieved from former responsibilities by the changes EMU will bring about.

The discussion of monetary integration and EMU starts in Chapter One with a '*témoignage*' to the merits and pitfalls of the European Monetary System. The recent turmoil on the financial and exchange-rate markets has proved that EMS and EMU seem to be strongly linked both content-wise and strategically. The first Chapter by *Gretschmann, Kotz* and *Sleijpen* addresses this question and asks to what extent the EMS has been determined from its inception more by a political art of fencing than by economic reasoning. It seems that the blend of political and economic elements stands at the same time for EMU's strengths and weaknesses. The contribution translates the EMS experience into conclusions to be drawn for EMU and it asks whether EMU can get off the ground if its natural parent EMS is dying a slow death? The inevitable question to be raised is whether a reform of the EMS is necessary or whether a speedier transition to EMU could overcome the current difficulties.

At the time when the Intergovernmental Conference on EMU was convened, back in December 1991 in Rome, the 'Europe of the Money' still seemed to be benefiting from the *'Pax Pecunia'*, with stability in the EMS at its height. Starting from these special circumstances, *Italianer* describes in Chapter Two in detail the long and breathtaking negotiation process and the economic arguments and political compromises involved, that have led to the signing of the Maastricht Treaty in Maastricht in February 1992. And once again politics seems to have prevailed over economics. The aim of *Italianer's* contribution is to give an insight into the various and often conflicting positions of the actors involved, like Member States, Community bodies, central bank governors, expert groups and Council Presidencies. Against this background, it does not come as a surprise that the final outcome of the negotiations drawn up in the Maastricht Treaty does not represent a perfectly consistent and monolithic entity, but rather resembles a 'package deal', with varying degrees of significance attached to its components by the individual actors. For the making of a 'Monetary Europe', many steps are still necessary, therefore the measures to be taken in order to fully open the gate towards the final stage of EMU are also discussed.

'Monetary Union: a goldmine rather than a minefield' was the keynote at the European Council in Maastricht. This holds true not only for Community members, but also for potential 'insiders' and members-to-be of the EC, that were very prone to take on the Emperors' new clothes. In the third Chapter of this volume, *Dörfel, Eggl* and *Schubert* discuss both the economic and political interest and the monetary operations of Austria, the informal 'insider', which have made it *de facto* a part of European monetary integration. The Austrian monetary authorities have pegged their *schilling* to the *Deutsche mark* and have, therefore, already profited from the *Bundesbank*'s policy. It goes without saying that Austria would also want to reap the potential benefits of EMU. The contribution discusses Austria's indirect experience of the EMS as well as the pros and cons of formal EMS membership. Since Austria presently fulfils all the criteria for participating in EMU, except the formal EMS membership, the Austrian authorities are not required to make major changes. The Austrian example shows that a formally considered outsider can become a *de facto* insider of the EMS, which performs so strongly in the EMS that it may be expected to strengthen the case for EMU.

From the economic and political boundaries of the EC dealt with in the preceding Chapter, we turn to the institutional heartland of Economic and Monetary Union in the second part of this volume, which deals with the construction and significance of a European Central Bank and its concepts and instruments. In the first Chapter of this Section, *Harden* covers the institutional and constitutional aspects of the ECB. He investigates the causes and consequences of the repartition of competences between the future ECB and the national central banks and he analyzes the significance of central bank autonomy for the

ECB as well as the ECB's institutional structure and constitutional foundation which are to safeguard independence from political instruction. The general picture he paints reveals that the legal setting of the European Central Bank as well as its constitutional strength would turn the ECB into a sort of 'economic government' of the Community, as the Treaty confers the necessary powers and since its independence removes any powerful outside control. The conclusion is, therefore, that a monetary union of this kind strongly requires a political union to counterbalance the lack of democratic control.

Harden's contribution focuses on the constitutional and institutional features of EMU and leaves aside the issue of policy instruments and day-to-day monetary policy-making. In contrast, *Eijffinger*, in the second Chapter of Section 2, moves ahead to an overview of the monetary policy practice and convergence (or divergence) involved in three EC Member States, Germany, France and the United Kingdom. From the comparison made by the author, it appears that, although some convergence in monetary-policy objectives and instruments has been achieved since the second half of the eighties, notably between Germany and France, much still has to be done. Efforts to harmonize the approach and tools of monetary operations in the EC seem to be warranted. Whereas the convergence in monetary policy making between France and Germany has reached an advanced level, the UK is still lagging behind and also the monetary instruments used there are very much out of line with those used in other EMS countries. In the author's view, the British and also other Member States still have a long way to go to develop convergent monetary policies.

The central bank which has the most to lose in EMU, but which is at the same time best equipped for the transition, is probably the German *Bundesbank*, not only because of its influence on European monetary affairs, but also because of its achievements in terms of price stability and independence. Despite being itself a bestseller in terms of monetary policy, the *Bundesbank* has always supported the idea of '*a strong and independent European Central Bank*'. The *Bundesbank*'s stance in the debate on EMU in general and the ECB in particular is expressed in the third and last Chapter of Section 2. *Jochimsen's* contribution reflects the 'critical undertones' of the German central bank with respect to possible complications and pitfalls as well as potential advantages of an ECB taking over from the *Bundesbank*. The sceptical melody mainly concerns the automatism leading to EMU's final stage, the political leeway in the determination of the necessary convergence, the concerns that the ECB might not be independent enough to pursue an anti-inflationary policy, and the role of the Council in the management of external exchange rates in EMU. Therefore, *Jochimsen* argues to apply rigorously the principle of subsidiarity to the area of monetary integration, without jeopardizing the objective of price stability. He recommends using the experience of the German federal bank structure (*Bundesbank vis-à-vis Landeszentralbanken*) as a blueprint for the further construction of the European System of Central Banks.

The third and last part of this volume goes beyond the boundaries set in the Maastricht Treaty and tries to make an assessment of the impact of EMU on other economic variables and policies. However, this assessment does more than look into the crystal ball. It seems that certain areas could turn out to be swampland for the further implementation of EMU. With the negotiations on the Community budget and the waking up of the Italian, Spanish and UK governments in the twilight of the EMS, the question as to whether EMU will endanger social and economic cohesion in the Community is now more topical than ever. In the first Chapter of Section 3, *Molle, Sleijpen* and *Vanheukelen* give an overall picture of the possible effects of EMU on relative income disparities between regions and Member States in the Community. It seems that in a longer term perspective the so-called 'cohesion countries' are the ones that will benefit the most from EMU; however, these countries in particular will suffer from the harshest adjustment costs. Notably the loss of the exchange rate as a policy instrument could deteriorate the possibilities of those countries to adjust. The experience in the EMS has proved that this conclusion is true. However, with or without EMU, the necessity for adjustment in terms of the adaptation of economic structures and policies (especially budgetary and fiscal policies) is unavoidable in the 'cohesion countries'. Taking this into account means acknowledging that the journey towards EMU involves many cliffs for the poorer members of the EC; cliffs that have to be avoided but which could also be made less dangerous by Community efforts to strengthen the existing pallet of regional and structural policies.

As pointed out in *van den Bempt's* contribution, macroeconomic, especially fiscal and budgetary policies could also run into trouble in EMU, as it is foreseen that Member States should coordinate their policies and curtail their deficits. Coordination seems necessary as the EC does not have any instruments ready to counterbalance macroeconomic shocks. This may imply more difficulties for some Member States than for others. Notably the 'deficit countries', like Italy, Greece and Belgium, will have to invest great effort in complying with the strict budgetary limitations required. The Member States which can fulfil the budget requirement will at the same time have relatively large autonomy in the implementation of fiscal policies (perhaps even greater than is currently the case). Whereas this picture is very attractive for national governments, it remains to be seen whether the division of labour between monetary and fiscal authorities will lead to conflicting or unstable policy objectives or not.

In the concluding Chapter, *Gretschmann* asks whether the economic policy-makers in EC Member States will be EMUsed. It goes without saying that a centralized supranational monetary policy will have serious consequences for other economic policy areas which will remain under national responsibility, such as fiscal policy, labour market and employment policies, incomes policy and regional policy. The author points out a paradox: in principle, in the face of a centralized monetary policy, national policies should be more flexible in order to be able to respond to national and regional requirement. In reality, however, it will probably not be possible to combine a single monetary policy with twelve different national fiscal, employment, incomes policies, etc. In order to guarantee a reasonable policy mix in an EMU, strict coordination and even harmonization is therefore required in other economic policy areas. This may ultimately promote a tendency to proceed from a monetary union to an economic union, fiscal union, social union, etc. Such a creeping process will be accompanied by new tasks for policy-makers. The constellations with which policy-makers will be confronted will be more complex and difficult to handle. Moreover, an institutional mechanism for coordinating Community policy and national economic policies is not in sight. So EMUsement of national policy-makers will be limited.

REFERENCES

Bean, Charles (1992), Economic and Monetary Union in Europe, *Journal of Economic Perspectives*, Vol. 6, pp. 31-52.

Commission of the European Communities (1990) *One Market, One Money. An Evaluation of the Potential Benefits and Costs of an EMU*, European Economy No 44, Brussels.

Commission of the European Commission (1992), *The Operation of the Community's Internal Market After 1992*, SEC (92)22773, Brussels.

Eichengreen, Barry (1990), *Is Europe an Optimum Currency Area?* CEPR Discussion Paper No 478, London.

Feldstein, Martin (1992), The Case Against EMU, *The Economist* June 13th, pp. 19-22.

Fleming, Marcus J. (1971), On Exchange Rate Unification, *The Economic Journal*, Vol. 81, pp. 467-488.

Fratianni, Michele; Hagen, Jürgen von (1992), *European Monetary System and European Monetary Union*, Boulder: Westview.

Goldstein, Walter (1992), Europe After Maastricht in: *Foreign Affairs* Winter 92/93, pp. 117-132.

Goodhart, C. (1991), An Assessment of EMU, *The Royal Bank of Scotland Review*, No 170, pp. 3-25.

Gros, Daniel; Thygesen, Niels (1992), *European Monetary Integration*, London: Longman.

Hasse, Rolf (1990), Europäische Wirtschafts- und Währungsunion: Bilanz der Koordinierungsdefizite, in: Hasse, R., Schäfer, W. (eds.), *Europäische Zentralbank*, Göttingen: V&R, pp. 74-85.

Lipp, Ernst-Moritz; Reichart, Horst (1991), Konfliktfelder auf dem Weg zur Europäischen Währungsunion, in: M. Weber (ed.), *Europa auf dem Weg zur Währungsunion*, Darmstadt: WBG, pp. 31-48.

Minford, Patrick et.al. (1992), *The Price of EMU Revisited*, CEPR Discussion Paper 656, London.

Mundell, Robert A. (1961), A Theory of Optimum Currency Areas, *American Economic Review* Vol. 51, pp. 657-665.

Padoa-Schioppa, Tomaso (1988), *Efficiency, Stability and Equity in the EC*, Oxford, University Press.

Williamson, John (1993) Exchange Rate Management, *The Economic Journal*, Vol. 103, pp. 188-197.

SECTION 1:

FROM EMS TO EMU: THE WINDS OF CHANGE ARE BLOWING HARD

THE EUROPEAN MONETARY SYSTEM:
THE GEOGRAPHY OF ECONOMICS VERSUS THE
POLITICS OF MONEY?

Klaus Gretschmann, Hans-Helmut Kotz, Olaf Sleijpen*

Europe's Monetary System: Economic Reality versus Political Voluntarism?

Being an expression of the relative value of national currencies, the exchange rate clearly represents more than expectations about developments of a purely economic content. Economists' preaching notwithstanding, this ratio is the most important price of a nation's economy. Otherwise it would be difficult to understand comments from well-known circles in London's Threadneedle Street describing the day when the British Pound left the European Exchange Rate Mechanism, (i.e. Black Wednesday), as a 'national day of humiliation'. After the lira realignment on 14 September 1992 triggered the run on the EMS, the almost pan-European eruption of mutual contempt – with the clear focus on the German *Bundesbank* – makes it palpable that one should not sideline politics in this play. German pundits also do not tire of telling us that the mythological *Deutsche mark* is the founding stone of the Germans' *national identity*. '*Changer ses devises*' does not come easy for the French either. Therefore, in a way, the foreign exchange markets by their buy and hold decisions seem to dabble in deep-rooted symbols of national pride. Against that background, the whole 'Maastricht process', aiming at a single European currency, went against the grain of a politically and economically quite diverse Europe. It was doomed to failure from scratch, or was it?

We have an ambiguous answer to that question. And that is why we will start at the beginning, when a coordinated monetary policy or even a European *numéraire*, as a matter of fact, were not very important. With the exception of some broad-brush guidelines for macroeconomic and monetary policy coordination and the setting up of a Monetary Committee, the Treaty establishing the European Economic Community in 1957 did not spend much ink on thoughts about how to bring about monetary cooperation within the European framework.[1] To be sure, this was conceptually not very consistent: eliminating

---

* The views expressed in this chapter are those of the authors. The chapter was completed in autumn 1992.

K. Gretschmann (ed.), Economic and Monetary Union: Implications for National Policy-Makers, 27–49.
© 1993 *European Institute of Public Administration. Printed in the Netherlands.*

– *within* a fixed exchange-rate context – impediments to the free cross-border flow of goods, services, capital and people, as the Treaty proposed to achieve by 1970, meant *implicitly* the waiving of an autonomous monetary policy. However, in the following decade, the widespread use of capital controls was helpful in rounding the edges of what Padoa-Schioppa later called the 'inconsistency quartet' (Padoa-Schioppa, 1982). In these early days, moreover, incentives for a closer monetary integration were definitely scarce: the European economies were growing at a rapid pace, inflation rates were (still) low, showing no great dispersion. Therefore, Member States decisions to peg their currencies to the US dollar parity was reasonable and credible and, as a consequence, exchange rate uncertainty was almost nil.

On the face of it, thus, the major objectives of the Treaty of Rome were in the domain of the real, goods-producing heart of the economy: the establishment of a Customs Union and the creation of common policies, notably in the areas of external trade and agriculture. This was in line with Monnet's functional integration approach, namely to begin cooperative efforts with institutional underpinning in well-defined sectors: agriculture, energy, transport, etc. However, a list of the 'real', i.e. economic reasons for the inception of the EEC, underlining its dominantly economic mission, conveys an incomplete impression. It is abundantly clear that *political visions* have contributed decisively to the coming into existence of the European Communities and to their institutional make-up. The conceived view is that the political vision of the founding fathers is strictly linked to the experiences preceding the second World War both in terms of domestic economic policies and with respect to foreign power-politics.[2] Here is a major point, which we have to stress: politics, not just policy, i.e. the implementation of sober, politically 'untarnished' economics, has been the decisive ingredient in the European process from the outset. It also means in the context of European integration that *there is no such a thing as unpolitical money!*

Despite or even because of this fact, monetary integration and, as a consequence, monetary institution-building were not a priority in the first two decades of the Community.[3] Within the Bretton-Woods System, perceived as a healthy and sustainable arrangement, Europe took its monetary clues from the outside. Therefore, according to the consensus view on this point, the perception of things concerning European monies as being problematic and thus their definition as political problems began with the slow-motion erosion of the dollar standard in the course of the 1960s. There is a minor quirk with regard to that view because, as a matter of fact, the European Commission proposed under its Chairman Walter Hallstein in October 1962 three stages towards the creation of a monetary union by 1971. However, this approach never got off ground since, among others, Germany could not warm to the idea of a regional monetary scheme and, in addition, feared for its capacity to control internal liquidity in the face of looming intervention obligations.

Conventional wisdom claims that monetary integration became an issue on the EC agenda for the first time at the Hague Summit of 1969.[4] Its upshot was the Werner Report, aiming at a common monetary policy by 1980 and borrowing the magical three-stage process from Hallstein's concept. Against the background of a dissolution of the international monetary system, combined with the different national ways of absorbing the shock waves sent to the system of relative prices by the quadrupling of oil prices, the ambitious Werner Plan ushered in a scaled-down version – the 'snake-construct'. Therefore, the real starter towards monetary integration in Europe was the birth of the European Monetary System (EMS) on 13 March 1979. Again, just looking at the economics does not suffice to come to grips with the creation of the EMS. Firstly, the Giscard d'Estaing-Helmut Schmidt initiative for the creation of an EMS had to be pushed through politically against the rigid, economic stance of the central banks. Secondly, what is more, the dialectical dynamics between politics and economics led, over time, to a redefinition of the EMS's goals and structures.[5]

As regards the Maastricht Treaty and its centrepiece EMU, to frontload our story, the process towards 'Maastricht' took its impressive momentum from history shifting into high gear: on the level of European union, Treaty provisions are designed to serve as a device to handle the political ramifications of the meltdown of the Soviet Empire; on the economic level, they were conceived as a means to cope with German unification. In line with this view, the sacrificing of the *Deutsche mark* on the European altar, i.e. the perspective of an Economic and Monetary Union (EMU), with one single currency and one European Central Bank, lessened particularly the French preoccupation about a Germany possibly drifting away towards the East, while still dominating Western Europe through its economic and political power. Against this background of the dialectics between politics and economics, monetary union without a commensurate political superstructure appears, as a matter of fact, to be a working option in the textbooks only. Thus, the fairly simple juxtaposition of 'economic realism versus political voluntarism' would impose an ill-conceived structure on our analysis of monetary cooperation in Europe.

Therefore, in this chapter, building on a brief historical and functional sketch, we will try to make sense of current developments in Europe and attempt to gauge what is in store. Consequently, our emphasis is not on policy but on the *'politics of monetary economics'*. The following narrative has a chronological structure: in the first section – 'history' – starting with the snake prelude and thus spanning two decades, the performance of the EMS will be discussed. Its track record was fertile ground for relaunching monetary union concepts at the end of the 1980s. We will deliberately omit discussions and subjects within the time span leading to the Maastricht Treaty since they are dealt with in other contributions to this book. Instead, by sticking with our focus on the context of Maastricht, the third section will deal with a brief and nevertheless decisive moment, the crisis in the EMS in the summer of 1992, culminating in the suspension of the Italian lira and the British pound from the EMS, i.e. the 'present'. Finally, we will ponder – in the light of linkages between EMS and EMU – the 'ifs' of 'Maastricht', which should be written with capital letters. Does a perhaps reformulated 'Maastricht' have a 'future'?

Rooting and Legitimizing the EMS: The Quest for Political and Economic Stability in a Volatile Environment

After a decade of accumulating deficits in the US current account, the dollar lost its shine in the course of the 1960s. Behaving according to the rules of the Bretton-Woods game implied accepting a monetary policy which was deemed too inflationary in Europe. As a consequence, the shivering US dollar anchor induced the search for a European alternative. In a final attempt to save the international fixed-rate system, the Smithsonian Agreement of December 1971 had widened the variation margins for the exchange rates against the US dollar to 4.5 per cent. For the European cross-rates this translated, at the extreme, into permissible divergences of up to 9 per cent. And this was thought to be incompatible with a healthy functioning of the common market, and it was believed to be particularly disruptive for the common agricultural policy.

THE WERNER REPORT'S EMU: A LAUNCHING PAD FOR...

It is here where, from an institutional perspective, the so-called Werner Report becomes the *référence obligée* (Mathieu/ Sterdyniak 1989, p. 110). At the Hague Summit of December 1969, the Heads of State and Government of the Community, thereby following the Barre Report of February that year, agreed to the creation of an Economic and Monetary Union. For that purpose the Commission established a study group chaired by Pierre Werner, then Luxembourg Prime Minister, to prepare the blueprint for such a venture. The Werner Report, which was adopted in 1971, came up with a three-tiered approach, calling for the attainment of irrevocably fixed parities, a complete liberalization of capital movements and, perhaps, a common currency by 1980. Therefore, the introduction of reduced fluctuation bands *within* the Smithsonian scheme – it is here where the 'snake in the tunnel' metaphor comes from – marks the birth of a distinctly European policy towards international monetary cooperation. With the final demise of the Bretton-Woods System, i.e. the floating of the US dollar, this became the 'snake in the lake'. Therefore, the unravelling of the Bretton-Woods System was conducive to making the *first* stage of the proposals operational in the spring of 1972.

The set-up of the snake mechanism, designed as a bilateral pegging of rates, was asymmetric: with n currencies there are n x (n-1)/2 exchange rates. Except for the nth country, this implied that the other snake members lost one instrument of economic policy, namely the monetary lever, which was devoted to exchange-rate targeting. Germany, since it held out the prospects of the most inflation-adverse stance, filled the role of determining monetary policy within the snake. And this translated, against the diverging shock absorption capacities within the snake countries, into the need for frequent exchange rate adjustments and fluctuating memberships. The complete Werner design however, namely stages two and three, never got a real chance because of the unfavourable economic environment, i.e. the first oil-price shock with the upshot of high and diverse inflation rates in the countries involved. As a consequence, there were no signs whatsoever that European politicians were really interested in turning the 'snake cottage' into the 'EMU castle'. Rather, they chose individual strategies for coping with the economic problems as shown by the withdrawal of most Member States from the 'Snake': by 1978 (one year before the inception of the EMS) only five currencies remained.

Recalling the basic tenets of the Werner Report begs the question of how far it was a prelude to the Delors Committee's deliberations. Both advocated the development of EMU in three stages and a transfer of competences in the field of monetary and macroeconomic policy-making from the Member States to the Community. This did not really bode well for the Maastricht Treaty on EMU because, this time round, there was again a serious shock to the system: German unification, with diverging effects on the European economic and political landscape still characterized by remarkable idiosyncrasies. However, in order to understand how a no less ambitious project for forming a monetary union in the EC re-emerged nevertheless from the mothballs, we have to tell the story of the EMS.

...THE LESS AMBITIOUS EMS EDIFICE

The former German Chancellor Helmut Schmidt recalls that the idea for the implementation of a 'zone of increasing monetary stability within Europe' was conceived in a talk he had with the then President Valery Giscard d'Estaing in 1978. The focusing idea was a predominantly defensive one, viz. to shield the European economies from the vagaries of the US dollar thereby establishing a calculable context for intra-European trade. He refers to informal discussions during 1977 with a negative attitude by the former *Bundesbank* President Emminger and a positive one by the President of the EC Commission Roy Jenkins.[6] Deliberately, the Giscard-Schmidt initiative was started secretly and initially conceived outside the EC procedures. The concept, as fleshed out by

Bernard Clappier, then Governor of the *Banque de France*, who had already worked on the Schuman Plan, and Horst Schulmann, Schmidt's economic sherpa from the Federal Chancellery, was presented to the prospective and surprised partners in the project by the Giscard and Schmidt duet orally at a leisurely meeting of the European Council in the late spring of 1978 in Copenhagen. A hard-copy version of the Clappier-Schulmann-concept was however distributed just the evening before the Bremen meeting of the European Council on 6 and 7 July 1978. At the end of the day, the essentials of the initiative survived the horse trading concerning the asymmetry of the intervention mechanism and the more symbolic role of the European Currency Unit (ECU). The system started in March 1979.

On a timescale, three periods can be distinguished representing different far-reaching political goals. The years between 1979 and 1983 represent the adjustable peg phase, mainly directed at producing the international public good of orderly foreign exchanges for Europe. After 1983 and the failed experiment of a pump-priming Keynesianism in France, the system was used as a disinflation mechanism. Then, with the prospects of ever closer convergence of inflation and interest rates and the Basle-Nyborg agreement in September 1987 on buttressing the intervention and monetary cooperation capacities, the phase of a hardening exchange-rate commitment began. The years 1989 and 1990 saw the entry of the peseta and the British pound into the Exchange Rate Mechanism (ERM). And, as we know from hindsight, with its close to irrevocably fixed parities, the transitional phase one of Maastricht began in earnest. The underlying theory legitimizing this political stance was based on the *reputation thesis*. It held that a disinflation within a credible fixed-parity environment changes the wage-price dynamics and therefore makes price stability a less expensive good in terms of output and inflation foregone.

On a clean sheet, such a venture would have been guided by the prevailing economic arguments concerning the relative evaluation of exchange rate regimes. Basically, the starting assumption of those who advocate fixed exchange rates is that markets are in a habit of temporarily indulging in destabilizing, fundamentally non-motivated speculation. They consequently hold that these fluctuations are 'pointless and costly',[7] if you like: pure waste. Therefore, the traditional and thus politically relevant argument for fixing rates in a regional dimension evokes the positive effects that flow from the elimination of an additional element of uncertainty. More recent arguments firstly hold that fixing rates demonstrates the involved governments' resolve for macro-discipline and, secondly, deliver an automatic device for international monetary cooperation.

– Market-determined exchange rates, as far as they are taking leave of their fundamental determinants, might come at a cost: they could have negative effects on trade and investments and thus on overall economic growth. As far as anomalies, i.e. inexplicable things in foreign exchange markets happen, these increase the risks associated with those cross-border trades that have different time structures of delivery and payment. Importers, or exporters for that matter, have to deal with the uncertainty of the price they have to pay or they expect to receive. That should reduce trade volumes and thus narrow the scope for the welfare enhancing gains from international exchange. Moreover, covering this risk in the derivative markets comes at a cost. However, empirical results on the validity of these arguments are far from conclusive (CEC, 1990) and, if the relationship between exchange rates and trade volume is significant, the impact appears to be rather modest (De Grauwe, 1987). Still, since the liquidity of forward-looking instruments decreases as one tries to hedge further into the future, the power of this point raises along the time scale. As a consequence, exchange-rate uncertainty should be particularly harmful for long-term engagements with their inherent higher degree of pay-off volatility. This should raise the discount factor for investments, leading to an additional risk premium in interest rates. Thus, a potentially more relevant adverse effect might come from 'the decision-delaying effects of uncertainty' (Krugman, 1989, p. 68). This puts a premium on adjustment to changes in real exchange rates and makes for a very cautious attitude. Alas, because we are in lack of proxies, we end up with inconclusiveness. This, however, does *not* speak for a resounding endorsement of floating within Europe. The ominous data leave us, as usual, with some uneasy agnosticism.

    – The second pro-argument, which has been influential particularly in the European context, holds that a credible exchange-rate target adds some further credibility to the pursuit of a disinflation effort. This should change the wage-price formation since an accommodating stance of monetary policy becomes less probable. Again, the data seem to be not very friendly to the pro-view as disinflation appears to be a generalized phenomenon: the 1979-1983 experience in industrial countries shows that price stability can be restored without fixed exchange rates (IMF, 1984). And, as Dornbusch reasons, the correlation of the EMS and non-EMS countries quarterly inflation performance rose significantly during the 1980s. He correctly remarks that mining the data, again, is not a helpful approach to deciding on how far the EMS was causal for the European disinflation experience (Dornbusch, 1991). And, clearly Austria, which because of its *Deutsche mark*-orientation has been an informal EMS member since the early 1970s, is not the counterfactual that could elucidate the position of what would have happened if there had been no EMS. Coming again to an equivocal economic reasoning, we are inclined to buy the discipline argument because otherwise we would have had problems in coming to grips for instance with the clear-cut reorientation of economic policy in France or, as a further example, the bold elimination of the *scala mobile* in Italy.

    – The third argument builds upon the idea that fixed exchange rates are an institutionalized means of taking account of international interdependence.

Such a system would create more scope for mutually beneficial policy coordination. And this, in turn, should decrease the probability of competitive devaluations with a 'beggar-thy-neighbour flavour'. On the other hand, against different objective functions and diverging interpretations about how the world really works, it is very hard to argue the case for concerted policy consistently.[8] Our point, however, is that the institutions are a learning device with an impact on the objective function.

After all, there are no unambiguous answers on the shelf. And therefore one usually finds economists on both sides of the battlefield. What does a politician make of all this? If economics cannot settle the question, he takes his clues from non-economic criteria. To be sure, the former German Chancellor did not think of himself or Giscard d'Estaing as minor experts. And, clearly, they were aware of the abovementioned standard reasoning on the respective merits of floating versus fixing the exchange rate. Again, the decision could not be anything but politically motivated. According to Schmidt, the new start in the area of exchange rate management within Europe rested on the belief that the European economies were not in a position to cope individually with the turbulent external environment. In addition, Giscard d'Estaing and Raymond Barre, who were under heavy domestic fire since they were subjugating the French monetary autonomy in exchange for a deflationary policy, were particularly interested in the disciplinary features of the EMS.

Thus, if we reinterpret the economic situation prevailing around 1978, the arguments are so finely balanced that we can find no unequivocal economic justification for the creation of the EMS. Economic growth had regained its momentum after the recession of 1973/1975 and inflation rates, though still high, had started to decline relative to the accelerating price levels as an upshot of the first oil shock. Interestingly, the nagging unemployment problem was in some quarters even deemed to be less intractable under the auspices of European monetary cooperation: according to that view, it should enhance the scope for a more expansive demand management. Hence, the EMS was not perceived as a single-purpose device, viz. to combat inflation.

It is uncontroversial to state that the architects of the EMS were mainly interested in achieving political goals and, not in the last place, in conserving the 'European spirit' which seemed to have lost ground after the successful completion of the Customs Union. It should not go without notice that perhaps a major EC policy, the Common Agricultural Policy (CAP), could also have had a hand in the creation of the EMS. A large part of the EC budget for the CAP was absorbed by so-called Monetary Compensatory Amounts (MCA): a system of levies and restitutions designed to eliminate sudden price differences on the markets for agricultural products (Molle, 1990). The intervention prices were expressed in ECU and then had to be recalculated in national currencies, as the ECU was not legal tender, and fluctuations in the exchange rates impacted differently of course on the prices expressed in national currencies. As this would be incompatible with the notion of a common agricultural market, the MCA were set up. The MCA were abolished in line with the Mansholt Plan and, in a way, the EMS could be seen as an arrangement to replace the MCA as it (partially) fixed the EC exchange rates. One should not underrate this argument, firstly, because the CAP comprises two-thirds of the EC budget and, secondly, because France in particular (one of the two 'EMS architects') has always benefited more from the CAP than most of the other Member States.

EMS MARK I: PRODUCING ORDERLY MARKET CONDITIONS (1979-83)

The experience acquired in the first four years of the existence of the EMS, shows that discipline among the Member States in order to stabilize the exchange rates was far away. Table 1 gives an overview of the most important dates of the System. In the period 1979 until 1983 seven realignments took place, the largest on 22 March 1983 affecting all EMS currencies. The outcome of these realignments led to the creation of two currency blocks: one headed by the *Deutsche mark* with, in its footsteps, the Dutch guilder and the second, the so-called 'soft currency' block, of the French franc and the Italian lira, to a lesser extent followed (at least until the sixth realignment in 1982) by the Belgium franc, the Danish krona and the Irish pound. These developments reflected the diverging macro-policy stances in the countries involved.

From an economic point of view, the realignments were appropriate. When the economic fundamentals (e.g. prices) underlying the exchange rates change, the exchange rate itself should budge. For a currency which is a member of a managed exchange rate regime, there are two ways to cope with an excess of domestic inflation relative to the anchor currency: a hike in interest rate in order to fend off pressure on the currency or an offsetting devaluation which restores competitiveness to the original level. The latter policy reaction was preferred, especially during the early years of the EMS. There were no signs that devaluations were perceived as overly undesirable or costly in political terms (a notion that undermined the reputation hypothesis argument for the inception, however not the evolution of the EMS). But this option on flexibility, i.e. the possibility of realignments, came at a price: it was reflected in interest spreads across currencies and particularly harmful in countries with high public sector deficit ratios.

The frequent parity adjustments in the first four years provided grounds for the critics of the EMS to assume that the system in one way or another would collapse. They referred to the incompatibility of fixed exchange rates and the liberalization of capital flows, the latter being a clear Treaty obligation. It was assumed that the economic fundamentals were not in line and that only capital controls, as they existed in France, Italy and Belgium, could secure the smooth

Table 1:
The Chronology of the EMS

	Date	Currency	% Realignment
1979	13 March	Start of the EMS	
	24 September	DEM	+2
		DKK	-2.9
	3 December	DKK	-4.76
1981	23 March	ITL	-6
	5 October	DEM, NLG	+5.5
		FRF, ITL	-3
1982	22 February	BEF	-8.5
		DKK	-3
	14 June	DEM, NLG	+4.25
		ITL	-2.75
		FRF	-5.75
1983	22 March	DEM	+5.5
		NLG	+3.5
		DKK	+2.5
		BEF	+1.5
		FRF, ITL	-2.5
		IEP	-3.5
1985	22 July	BEF, DKK, DEM, FRF, IEP, NLG	+2
		ITL	-6
1986	7 April	DEM, NLG	+3
		BEF, DKK	+1
		FRF	-3
	4 August	IEP	-8
1987	12 January	DEM, NLG	+3
		BEF	+2
1989	19 June	Entry of ESP	
1990	8 January	ITL (narrow band)	-3.7
	8 October	Entry GBP	
1992	6 April	Entry PTE	
	14 September	ITL	-7.0
	16 September	ITL and GBP withdraw	
		ESP	-5.0
	22 November	PTE, ESP	-6.0

Source: Bank of England, 1992.

functioning of the EMS. Even the *Deutsche Bundesbank* expressed its concerns on this matter as it feared that the liberalization of capital flows in Germany would put high external constraints on its monetary policy. The opposite would come true as the non-German central banks increasingly experienced the anti-inflationary policy of the *Bundesbank* as an external constraint on their policy leeway. However, the nightmare (or for some, perhaps, a sweet dream) that the gradual liberalization of capital flows would imply the end of the EMS was, for the time being, not borne out. The main reason was the relative ineffectiveness of capital controls. Figures 1 and 2 show the development of off-shore and onshore interest rates.[9] If capital controls were to be effective, the interest rate differential ought to be persistently large. However, the differential is mostly close to zero, with the exception of some large peaks that coincide with the periods immediately proceeding realignments, but in a way these 'peaks' do nothing more than express the financial markets' concern about 'fundamentals' and about EMS parity rates not being in line. One reason for the possible ineffectiveness of capital controls are the incentives to shift terms of payments, the so-called 'leads and lags' (Gros and Thygesen, 1988): if interest rates are higher abroad, the exporters in the country expecting a devaluation have an incentive to delay ('lag') the repatriation of their revenues in foreign currency, while importers have an incentive to pay ('lead') their deliveries as soon as possible. However, since exchange rates are mainly driven by asset allocation decisions, the fragile, ever-changing equilibrium of expectations concerning the future course of policies appears to be more important.

EMS MARK II: THE DISINFLATION DEVICE (1983-1987)

The turning point in the more or less Shakespearean 'As you like it' policy which has characterized the EMS since its inception was the dissolving of the 'economic experiment' of the French socialist government. In 1981, François Mitterand was elected President and his socialist government embarked immediately on an expansionary fiscal policy. The hoped for upsurge in economic growth was not particularly impressive as most demand effects were exported abroad through higher French imports. As a result, the French current account deteriorated and hefty devaluations of the French franc in 1982 and 1983 became inevitable. After acknowledging the unsustainability of its programme, the French government made a policy orientation U-turn and, in order to steady the new course, committed itself to the EMS exchange rate target. Though less pronounced, similar reorientations in policy also took place in Belgium and Denmark. As a consequence, the 'soft currency' part of EMS shrank to the Italian lira and the Irish pound. This change in economic policy reflected to a large degree a tidal shift away from demand management strategies towards a more supply-oriented approach. The political reorientations in the

Figure 1:
Offshore/Onshore Interest Rate Differential (Italy)

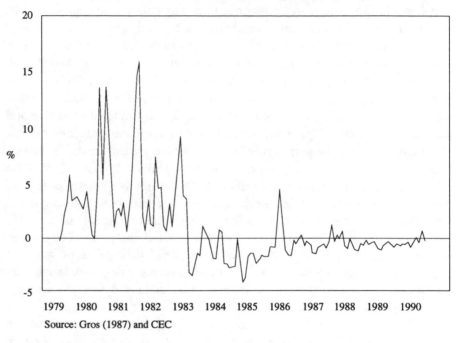

Source: Gros (1987) and CEC

Figure 2
Offshore/Onshore Interest Rate Differential (France)

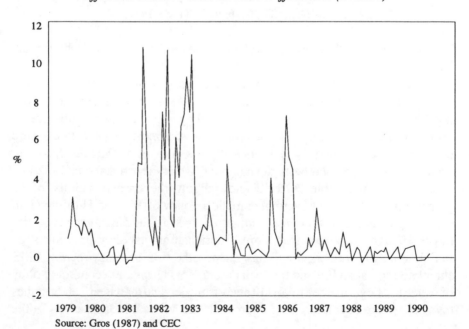

Source: Gros (1987) and CEC

United States and the United Kingdom, relying primarily upon markets – dubbed Reaganomics or Thatcherism – and aiming at long-term structural adjustments to the economy plus greater price stability, had their impact on other countries. In most of Europe, conservative governments were in power. By adding a strong dose of reliability to this pledge, viz. the explicit tying to the *Deutsche Bundesbank*'s approach, it was believed that attaining price stability would come at lower cost. Aiming at the EMS exchange rate targets which were determined by the strongest currency in the parity grid, the *Deutsche mark*, set the central banks free from *ad hoc* political interference and signalled that the accommodating of accelerating wage and price inflation was a thing of the past. As a result, the number of realignments decreased: between 1983 and 1987 there were only 4 realignments, most of them reflecting the weak position of the Italian lira. It seemed that all Member States had entered the same harbour, following the German flagship: convergence of inflation rates and interest rates was the result.

The economic theory underlying these developments was the *credibility or reputation hypothesis*, claiming that the exchange rate constraint dictated by the adherence to the *Bundesbank*-dominated ERM influenced inflation expectations in the private sector. The enhanced credibility of the commitment should accelerate the disinflation's speed while at the same time reduce its costs sharply, as measured in foregone output and employment. The potential gains to be reaped from relinquishing the national instruments in the monetary tool box by tying one's lot to the *Bundesbank* led also non-EMS countries to shadow the ECU (or the *Deutsche mark*). Empirical results on the validity of the credibility hypothesis, however, do not find too much evidence to support this view (Weber, 1991, Egebo and Englander, 1992). Still, the ERM was a device that fostered the reorientation of political priorities.

Between 1983 and 1989, the EMS experienced a significant change in substance. The system became more asymmetrical: the *Bundesbank* determined the monetary thrust within the ERM and the other n-1 Member States followed suit in order to stabilize their parity (Giavazzi and Giovannini, 1986 and 1989, Mastropasqua et al., 1988 and Bini Smaghi and Micossi, 1989). The existing yield spreads mainly reflected the respective devaluation expectations. And these were predominantly caused by the diverging anti-inflation performances. In other words, the EMS exhibited a comparatively low degree of real exchange rate variability. As a consequence, those members who had to cope with a credibility *malus* were struggling with higher, growth-dampening real interest rates. Nominal yield convergence therefore came at the price of a reduction in economic activities and thus higher unemployment. Against the background of sticky prices and some persistence in price-level movements, the idea of a trade-off between an anti-inflationary stance and the goal of a sustainable level of employment (i.e. the 'Philips curve argument') has re-entered the scene. Table

2 below produces some tentative data on the sacrifice ratios (i.e. the short- to medium-term loss of employment caused by disinflation) for two subsequent periods for ERM and non-ERM countries.

Table 2:
Sacrifice Ratios[1] in Two Periods of Disinflation
Own computations, based upon OECD data

INITIAL ERM COUNTRIES	1974-1978	1981-1989
Belgium	-2.4	-10.5
Denmark	-2.5	-3.2
Germany	-1.8	-10.5
France	-1.4	-2.7
Ireland	-1.5	-4.7
Italy	-0.6	-1.9
Netherlands	-1.6	-7.8
SOME NON-ERM COUNTRIES	**1974-1978**	**1981-1989**
United Kingdom	-1.3	-3.2
Japan	-0.1	-0.7
United States	-1.7	-0.2
Austria	-0.2	-3.8
Switzerland	-0.1	-3.0
Finland	-1.0	-0.3
Norway	-1.0	-1.7

[1] The sacrifice ratios give the cumulative rise in unemployment rates in each period necessary to reduce inflation by one percentage point.

This table tentatively suggests, firstly, that the original EMS countries in the period 1981-1989 compared to the years between 1974-1978 appear not to have been able to contain the disinflation's nasty side-effects. Secondly, the table tells us as well that the EMS countries did not perform significantly better than the non-EMS countries, as evidenced by comparing the upper and lower halves.

Hence, in the data above, no supporting piece of evidence for the credibility hypothesis is detectable.

What is more, the relatively long time it takes interest rates to converge seems further to confirm the slow-motion build-up of credibility in the system. It appeared that the financial markets were not very confident of the 'follower' policy of the EMS central banks and they demanded a quite substantial risk premium on investments in currencies other than the *Deutsche mark*. How could they? After all, this was the phase when the EMS was predominantly conceived as a fixed, but still adjustable peg. As a matter of fact, the tight monetary policy of most central banks and, consequently, the forthcoming high (nominal) interest rates were a drag on the economic performance of the non-German EMS countries. Devaluations to cream the upward drift on interest rates would, however, have been self-defeating in the reputation building context. In the long-run, as experience overwhelmingly teaches us, a devaluation of the currency usually turns out to be counterproductive. The Netherlands' experience, for instance, is no exception to that rule. In the 1983 realignment, the Dutch guilder was only revalued by 3.5 per cent compared to a 5.5 per cent realignment of the *Deutsche mark*. This slight relative devaluation of the Dutch guilder perhaps benefited competitiveness in a short-term dimension. It came, however, at the cost of adding a further credibility *malus* to the Dutch interest rates and thus lengthened the path towards nominal convergence.

EMS MARK III: NO MORE REALIGNMENTS

Indeed, the circumstances under which the EMU debate started again in the second half of the 80s were characterized by a shift in consensus on the ends and means of economic policy. But there is more to it than that: the story has a real side too. Monetary union, says Jacques Delors, would put a second tiger in the European tank, the first being the Single Market, the '1992 Project'. In 1985, the White Paper on the completion of the internal market was adopted by the European Council in Milan. And this common market, with its free flow of goods, capital, people and services, was wetting the appetite for more. The President of the Commission relaunched the idea of an Economic and Monetary Union in Europe as a follow-up to the '1992 programme': one market needs one money. In the Delors Report of 1989 on Monetary Union as well as in the Treaty of Maastricht itself, the EMS was assigned an active role in the transition towards the final stage of EMU. The up to then successful strategy of creating points of no return – the journey to EMU is indeed designed as a step-by-step evolution of ERM – produced a situation where Europe apparently could only advance towards a common currency or face retreat, i.e. a vicious tendency towards fragmentation. EMS Mark III and EMU appear to be fatally linked.

Add to this the German unification in 1990, which produced dramatic effects in our dialectically intertwined spheres of politics and economics. Fears of political domination by the new colossus, as Germany was perceived, led to the conclusion that an acceleration and intensification of the European unification process were the only means to cope with the looming political disequilibrium and to tie Germany down. In the economic field, the unification amounted to a deficit-financed boost to an economy working close to capacity. The *Bundesbank*, determined to contain the inflationary consequences of this development, raised its interest rates in order to avoid a persistent deterioration in the *Deutsche mark*'s purchasing power. The ensuing tightening of the monetary stance led to a real appreciation *vis-à-vis* the US dollar. In the US, in turn, the Fed. had for years been cutting interest rates to revitalize demand and investment. This divergence caused the *Deutsche mark* to rise and the US dollar to plunge, putting weaker currencies in the ERM under strain.

In the beginning of the 1990s, worldwide economic growth began to falter. Economic hopes had to be discounted with the incoming quarterly crop of data. The nominal convergence within the EMS came to an end and since 1989 even a divergent trend can be observed. This was a potentially destructive source of further stress in the EMS. We will take up this point below. On the other hand, politics tried to overcome the turbulences and spillovers from Eastern Europe by deepening Western European integration particularly, but not exclusively, in the economic and monetary area. Resorting to the EMS as a launching pad, the EMU designers have taken into account the potential fragility of the EMS arrangement. The result was the setting of tough criteria with regard to the fight against inflation, sustainable public finances and bond market convergence.

Losing Momentum: EMU's *finale tragique* in the Summer of 1992?

Concerning the economics and politics of 'Maastricht' in EMU, we turn elliptical, since these crucial questions will be thoroughly addressed in the following chapters. What is important to us, however, is the establishment of a belief, even ahead of the signing of the Maastricht Treaty in December 1991, that a criteria-based process towards an Economic and Monetary Union (EMU) had been credibly launched. Capital markets as aggregators of profit-minded investors are in the business of deciphering the future as far as it has a bearing on the pricing of financial assets. Such forward-looking institutions thus influence, by acting on anticipated developments, what is happening in the respective present. Therefore, from a bond valuation point of view, the set-up of the prospective European System of Central Banks (ESCB) and the membership qualifiers with regard to the enforcement of macro-discipline in the domain of fiscal and monetary policy were decisive for the allocation across countries. EMU, since it held out the perspective of a monetary authority as independent and as inflation averse as the *Bundesbank*, promised a significant and differentiated fall of inflation rates in the participating countries – finally towards the German level. As a result, bond yields should fall as well and converge, again towards the German floor. Therefore, from an allocation point of view, this emphasized the attractiveness of markets where the divergence from the anchoring *Deutsche mark* was greatest. Of course, a substantial part of the yield spread relative to the *Deutsche mark* was an expression of the expected realignment risk in the respective currency. However, since the 'Maastricht process' hardened the commitment to the exchange rate target – prospective members were required to remain within the parity grid without severe tension and without devaluation two years prior to stage three – the convergence process as an investment theme gained momentum.

We would like to propose that the changing appraisal of the credibility of this story is a crucial element in the run up to the EMS crisis in the late summer of 1992. Here we rely on anecdotal evidence, but we believe that for this type of evaluation the dialectic between economics and politics is of literally critical importance. In other words, the changing fortunes of 'Maastricht' in the public debate and thus the varying probability of its actual implementation were closely reflected in the pricing of bonds denominated in Europe's different monies, including the basket dubbed ECU.

Arguably and nicely in line with our main point, the acceleration of European history, and particularly German unification – thus, pure politics – contributed decisively to relaunching the EMU concept.[10] However, as the Werner Plan failed due to a turbulent international environment, the economic implications of the unification shock seemed to have undermined the 'Maastricht plot'. Economically, German unification translated into a dramatic decline in Eastern German output. However, consumption and capital expenditures in the five new *Länder* was held up on the basis of massive deficit-financed transfers. The implicit large gap in the regional current account was primarily reflected in a huge hole in Germany's public sector budgets (in all their guises) plus a dramatic swing in the current account. It translated into a shift in aggregate demand mainly in favour of German goods. In the first round, the positive spill-overs from the buoyed aggregate German demand had positive impacts on those EMS partners that were economically closely linked to the German economy. After a while, the dampening effects of the levelling up of (ex-post) real interest rates in a more or less depressed economic environment scaled down the activity level in the EMS countries. The boost to an economy already steaming at full capacity added significantly to the underlying inflation. This, however, was unacceptable to the *Bundesbank* which tightened its monetary reins. In the textbook world of flexible rates, such a set-up of monetary and fiscal policy would initially prop up real interest rates, lead to a real appreciation and a deterioration in the current account. (Then, after an extended medium run, to ensure a rebalancing of capital flows towards a level reflecting the underlying relationship between productivity of capital and domestically generated savings, the real exchange rate should depreciate.) Relative to the non-EMS world, the first part of this story has more or less materialized. However, within the ERM, the contained real appreciation and ratcheting-up of real interest rates in the face of a world recession and an ever softer US dollar created increasing tensions.

Here we have one of those shocks that impact asymmetrically on the ERM region and where, as a consequence, a revaluation of the *Deutsche mark* would be economically well advised. As a matter of fact, the *Bundesbank* clamoured to no avail and ahead of 'Maastricht' for a realignment. This, however, would have amounted to a hefty discount of the investments in credibility that supported the current ERM cross-rates, the political freezing of which (i.e. the lack of political will to adjust rates) had made realignments impossible in the years before. Furthermore, it would have signalled to the price-setters that, after all, some accommodation was still possible. In other words, it would have been tantamount to a loosening of the institutionalized disinflation squeeze. Moreover, it would have stressed again, and this is a political point, the '*superiorité éclatante*' of German monetary policy. On balance, here again, muddy politics overcame pure economics. However, with the petering out of the demand boosting and growth-driving spillovers from German unification in the ERM area, the locking into an unsustainably high-interest environment (real rates far above potential growth) became ever more crippling. Thus, the faltering public support and an emerging zapping of the momentum towards EMU finally reminded the markets that there was no such thing as a permanently fixed parity.

It is noteworthy, however, that in the autumn of 1991 and then for more than half a year – a historical dimension for short-lived activities in capital markets – the EMS straitjacket appeared to loosen. On 5 May 1992, in a front-page piece, *Le Monde* even launched the idea of a French franc revaluation – after 14 depreciations since 1944 as the journal recalled on 7 July 1992. Finally, the French paper added, France behaved more reasonably relative to a Germany that was handicapped by its unification, in all the relevant dimensions: be it inflation performance, fiscal policy or external trade. The *Financial Times* piggy-packed on that idea and wrote in a leader on 6 May 1992 that 'Mr Major's finest hour might be at hand' because the just installed Conservative government might lead a cut in European interest rates and possibly start the process towards a dipping below the German (interest) line. The background melody to this tune was a nasty public sector strike in Germany. The famous consensus seemed to evaporate. A cohesion wearing thin, to be sure, would add significantly to the problems emanating from unification. And on the premise that the *Bundesbank* would be forced into accommodation, at long last, there seemed to be a real chance that the German interest rate floor could be pierced, due to 'Maastricht'.

Then, however, came the Danish *Nej*. This was from a capital markets' perspective decisive since it spoiled the prevailing investment theme: with an increasing emphasis international investors had overweighted their positions in those currencies that were expected to profit most from a convergence towards the German level of interest rates. The reasoning behind this repositioning was that for those who wanted to participate in EMU from scratch, 'Maastricht' implied a hardening of the constraints imposed by the Exchange Rate Mechanism and this increasing credibility ultimately implied an outperformance in currencies with higher yields. The ECU market took as well a bet on the qualifying participants: this basket of currencies (and the potential European currency) traded since the beginning of 1991 significantly below the theoretical yield as a weighted average of its components. As a consequence, in the wake of the Danish referendum, the 'Maastricht story' became implausible. Therefore, spreads over German rates again rose significantly.

The increasing reluctance towards 'Maastricht', combined with one or two domestic reasons, led President Mitterand briefly after the Danish vote to call a referendum on the French decision as well. On 16 July, in the face of an overshooting money supply, the *Bundesbank* tightened its squeeze a further notch. It conspicuously used the discount rate with less of a cross-border effect. However, the heat in the European monetary kitchen was increasing. Unfortunately, the probability of a positive outcome of the French referendum for the 'Maastricht' supporters drew continuously smaller. In order to stop the tide, a peculiar marketing to sell the 'Yes to Maastricht' developed: 'Maastricht' was according to some synonymous with a 'Versailles without a war' *(Le Figaro,* 18 September 1992) and to others the rejection would be comparable to a *'Munich politique'* (*Le Monde*, 3 September 1992).

Finally, the French voted with a very slim *oui*. In the meantime, however, the market had just lost its faith. This forced the *Bundesbank* to intervene heavily in order to keep the ERM afloat. Overwhelmed by the selling pressure, the *Bundesbank* appeared at long last to give in when it struck the unfortunate deal of 14 September 1992: lira devaluation in exchange for a small reduction in its Lombard rate to 9.5 per cent. The ensuing speculative attack on the lira and then the British pound became irresistible. Markets engaged in this one-way bet, because the profits to be reaped in testing the guts of the implied administrations were tremendous. On Black Wednesday alone, a major UK bank's dealing in the British pound rose more than fivefold. And to raise interest rates in the face of the deepest slump since the thirties to unsustainable heights was not an option bought by the market. The suspension of the British pound from the ERM meant for the British government that it was left without its economic script. This was, perhaps, the most important reason for the ensuing 'war of words' between the British and the Germans and the ferocious attacks on the nearest European scapegoat, the *Bundesbank*.

Then, however, endowed with the profits from the attack on the British pound, markets turned towards the French franc. *Le Monde* (on 23 September 1992) saw German solidarity put to a crucial test. Fortunately, with the help of tremendous intervention, 'Germany and France (held) the Maginot Line' *(Wall Street Journal,* 28 September 1992). At the end of the day, the *Bundesbank* decided to give up on its intermediate money supply target and opted for an interest stabilization programme with short-term rates some 100 basis points below their level before the currency upheavals. It made very clear its resolve to defend the hard core of the system – and put its money where its mouth was. This has been, as those who watch the *Bundesbank* can evaluate, no minor shift of tack.

The New Synthesis between Economics and Politics – A Scaling Down of EMU Ambitions

To sum up with a rough answer to a brief question, which will be taken up at the end of this book, namely: What's next? After the turmoil, it is clear that a comprehensive concept of 'Maastricht', viz. an encompassing monetary union for all EC members, has been hit for a long shot or even gone for good. However, this does not necessarily entail a swing of the pendulum towards monetary fragmentation. We are left with the defended core of the ERM. And this makes markets ponder and bet on a smaller monetary union (SMU). Such an SMU should not come as a great surprise, since 'Maastricht' on a realistic interpretation incorporated a multi-track approach. Nevertheless, an SMU, as one might sketch it along pure economic lines of reasoning, seems implausible on political grounds. Mainly because, from a French perspective, it would amount to participating in a German dominated block. France's entire mission in pushing for EMU to get the Germans out of the driver's seat and to regain influence over Europe's monetary policy would have failed.

While the odds are in favour of an ultimate ratification of the Maastricht Treaty, however, to accommodate the Danes and the British, in an attenuated version, the automatism foreseen for the gradual move from freezing the ERM to setting up EMU will not work the way it was conceived. Therefore, the fall-back position is the ERM. Of course, with its asymmetric features, it is a politically fragile construct (Bofinger, 1992, p. 457). On the other hand, the alternative, namely regressing towards a flexible system of floating exchange rates within Europe, is clearly less than enticing. Therefore, the most plausible scenario entails a relaunching of monetary integration, however on a deferred time-scale and patterned along a hardening strategy which is the lesson of the most recent developments within the EMS. A fully fledged EMU seems to be an option far out of the market. It would, therefore, be surprising if we were to witness such a development on this side of the year 2000 horizon.

NOTES

1. Art. 104 to 107, EEC Treaty.
2. See on this point Delors, Jacques (1992, pp. 280).
3. For a comprehensive overview, see Molle (1990); for summaries, see also Ungerer et al. (1990), appendix III, Kindleberger 1984, Ch. 24 and Gros/Thygesen (1992), Ch. 1 and 2.
4. Here we indulge in the debatable habit, though customary in monetary integration literature, of disregarding reform proposals concerning the longer-side of the financial system. In this area, which is interestingly regarded as belonging to the real side of the story, the Segré-Report of the mid-sixties was a precursor to financial integration as conceived in the internal market project.
5. Here conclusive anecdotal evidence is produced in the recently published memoires of two major players, i.e. Valéry Giscard d'Estaing and Helmut Schmidt (see his 1990 book, pp. 247-72).
6. Schmidt here is probably alluding to the speech at the European University Institute in Florence in 1977.
7. See for a very concise reasoning, Krugman, Paul (1989); see also Krugman, Paul and Maurice Obstfeld (1988, Ch. 19).
8. Moreover, policy coordination as such can also take place in a system of floating rates or, to be more precise, in a system of dirty floating.
9. Differential between the interest rates of three-month deposits in FRF and ITL on the domestic interbank markets and the Euro-markets.
10. See on this point, from a French perspective, Vernet, Daniel (1992) and Giesbert, F.-O. (1990). Actually, M. Bérégovoy proposed this speeding up of the European integration a few days after the fall of the Berlin Wall in a speech given in Frankfurt.

REFERENCES

Bank of England, *Fact Sheet*, July 1992.

Bini Smaghi, L., and Micossi, Stefano, 'Managing Exchange Rates in the EMS with Free Capital', *Banca Nazionale del Lavoro Quarterly Review*, no. 171, 1989, pp. 395-430.

Bofinger, Peter, 'Europäische Zentralbank versus Europäisches Währungsystem', *Wirtschaftsdienst*, 9, 1992, pp. 457-463.

Commission of the European Communities (CEC), 'One Market, One Money: An Evaluation of the Potential Benefits and Costs of Forming an Economic and Monetary Union', *European Economy*, no. 44, (Brussels: 1990).

De Grauwe, Paul, 'International Trade and Economic Growth in the European Monetary System', *European Economic Review*, no. 31, 1987, pp. 389-398.

Delors, Jacques, '1992 et l'héritage de l'histoire', 1989, in Delors, Jacques, *Le Nouveau Concert Européen* (Paris: 1992).

Dornbusch, Rudiger, 'Problems of European Monetary Integration', in Giovannini, A. and Mayer, C. (eds), *European Financial Integration* (Cambridge: 1991), pp. 305-327.

Egebo, Thomas and Englander, A. Steven, 'Institutional Commitments and Policy Credibility: A Critical Survey and Empirical Evidence From the ERM', *OECD Economic Studies*, no. 18, 1992.

Giavazzi, Francesco and Giovannini, Alberto, 'The EMS and the Dollar', *Economic Policy*, vol. 2, 1986, pp. 455-485.

Giavazzi, Francesco and Giovannini, Alberto, *Limiting Exchange-Rate Flexibility*, (Cambridge, Massachussetts: MIT Press, 1989).

Gros, Daniel, 'The Effectiveness of Capital Controls: Implications for Monetary Autonomy in the Presence of Incomplete Market Separation', *IMF Staff Papers*, no. 34, (Washington DC: International Monetary Fund, 1987), pp. 621-642.

Gros, Daniel and Thygesen, Niels, 'The EMS: Achievements, Current Issues and Directions for the Future', *CEPS Paper*, no. 35, (Brussels: 1988).

Gros, Daniel and Thygesen, Niels, *European Monetary Integration. From the European Monetary System to European Monetary Union* (London: Longman, 1992).

International Monetary Fund, 'The Exchange Rate System: Lessons from the Past and Options for the Future', *Occasional Paper*, no. 30, (Washington DC: IMF, 1984).

Kindleberger, Charles P., *A Financial History of Western Europe* (London: 1984).

Krugman, Paul, 'The Case for Stabilizing Exchange Rates', *Oxford Economic Review of Economic Policy*, vol. 5, 1989, no. 3, pp. 61-72.

Krugman, Paul and Maurice Obstfeld, *International Economics, Theory and Policy* (Glenview: 1988).

Mastropasqua, Cristina, Micossi, Stefano, and Rinaldi, Roberto, 'Intervention, Sterilization and Monetary Policy in European Monetary System Countries 1979-1987', in Giavazzi, Francesco (ed.), *The European Monetary System*, (Cambridge: Cambridge University Press, 1988), pp. 252-291.

Mathieu, Catherine and Henri Sterdyniak, 'Vers une monnaie commune en Europe?', *Revue de l'OFCE*, January 1989.

Molle, Willem, *The Economics of European Integration (Theory, Practice, Policy*, (Dartmouth: Aldershot, 1990).

Padoa-Schioppa, Tomaso, 'European Capital Markets Between Liberalization and Restrictions',1982, in CEC (1985): 'Money, Economic Policy and Europe', *The European Perspectives Series* (Brussels: 1982).

Schmidt, Helmut, *Die Deutschen und ihre Nachbarn* (Berlin: 1990).

Ungerer, Horst et al., 'The European Monetary System: Developments and Perspectives', *Occasional Paper*, no. 73 (Washington DC: IMF, 1990).

Weber, Axel, 'Reputation and Credibility in the European Monetary System', *Economic Policy*, no. 12, April 1991, pp. 57-89.

MASTERING MAASTRICHT:
EMU ISSUES AND HOW THEY WERE SETTLED

Alexander Italianer*

Introduction

The Treaty on European Union,[1] which was signed in Maastricht on 7
February 1992 after a political agreement was reached on 10 December 1991,
is the conclusion of the work of two parallel Intergovernmental Conferences:
one on European Political Union (EPU), and one on Economic and Monetary
Union (EMU). Although a number of articles in the new Treaty can be
considered as horizontal, i.e. linked both to EPU and EMU, the EMU part is
clearly distinct from the rest of the Treaty.[2] The new Treaty has been
submitted by the governments of the Member States to their national
parliaments for ratification, and will enter into force after ratification by all
Member States, but not earlier than 1 January 1993. A difference between the
EPU and the EMU parts of the Treaty is that some provisions on EMU are
applicable at a later date than the Treaty itself. This is due to the fact that EMU
is to be achieved in three stages, and the provisions concerned are only
applicable in the later stages. Stage one started on 1 July 1990, but stage two
will only start on 1 January 1994, while stage three will start at the latest on
1 January 1999 (see Table 1).

Whereas the formal EMU negotiations took less than one year (the
opening meeting took place during the European Council meeting in Rome
on 14-15 December 1990), the EMU Treaty must be seen as the fruit of very
long preparations which started more than 20 years ago and received fresh
impetus from the Delors report published in April 1989.[3] This long preparation
should at least have provided the opportunity to reach a large degree of
consensus before the actual start of the negotiations. Indeed, one may say that
this was the case for a number of issues, but certainly not all. The question is:

---

* Helpful comments from Helmut Wittelsberger, Pieter Jan Kuijper and Alison
  Molders are gratefully acknowledged. The views expressed in this chapter are
  those of the author.

K. Gretschmann (ed.), Economic and Monetary Union: Implications for National Policy-Makers, 51–113.

Table 1:
Overview of Stages of EMU

Stage 1 – Before ratification of new Treaty (from 1 July 1990):

– Liberalization of capital movements inside Community
– Multilateral surveillance procedure for economic policy coordination
– Strengthened monetary cooperation

Stage 1 – After ratification of new Treaty (1993):

– Freezing of currency composition ECU basket
– Irrevocable commitment to single currency (ECU)
– Reinforced multilateral surveillance in the context of broad guidelines for economic policies and convergence programmes of Member States

Stage 2 – From 1 January 1994:

– Liberalization of capital movements to or from third countries
– Prohibition on direct access to central banks and on privileged access to financial institutions for the financing of public deficits
– No bail-out rule for Member States
– Start of procedure to avoid excessive public deficits (non-binding)
– Continued balance-of-payments support
– European Monetary Institute (EMI) set up, prepares complete framework for stage three
– Start of process leading to independent central banks

Stage 2 – After decision on start date Stage 3 (before 1 July 1998):

– Establishment of ESCB and ECB and adoption of necessary legislation

Stage 3 – 1 January 1999 at the latest:

– Irrevocable fixing of exchange rates, followed by introduction of ECU as single currency
– Single monetary policy conducted by independent ECB
– Single exchange rate policy determined between Council of Ministers and ECB
-- Binding procedure (including sanctions) aimed at avoiding excessive public deficits.

'Why not?' With the benefit of hindsight, several reasons may be invoked why in some cases agreement was only reached at the last minute. This chapter will not give a day-to-day 'when' of certain agreements. In some sense, nothing was agreed until the Heads of State and Government reached their overall accord in Maastricht on 10 December 1991: even a complete EMU agreement could, at the last minute, have been stalled in the absence of an agreement on Political Union. Rather than concentrating fully on the time perspective, the chapter tries to give an account of the 'why' of the most important Treaty provisions. In doing so, a certain time perspective is indispensable, but it will be limited to some of the 'landmarks' of the process leading to EMU, which are given in Table 2, and which will be used to structure the content of the chapter.[4]

Table 2:
Main Steps in EMU Negotiations

February 1988	Memoranda from Balladur (1988) and Genscher (1988)
June 1988	European Council in Hanover gives mandate to Delors Committee
April 1989	Publication Delors report[1]
June 1989	Delors report accepted by European Council in Madrid as a basis for the Intergovernmental Conference
October 1989	Guigou report
July 1990	Report of the Monetary Committee[2]
August 1990	Commission communication on EMU[3]
October 1990	Conclusion of European Council in Rome on mandate for EMU IGC
November 1990	Draft statutes of the ESCB and the ECB[4]
December 1990	Draft Treaty of the Commission[5]
	Opening of IGC in Rome during European Council meeting
June 1991	Draft Treaty non-paper presented by Luxembourg Presidency[6]
October 1991	Formal EMU Treaty proposal of Dutch Presidency[7]
February 1992	Signing of Treaty on European Union in Maastricht

(1) Committee for the study of Economic and Monetary Union (1989).
(2) Monetary Committee (1990).
(3) Commission of the EC (1990).
(4) Europe Documents, no. 1669/1670, 8 December 1990.
(5) Intergovernmental Conferences: Contributions by the Commission, Bulletin of the European Communities, Supplement 2/91.
(6) Europe Documents, no. 1722/1723, 5 July 1991.
(7) Europe Documents, no. 1740/1741, 4-5 November 1991.

In order to understand the 'why' of the EMU Treaty, one has to recognize that it constitutes a multidimensional representation of the interests of certain groups, each of which was more or less successful in ensuring that its views were taken into consideration.

– The *Community*: the interest of the Community can be considered as both the starting point and the end of the negotiations, due to the strong political will to further deepen European integration and to conclude the negotiations successfully.

– The *EMU conference* itself: due to the parallel conference on Political Union, certain horizontal issues came up which needed coordination of views between the two conferences.

– The *Community institutions*: the EMU Treaty was negotiated by representatives of the Member States and was therefore implicitly in the hands of the Council of Ministers. Due to the participation of the Commission in the negotiations and as a result of the interinstitutional conferences held between the Council, the Commission and the European Parliament, the institutional equilibrium between these institutions and other bodies involved was an important negotiating issue.

– The *ECOFIN Council*: since the EMU Treaty was negotiated by the finance ministers, who usually meet in the Council on Economic and Financial Affairs (ECOFIN Council), they wanted to secure, in some instances, a proper role for the ECOFIN Council, as opposed to other compositions of the Council, or as concerns the Heads of State and Government.

– The *Member States*: the political or economic interests of the Member States were undoubtedly the preponderant factor in shaping the result which was finally reached at Maastricht.

– The *advisory committees*: the Committee of Governors of the Central Banks of the Member States and the Monetary Committee played an important advisory role which was interlinked with their own interests.

– Different *authorities inside the Member States*: in some instances, differences of interest between finance ministries and the national central banks or between central and local government played a role.

– The *markets*: the reactions of the markets, notably financial markets, were to some extent a factor which was taken into account in the negotiations.

– The *academic world*: the EMU process launched a vivid debate on many different aspects of EMU, some parts of which re-appeared in the negotiations.

– The *citizens*: the smallest of the units representing an interest were not forgotten in the negotiations.

The mere existence of these players of different sizes and characteristics makes an accurate description of the 'why' of each of the Treaty provisions an impossible task, if only because views will differ on the main driving force behind certain articles. Nevertheless, the possible interests of particular players may be recalled in certain specific cases.

The remainder of this chapter is organized as follows: the second section gives a brief historical account of monetary integration in the Community up to the Delors report. The third section describes the EMU discussions up to the start of the negotiations, in particular the conclusions of the October 1990 European Council in Rome, and the Commission's draft Treaty. In the fourth section, the results of the negotiations under the Luxembourg Presidency are outlined. This led to a draft Treaty text presented in June 1991, which formed the basis for the remainder of the negotiations. The fifth section starts by discussing the first part of the negotiations under the Dutch Presidency which culminated in a formal treaty proposal on 28 October 1991. This still left a considerable number of outstanding issues which were only finalized just before or during Maastricht, which are also discussed in this section. In the final section, some issues will be raised that are still outstanding in the run-up to establishing a single currency before the end of the century.

Monetary Integration in Europe up to the Delors Report

Monetary integration in the Community is an issue which is almost as old as the Treaty of Rome. As early as 1961, the Commission proposed a monetary union as part of its action programme for the second stage of the Common Market.[5] The achievement of the Customs Union ahead of schedule in July 1968 was followed in February 1969 by a Commission memorandum proposing Economic and Monetary Union (EMU). On the basis of this memorandum, the summit in The Hague in December 1969 decided to draft a plan through which the Community would develop by stages into an EMU, and it instructed a group, chaired by the Luxembourg Prime Minister and Minister of Finance, Pierre Werner, to draw up this plan. On the basis of the Werner Plan,[6] which envisaged the creation of EMU in three stages before the end of the 1970s, a resolution of the Council and of the representatives of the Member States was adopted in March 1971, expressing their political will to establish an EMU in the coming decade.[7] In April 1972, an exchange rate agreement ('the Snake') began, which was to lead a rather turbulent and unsuccessful existence.[8] In October 1972, the Heads of State and Government reaffirmed their political resolve to move to EMU with a transition to the second stage on 1 January 1974, and its complete realization by 31 December 1980 at the latest,[9] and a European Monetary Cooperation Fund was set up.[10] Later, in 1974, the Council adopted a decision aimed at the convergence of economic policies which was to serve as the basis for economic policy coordination.[11] Until the end of the decade, these were the main concrete achievements of an EMU which did not develop any further.

Several factors may be deemed responsible for the failure to achieve EMU before the end of 1980, as originally planned. As regards the EMU process itself, the most important factor seems to have been the absence of a credible commitment in terms of legal texts and agreements. The major difference in this respect with the current EMU Treaty is that the latter is not a political statement from which governments can deviate according to circumstances, but a strong legal commitment to a single currency in the form of an international treaty. The second factor which impeded a successful transition to a full-blown EMU by 1980 must be found in external circumstances. In particular, the demise of the Bretton Woods system with the move to flexible exchange rates, the oil price shock of 1973/74 and the 1975 recession, created extremely unfavourable circumstances for establishing a system of irrevocably fixed exchange rates. Some of these factors were cyclical (although perhaps provoked more directly by non-cyclical factors such as the Yom Kippur war), but others were clearly fundamental changes in the economic system, or changes in 'regime'. Moreover, it is clear that the Member States had different policy preferences regarding the output-inflation trade-off. An important question, to be discussed below, is indeed whether similar factors could again turn up in the 1990s and hamper or accelerate the achievement of EMU agreed upon in Maastricht.

Monetary integration in Europe was launched again, inspired by a speech from the President of the European Commission, Roy Jenkins (1977), through the Schmidt-Giscard d'Estaing initiative on the creation of the European Monetary System (EMS), formalized in the March 1979 agreement[12] linking the exchange rates of – the then – eight Member States, excluding the UK, through a system of fixed but adjustable parities with limited fluctuation margins in the Exchange Rate Mechanism (ERM), with at its centre the European Currency Unit (ECU), a basket of all Community currencies.[13]

In its early stages, most observers were very sceptical regarding the EMS. This scepticism was fuelled by the second oil crisis at the end of 1979 and the rekindling of inflation. Gradually, however, there was a basic change in attitude towards inflation and towards the devaluation instrument, and a readiness emerged to accept the *Deutsche mark* as an anchor. Consequently, the role of the EMS as a modest attempt in the direction of more stable exchange rates was reinforced during the 1980s, such that it became increasingly the framework for monetary stability. This attracted new members into the ERM and saw a decline in both the number of realignments and the extent to which price differentials were compensated.[14] On the economic side, this enhanced monetary cooperation was joined in 1985 by the Commission's White Paper[15] proposing the completion of the internal market before the end of 1992, which became the basis for a large number of legislative proposals adopted by new procedures resulting from the Single European Act signed in 1986. A few years after the take-off of the internal market programme, its success became clear and this, combined with the success of the EMS, led the Hanover European Council in June 1988 to conclude that the internal market process was 'irreversible', and to ask a committee of experts, chaired by Jacques Delors, President of the European Commission, to study and propose 'concrete stages leading towards Economic and Monetary Union'. This decision of the European Council was certainly inspired by the memoranda from the German Minister for Foreign Affairs, Genscher, and the French Minister for Economic and Financial Affairs, Balladur.

For an understanding of the recommendations in the Delors report, it is important to assess the composition of the Delors Committee itself. It consisted of the twelve governors of the central banks of the Member States, three independent experts, and the President of the Commission, each person acting in a personal capacity. Notwithstanding this last fact, the strong presence of central bankers in the committee can be traced back in the report. It should also be noted, however, that the fact that the central bankers acted in a personal capacity meant that they could sidestep certain of their governments' views allowing, for instance, the Governor of the Bank of England to sign a report advocating a single currency without this being the objective of the British Government.

The structure of the Delors report is almost the same as that of the EMU Treaty, for which it served as a basis. It sets out the content of Economic and Monetary Union in the final stage of EMU and the institutional requirements, ending by describing the transitional stages to EMU, of which there would have to be three, as in the Werner Plan.

Monetary Union is defined in the report as consisting of complete currency convertibility, complete liberalization of capital flows, the integration of financial markets and the irrevocable fixing of exchange rates, leading to the introduction of a single currency. This would lead to a common monetary policy executed by a new institution, the European System of Central Banks (ESCB). The ESCB should have price stability as its primary objective, and should support general economic policy subject to that objective. It should be entrusted with the formulation and implementation of monetary policy, implement the Community's exchange rate policy, manage the pooled exchange reserves and coordinate banking supervision. The ESCB should have a federal structure, consisting of a Council, a Board, and the national central banks as executing branches of the system. Furthermore, it should be independent, but be accountable for its policy to the European Parliament and the European Council.

These recommendations of the Delors Committee seem strongly influenced by the presence of central bankers and, in particular, by German and Dutch ideas on monetary policy, given for instance the emphasis on independence and the primacy of price stability. The Committee, on the other hand, did not entrust the complete responsibility for exchange rate policy or for banking supervision to the ESCB, which must be seen as a reflection of certain national views on the attribution of powers in this field to the finance ministers or the central banks. Most of the Committee's recommendations on Monetary Union in the third stage have been incorporated in the EMU Treaty, albeit the arrangements for exchange rate policy give rather more power to the ESCB than was foreseen in the report, while its tasks in the field of prudential supervision are more limited and require unanimity of the Council in order to be extended.

Economic Union, in the third stage of EMU, was defined by the Committee as consisting of the completed single market with freedom of movement for goods, persons, services and capital, the strengthening of market mechanisms (e.g. competition policy), common policies aimed at structural change and development, and a high degree of macroeconomic policy coordination, including binding rules for budgetary policies. It was emphasized that possible imbalances required enhanced factor mobility and flexible prices, and the report recommended the use of additional, conditional and temporary financial support to intensify Member States' adjustment efforts. Macroeconomic policy coordination should be aimed at the definition of the Community policy mix and the Community's role in the international adjustment process, while governments should refrain from direct intervention in wage and price formation, in particular as a response to tensions caused by wage divergences. The binding budgetary rules should consist of limits on budget deficits per country, a prohibition on monetary financing and only a limited recourse to external borrowing. For Economic Union, the report did not see the need for a new institution as for monetary policy, and recommended that the Council should formulate broad guidelines for economic policy which should be implemented by the Commission and the Member States. The report advocated that new functions in the field of competition policy should be granted to the Commission and that there could be a need to extend regional and structural policies. The Council should formulate a medium-term budgetary policy framework, formulate the exchange rate policy of the Community and participate in economic policy coordination at international level. In the budgetary field, there should be a balance between rules and discretion.

The Committee's recommendations in the economic field seem to strike a balance between the views of central bankers and the views of those advocating a Community role in economic development. The former are represented by the insistence on binding budgetary rules, the strengthening of market mechanisms and supporting the absence of government involvement in wage and price formation. The latter is reflected in the recommendations on the extension of regional and structural policies and financial support for adjustment efforts.

The EMU Treaty has followed several, but not all of these recommendations. The Articles on competition policy were virtually left unchanged, albeit the Commission has been granted more power through the new merger Regulation which has been applicable since September 1990.[16] In the EPU Treaty, regional and structural policies are extended through the creation of a cohesion fund (aimed at transport infrastructure and the environment), the introduction of more flexibility in the Community's structural funds and the Protocol on social policy (which, however, does not apply to the United Kingdom). On the other hand, the financial assistance mechanism specified in the EMU Treaty seems not to cover the conditional and temporary financial support mechanism for intensification of Member States adjustment efforts that was advocated by the Delors Committee. In the field of budgetary policy, general rules setting identical criteria for national budget deficits instead of country-specific ceilings have been introduced, albeit subject to a discretionary political judgement. Also, monetary financing is prohibited, but nothing is said on limits of external borrowing by Member States.

In the institutional field, the Committee's report proposed, as part of the consultation procedures to obtain coherent monetary and fiscal policies, that the Presidents of the Council and the Commission participate, without voting rights, in the meetings of the ESCB Council and that the Chairman of the ESCB attends Council meetings of relevance to monetary policy. Furthermore, the report states that consideration should be given to the role of the European Parliament. These recommendations have all been taken into account in the EMU Treaty, albeit the role of the European Parliament and institutional procedures in general are rather diverse (see below), and the Commission may send any of its members instead of its President.

On the three stages leading to irrevocably fixed exchange rates and a single currency, the Committee said that there should be no fixed length for stages one and two, and that there should be flexibility concerning the participation of Member States in certain arrangements. By not fixing the starting dates of stages two and three, the central bankers' view that political 'convergence' should not prevail over economic convergence was clearly voiced. It is not surprising, therefore, that it was at two European Council meetings (first in Rome in October 1990 and then in Maastricht in December 1991) that specific dates were introduced for the start of the second stage and as a deadline for the start of the third stage, respectively, thereby overruling the Committee's position at the highest political level. Furthermore, derogations and therefore flexibility in participation were only introduced for the third stage, but this is linked to the content of the second stage and in particular to the fact that the

EMU Treaty does not require full participation of all Member States in the ERM under the same conditions, as advocated by the Delors Committee for stage one.

Most of the Committee's other recommendations for the first stage were taken up, such as strengthening the cooperation framework for economic and monetary policies. No treaty provisions are foreseen, however, for removing the impediments to the private use of the ECU nor for creating a European Reserve Fund, the latter being an option on which there was also no agreement in the Delors Committee.

The EMU Treaty itself is the result of the recommendation in the Delors report that a modification of the Treaty of Rome would be required for stage two of EMU. Rather surprisingly, the main reason why this was recommended by the Committee was the need to set up the ESCB by the beginning of stage two. According to the EMU Treaty, however, this does not happen until the starting date of stage three is known, although the precursor of the ESCB, the European Monetary Institute (EMI), is indeed established at the beginning of stage two. Although most of the Committee's proposals for economic policy in stage two have been introduced in the EMU Treaty (e.g. policy guidelines by majority decision, non-binding rules for annual budget deficits), the non-existence of the ESCB seems to have precluded most of the Committee's proposals for monetary policy in stage two. These, for instance, are the transition from coordination to a common monetary policy, the corresponding gradual transfer of power, the introduction of general orientations to be respected by national central banks, the pooling of foreign exchange reserves (allowed on a voluntary basis, however) and a reduction in the fluctuation margins. The latter possibility, also proposed by the Danish delegation during the negotiations, was not retained in the EMU Treaty.

The Committee's recommendations on the transition to the third stage do not say much more than what the content of that stage would be, which largely coincides with its definition of a full EMU, especially in the field of monetary policy. It is noteworthy, however, that in the economic field the report advocates, in addition to the binding rules on national budgetary policies, the possibility for discretionary changes in the Community's resources, in particular with a view to supplementing structural transfers in order to influence the Community's policy stance or for the use of conditional financial support for adjustment. This possibility was not retained, although it must be seen as a proposal aimed at creating the instruments for a harmonious development of economic policy in parallel with the introduction of a single monetary policy.

Concluding, one may say that the Delors report has been a decisive influence as a blueprint for the EMU Treaty as signed by the Member States. Due to the presence of the central bankers on the Committee, this influence must be deemed to be particularly strong in the design of Monetary Union in the final stage. In the economic field, the report has only been followed partially, while its views on the transition were, to an important extent, bypassed both as regards timing and content. Here, political considerations seem to have outweighed economic reasoning.

From the Delors Report to the Start of the Negotiations

The first decision taken by the European Council in Madrid in June 1989 after the submission of the Delors report, was to effectively call an Intergovernmental Conference (IGC), using the Delors report as a basis for the negotiations. In accordance with the conclusion of the Delors report that the first stage of EMU did not require a modification of the Treaty, it was furthermore decided that the first stage of EMU would start on 1 July 1990, coinciding with the complete liberalization of capital movements. It was clear that, although providing a useful guide towards EMU, the Delors report was not a treaty text nor was it sufficiently precise on a number of other issues such as the division of responsibilities on exchange rate policy or the precise content and timing of the transitional stages. Consequently, the European Council asked the competent bodies (Council, Commission, Committee of Governors, Monetary Committee) to carry out the necessary work for the preparation of the IGC. Very soon, a high-level working group chaired by Mrs Guigou, adviser to the President of the French Republic, was set up by the Council with the mandate to identify, analyze and list possible elements which could figure in the future EMU Treaty.

THE GUIGOU REPORT

The Guigou report, presented in October 1989, mainly consists of a list of questions raised by the implementation of an Economic and Monetary Union, taking as its points of departure the Delors report, the existing Community framework (or '*acquis communautaire*') and the political guidelines from the Madrid European Council: parallelism between Economic Union and Monetary Union, subsidiarity and the diversity of specific situations. As regards Economic Union, questions were formulated on the need for accompanying policies, economic and social cohesion, and on budgetary and non-budgetary macroeconomic policies. On the monetary side, the questions concerned the functions of the ESCB and the instruments at its disposal, as well as the choice between fixed exchange rates or a single currency. Furthermore, institutional issues and questions of coordination between Economic Union and Monetary Union were addressed. Finally, the report discussed some issues of method:

the need for one or more new treaties, the transition, the relationship between treaty and secondary legislation and the possibility of flexible participation.

Although concise, the Guigou report asked many questions which, later in the negotiations, became major issues. Other questions, however, were either settled rather easily or handled in the IGC on Political Union, which had not yet been called at the time the report was published.[17] Examples of the former are the questions on the number of treaties needed, a possible macroeconomic role for the Community budget or whether there should be a new institution for Economic Union. Examples of the latter are economic and social cohesion, or the issue of the accompanying policies for the internal market.

In March 1990, the Council adopted two further recommendations contained in the Delors report, namely a revision of the 1974 Council Decision on convergence of economic policies[18] and a revision of the 1964 Council Decision which created the Committee of Governors as the framework for monetary policy coordination.[19] The Convergence Decision was replaced by a Council Decision whereby a system of multilateral surveillance of budgetary and other economic policies was established, whereas the 1964 Decision was amended such that it reinforce monetary policy cooperation, in particular by creating a framework for *ex ante* consultation.

At the European Council meeting in Dublin in June 1990, it was decided to open not only one, but two IGCs before the end of 1990, thus shifting part of the attention to Political Union and leaving the preparation for EMU mainly to the finance ministers and their advisers.

REPORT OF THE MONETARY COMMITTEE

As part of the preparations for the IGC, the Council had asked the Monetary Committee for its advice, which resulted in a paper containing confidential recommendations which later became known to the public.[20] This report paid particular attention to the requirements of EMU for budgetary discipline. It concluded, by a large majority, that certain measures should be taken to reinforce market pressure on governments in financing their deficits, such as a prohibition on monetary financing and a no bail-out clause, but that such measures would need to be complemented by the principle that excessive deficits must be avoided, which should be enforceable by the Council.

OPINION OF THE COMMISSION

As early as their informal meeting in the spring of 1990 in Ashford Castle under the Irish Presidency, the finance ministers had discussed EMU issues on the basis of a Commission paper, of which a final version was published as a Communication in August 1990. This paper was the first formal contribution of the Commission to the EMU negotiations. It derived part of its importance from the fact that it added to, or departed from the Delors report in a number of respects. These differences from the Delors report are briefly spelled out in the following.

In the field of Monetary Union, the Commission introduced the name 'Eurofed' for the ESCB, suggested that the Chairman of the Council of Eurofed should be from among the members of the Board, emphasized that not only the Council of Eurofed but also the national central banks should be sufficiently independent, and proposed the ECU as the single currency. Except for the name 'Eurofed', all these recommendations were later included in the Treaty.

In the area of Economic Union, the Commission argued for accompanying policies in the field of competition, notably as regards state aids, further involvement of the Community in tax harmonization, and a balance between allocative efficiency and ecological efficiency as regards environmental policy. Only this last issue was the subject of a treaty modification, obtained at the IGC on Political Union.[21] For economic policy coordination, the Commission proposed introducing a no bail-out rule for Member States, but showed itself in favour of binding procedures rather than binding rules for budget deficits, by accepting the principle that excessive public deficits should be avoided, but referring the judgement on this principle to the multilateral surveillance procedure, using objective criteria only as a yardstick. The EMU Treaty follows this recommendation to a large extent, since criteria on budget deficits are not binding but have the reduced role of triggering a procedure which, after an overall assessment, could lead to a verdict by the Council of an excessive deficit. On the other hand, once an excessive deficit is established in this way, the Member State can be obliged by the Council to correct it under the threat of sanctions. Furthermore, in the same vein as the Delors report, the Commission showed itself in favour of a shock absorption mechanism linked to conditionality, which was later included in the Treaty but under strict conditions (unanimity decision except for natural disasters).

On the transition, the Commission was more explicit than the Delors Committee. The Commission proposed that the second stage should start on 1 January 1993, and that the transition to the final stage thereafter should be short for reasons of political and economic momentum and due to the risks of systemic instability in the EMS with free capital movements.

THE ROME I CONCLUSIONS

As reported in the press,[22] the proposal to start the second stage in 1993 raised objections from Spain since that country feared that its economic adjustment in the face of both its accession in 1986 and the internal market would not have advanced sufficiently in order to be ready, economically speaking, for a rapid transition to a single currency after 1993. Faced with the possibility of an uncertain timing for the transition to the second stage as a result of this position, the Dutch Minister for Finance proposed delaying the start of the second stage by one year, until 1994. This compromise proposal formed one of the elements of the guidelines given to the IGC by eleven countries (the United Kingdom formulated separate conclusions) in the European Council when it first met in Rome under the Italian Presidency on 27-28 October 1990.

The Rome I conclusions of the Italian Presidency provided an important impetus to the negotiations when the IGC started, and must be considered, despite the objections of the United Kingdom and the ambiguities it contained, as constituting political agreement on the first major building block for the later EMU Treaty. In particular, the Rome I conclusions provided for:

− a market-based Economic Union combining price stability with growth, employment and environmental protection and dedicated to sound financial and budgetary positions and economic and social cohesion;

− a Monetary Union with a new, independent monetary institution responsible for a single monetary policy based on a single currency with price stability as the primary objective;

− the start of the second stage on 1 January 1994 and the obligation for Member States before that date to have the largest possible participation of their currencies in the ERM, to start a process leading to the independence of the national central banks, to prohibit monetary financing and not to assume responsibility for each other's debts;

− in the second stage, the obligation for the new monetary institution to reinforce the coordination of monetary policies, to prepare for the single monetary policy and to supervise the development of the ECU;

− within three years after the start of the second stage, a decision on the start of the third stage, which should start within a reasonable period thereafter;

− the possibility of derogations both in the second and the third stages.

Immediately after the Rome I European Council, differences of interpretation were advanced by some Member States on two aspects. The first concerned the mention in the conclusions, after listing the obligations for the Community and the Member States before the start of the second stage, of the necessity for further lasting and satisfactory progress towards convergence, in particular for stable prices and the restoration of sound public finances. Some Member States interpreted this as implying a conditional, as opposed to an unconditional, start of the second stage, depending on further achievements in the field of convergence. A second difference of interpretation concerned the question of whether or not the monetary institution operating in the second stage was supposed to be the same institution as that of the third stage. Both these questions were only settled later in the negotiations.

DRAFT STATUTE OF THE ESCB AND THE ECB

On 27 November 1990, the Committee of Governors presented a draft Statute of the European System of Central Banks and of the European Central Bank (ECB) to the President of the ECOFIN Council for transmission to the IGC. This Statute provided a legal translation of the principles adopted in the Rome I conclusions as regards Monetary Union in the final stage of EMU, but remained open as to the role of the monetary institution in the second stage or on the arrangements for the transition to the final stage, in particular as regards the Member States with derogations. It also provided for a detailed description of the organization, the functions and operation of the ESCB, but left open a number of important questions concerning the relations of the ESCB and the ECB with third parties (prudential supervision, regulatory powers) and the financial provisions.[23] The Committee of Governors therefore provided an important input into the IGC as regards the legislation applicable inside the ESCB, while still leaving open a number of issues involving the dealings of the ESCB with the Council, market participants or other third parties.

Since the Committee of Governors not only had to perform a task by contributing to the preparation of the IGC and was also an interested party, its draft Statute contained some provisions which gave particular emphasis to the responsibilities of the ESCB and the ECB. Examples are the relative autonomy created in the field of exchange rate policy, the role foreseen for the ESCB in the field of prudential supervision and the requirement that coins be put into circulation by the ECB and/or the national central banks. No related articles survived unchanged in the final text. However, the main thrust of the Committee's draft was maintained.

DRAFT TREATY OF THE COMMISSION

On 10 December 1990, the Commission presented to the Member States, in the form of a working document, a draft EMU Treaty modifying the EEC Treaty. Apart from the Statute of the ESCB and the ECB, this draft Treaty provided a complete and concrete example of how the EMU Treaty could look. The strategy followed in the Commission's draft Treaty seemed to be to translate the Rome I conclusions into treaty language, adding for the rest the outline of EMU as formulated in the Commission Communication of August 1990. For instance, the starting date of 1 January 1993 for the second stage as proposed in the Commission's Communication was replaced by that of 1 January 1994 as in the Rome I conclusions.

The structure of the Commission's draft EMU Treaty is the one preserved in the text signed in Maastricht and corresponding to the Delors report. It contains a definition of Economic Union and Monetary Union in the beginning and the introduction of the ESCB as a Community body. In the chapter on the free movement of capital, the complete freedom of capital movements and payments is defined. In a new Title, labelled 'Economic and Monetary Union', four chapters contain the core provisions on EMU:

- economic policy;
- monetary policy;
- institutional provisions;
- transitional provisions.

In the chapter on *economic policy*, content is given to economic policy coordination in the form of a multilateral surveillance procedure operating in the framework of multiannual guidelines decided upon by the Council after deliberation by the European Council.[24] General and specific recommendations to Member States are conceived as the instruments for putting pressure on Member States to act consistently with the multiannual guidelines. For Member States in difficulties, a financial assistance mechanism is introduced.[25] Budgetary discipline is addressed by prohibitions on monetary financing, on privileged access to the capital market and on the granting of unconditional guarantees for the public debt (bail-out) of Member States. In addition, the principle that excessive budget deficits are to be avoided is introduced without, however, giving the Council binding powers of enforcement *vis-à-vis* the Member States. In the Maastricht text, all these provisions on economic policy were retained, although in modified form. In particular, financial assistance can only be granted by unanimity (except in cases of natural disasters), while there is an explicit procedure to identify excessive deficits and to enforce their correction, ultimately using financial sanctions.

The *monetary policy* chapter reflects the Rome I conclusions but introduces in addition the name 'Eurofed' for the ESCB, subordinates Eurofed to the guidelines of the Council in conducting foreign exchange interventions, involves the European Council and the European Parliament in the appointment of members of the ECB's Executive Board and specifies that the Community be represented in international monetary or financial bodies by the President of the Council, the President of the ECB and a member of the Commission. By contrast, in the Maastricht text, the name 'Eurofed' is no longer present and the ECB is given more responsibility in conducting exchange rate policy, whereas the Community's external representation is decided upon by the Council on a case-by-case basis.

The *institutional provisions* describe the cross-participation of the Community institutions in meetings of the Council of Ministers and of the Council of the ECB. The President of the Council and a member of the Commission may attend meetings of the Council of Ministers and of the Council of the ECB without voting rights, while the President of the ECB should attend meetings of the Council of Ministers dealing with the coordination of economic policies and multilateral surveillance recommendations. The democratic accountability of the ECB *vis-à-vis* the European Parliament is also described, as well as the slightly modified tasks of the Monetary Committee. In the EMU Treaty, the provisions on cross-participation between the institutions and democratic accountability were retained without major modifications. The Monetary Committee, however, is given more than its advisory status as proposed by the Commission: it will contribute to the preparation of most of the Council's work regarding EMU, using a formulation close to that of the Committee of Permanent Representatives, and will be replaced in the third stage by an Economic and Financial Committee. In addition, there is a new article according to which the Commission has to examine requests by the Member States or the Council that it make a proposal or recommendation. Altogether, it must be concluded that the transfer of more responsibilities regarding economic policy to the Community level is accompanied by supplementing the possibility for taking initiatives by the Commission with a changed role for the Council and the Member States, respectively.

In its *transitional provisions*, the Commission's draft Treaty describes the transition to and content of the second stage and the transition to and start of the third stage. With regard to the ambiguities in the Rome I conclusions on the convergence conditionality prior to the start of the second stage and the nature of the monetary institution in that stage, the draft Treaty makes clear choices. The start of the second stage is made unconditional on convergence, but it is specified instead that measures should be taken during the second stage to reinforce convergence, along the lines specified in the Rome I conclusions. In addition, the possibility is introduced of advancing some or all of the economic policy provisions from the third stage to the second stage. The EMU Treaty signed in Maastricht has shifted both provisions forward in time: Member States with convergence problems should adopt multiannual programmes *before* the start of stage two, whereas the multilateral surveillance enters into force upon ratification and all provisions aimed at avoiding excessive deficits, except the binding elements such as sanctions, are applicable in the second stage.

As regards the nature of the monetary institution in stage two, the Commission's draft Treaty takes the interpretation that this should be the Eurofed. In addition to the general tasks specified in the Rome I conclusions, the draft Treaty lists a number of specific tasks most of which ended up, either completely or in modified form, in the EMU Treaty. Although the monetary institution in the second stage was finally given a form different from that of the Eurofed, the Commission's draft Treaty proposals for the content of that stage were broadly retained. It should, however, be noted that the EMU Treaty does not specify the need for complementary legislation concerning the tasks of the EMI in the second stage, contrary to the Commission's draft Treaty. On the one hand, this is due to the fact that the EMI is given less executive powers in its tasks than proposed in the Commission's text. On the other hand, this shifts the right of initiative and of decisions away from the Commission and the Council to the EMI itself.

For the transition to the third stage, the Commission's draft Treaty follows the Rome I conclusions that the Commission and the monetary institution in stage two should report to the European Council on the results obtained in stage two and in particular on convergence. The European Council is given the role of establishing that the necessary conditions are met, after which the Council should take, by a special qualified majority of at least eight Member States voting in favour, the necessary decisions, in particular on derogations for Member States. Furthermore, the Council adopts by unanimity the irrevocably fixed exchange rates, the measures for introducing the single currency and, if necessary, the arrangements for national currencies to provisionally keep the status of legal tender. After these decisions, the Eurofed would fully exercise its powers and the third stage would have thus started. The majority of these provisions can also be found in the EMU Treaty, but with much more detail regarding conditions, procedures and content of derogations. They proved to be one of the most difficult parts of the Treaty on which to reach agreement.

Results Under the Luxembourg Presidency

The negotiations under the Luxembourg Presidency consisted initially of a close reading of the Commission's draft Treaty. Submissions by the Member States and, in a later stage, so-called non-papers of the Presidency, also played an important role. By the end of the Luxembourg Presidency, at the European Council meeting in June 1991, a reference document containing a complete draft Treaty was accepted as the basis for further negotiations under the Dutch Presidency.

ALTERNATIVE PLANS

Among the submissions from the Member States, four drew particular attention because of their comprehensiveness. Of these, the 'hard ECU' plan of the United Kingdom and the 'hard-basket ECU' plan of Spain focused on the role of the ECU in stage two, while France and Germany each presented complete draft treaties.

The 'hard ECU' plan of the United Kingdom,[26] while not containing a commitment to a single currency, provided an alternative to the second stage of EMU. Building on an earlier proposal for competing currencies,[27] the plan proposed to set up a European Monetary Fund (EMF) which would issue 'hard ECU' against currencies of the Member States. In case of a realignment in the EMS, the hard ECU would never be devalued against any of the participating currencies. Part of its hardness also derived from the obligation for Member States to buy back their own currency at the request of the EMF. The Spanish plan for a 'hard-basket ECU' provided for a change in the basket composition of the ECU at each realignment such that the ECU would never devalue against the strongest currency in the EMS.[28] The British and Spanish plans each tried to give substance to the idea of strengthening the ECU in the second stage of EMU. A third proposal was not to change the currency composition of the ECU any more. Since changes in the composition of the ECU (usually at 5-year intervals) tend to re-establish the weight of the most inflationary currencies, which usually diminishes because of a tendency towards depreciation, the freezing of the currency composition would at least provide for some kind of hardening of the ECU. It was this last proposal which was finally retained in the Maastricht Treaty.

The French draft Treaty was closely inspired by that of the Commission in its structure, but differed substantially as regards content. In particular, it proposed to give a strong role to the European Council as the highest decision-making authority in EMU and introduced the shared right of initiative for the Commission, the President of the Council and the Member States. In the field of economic policy, sanctions were foreseen if recommendations from the Council were not respected and there would be no financial assistance mechanism, whereas for monetary policy the Council would have more grip on the ESCB, for instance by having the power to introduce minimum reserve requirements and by having the responsibility for the definition of exchange rate policy. For the transition period, the French proposal was that all Member States should be in the exchange rate mechanism of the EMS in stage two, and that the EMS would become part of the Treaty. In the Maastricht Treaty, some elements of the French proposals can be traced back: the final responsibility of the Council for the exchange rate system, the possibility for the President of the Council to submit a motion for deliberation to the ECB, a role for the Heads of State and Government in drawing up the broad guidelines for economic policies and formal power of decision on the transition to the third stage, a stronger role for the Monetary Committee in the preparation of the work of the Council and the possibility for the Council or the Member States to ask the Commission to come forward with a recommendation or a proposal.

The German draft Treaty departed somewhat more from that of the Commission than did the French proposals. For economic policy, it proposed the introduction of some 'ground rules' such as the liberalization of prices, the indexation to price changes only subject to the approval of the ECB, a best-endeavours clause for privatization, freedom to conclude collective wage agreements, restriction on state aids and national responsibility for the results of economic policy. Of these 'ground rules', only the most important one, that of an open market economy with free competition, was retained in the Maastricht Treaty. For budgetary policy, the German draft Treaty proposed introducing the 'golden rule' that the budget deficit should not exceed government investment. Moreover, an excessive deficit would be deemed to exist if the public deficit or debt exceeded the Community average by a certain percentage. In such cases, the Council could impose a ceiling on the budget of a Member State, the non-respect of which could lead to sanctions such as the suspension of Community payments. Elements of these proposals can be traced back in Article 104c of the Maastricht Treaty, which gives criteria for excessive deficits in terms of the deficit-to-GDP and debt-to-GDP ratios, makes a reference to the level of government investment in relation to the public deficit and allows for sanctions against a Member State which does not correct an excessive deficit. In the field of monetary policy, the German proposal was that the Council could, by unanimity, decide on the exchange rate regime and on the central parities in such a regime, but that the ESCB would have the responsibility for interventions on the foreign exchange market. In the Maastricht Treaty, the limitation of the Council's final responsibility for the exchange rate regime was retained.

For the second stage, the German Treaty proposed a separate decision by the Council on the start of the second stage, in particular in order to verify the progress in the field of convergence. Furthermore, a Council of Governors of Central Banks of the Member States rather than the ESCB would be established at the start of the second stage, the rules concerning the composition of the ECU basket would have to be adapted such that the ECU could no longer be devalued (cf. the Spanish plan) and the Member States should already introduce the 'golden rule'. The decision on the passage to the third stage would be taken by the European Council by unanimity if it found that a majority of Member States met the economic conditions. The latter would mean that there should be price stability to a large extent, that budget deficits should be at acceptable levels and that interest rates should be close to each other. The requirement that a majority of Member States should meet the conditions and precise criteria in terms of inflation, interest rates and budget deficits were all included in the Maastricht Treaty, the decision being taken however by qualified majority.

RESULTS ACHIEVED

The results under the Luxembourg Presidency can be judged from making a comparison between the Luxembourg draft Treaty and the Commission's draft Treaty on the one hand, and between the Luxembourg draft Treaty and the Maastricht Treaty on the other.

A comparison with the Commission's draft Treaty shows that there are a number of areas where the Luxembourg draft Treaty introduced either slight changes or more detail, but did not deviate essentially from the Commission's draft Treaty. In other areas, however, new approaches were taken. Examples of the former are the multilateral surveillance procedure which was slightly modified, the more detailed definitions of the prohibitions against monetary financing, privileged access to financial institutions or the 'no bail-out' rule, the elaboration of a procedure aimed at avoiding excessive deficits, the introduction of an explicit list of articles in the statutes of the ESCB which could be modified through secondary legislation and more elaboration of the role of the Monetary Committee/Economic and Financial Committee. Most of these modifications were also retained in the Maastricht Treaty. However, the Luxembourg draft Treaty also contained new elements. For the excessive deficit procedure, the possibility of sanctions in line with the German and French proposals was introduced. For monetary policy, the ECB itself would no longer issue notes and coins, but would regulate the issue. The members of its Executive Board would be appointed with a non-renewable – rather than a renewable – mandate of eight years. For exchange rate policy, the notion of an 'exchange rate system' as in the German proposal was introduced, the possibility of guidelines for exchange rate policy being put into square brackets. The external representation of the Community in the field of EMU would be done on an *ad hoc* basis instead of by the Presidents of the Council and the ECB and a member of the Commission. In the institutional field, the French proposal that the President of the Council could submit a motion for deliberation to the Council of the ECB was introduced.

The strongest modifications which were proposed, however, concerned the transitional period. The debate interpreting the Rome I conclusions regarding the need for convergence as a condition for the start of stage two was solved by proposing that Member States would, if necessary, adopt multiannual convergence programmes before the start of stage two and that there would be a general assessment by the Council on the progress made with regard to convergence. The compromise contained in these proposals was also retained in the Maastricht Treaty. Another issue for discussion raised by the Rome I conclusions was whether the monetary institution to be set up at the start of the second stage was to be the ESCB or not. The Luxembourg draft Treaty aimed to solve this question by setting up, not at the start of stage two but immediately after ratification, a Board of Governors of Central Banks of the Member States, and by setting up the ESCB at the beginning of stage two which, however, would not start to operate before 1 January 1996. The tasks of the Board of Governors would be those specified in the Rome I conclusions, while in 1996 the ESCB would take over these tasks and, in addition, assume responsibility for the ECU clearing system, prepare the monetary instruments for the third stage and the integration of payment networks. To these tasks would be added, after the decision on the start of the third stage, supervision of the technical preparation of notes and coins in ECU, the possibility of addressing confidential or public recommendations to the central banks of the Member States and the management of exchange reserves on behalf of the Member States. This complex division of stage two into three sub-stages cannot be found in the Maastricht Treaty, although the idea of two different institutions, one of which would take over the tasks of the other, was clearly retained through the establishment of the EMI.

The Rome I conclusions also said that the greatest possible number of Member States should participate in the ERM before the start of stage two, and that the ECU would have to be strengthened further during the transitional phase. Concerning the latter, the Luxembourg draft Treaty proposed a provision saying that the Council and the Board of Governors should take the necessary measures for the ECU to become a strong and stable currency, without being more specific regarding the different proposals for reinforcing the ECU. This formulation was not kept in the Maastricht Treaty. Similarly, the Luxembourg draft Treaty was not explicit on the meaning of the provision that the greatest possible number of Member States should adhere to the ERM; it only specified that all Member States should take the measures necessary to enable them to take part in the ERM from the beginning of the transitional period. There was, however, the provision that as of 1 January 1996 Member States should respect the normal fluctuation margins of the ERM, albeit with the possibility for derogations as foreseen in the Rome I conclusions. This idea is contained in the Maastricht Treaty through the criterion for participation in the third stage, which specifies that there should have been a two-year participation in the ERM observing the normal fluctuation margins.

For the transition to the third stage, the Luxembourg draft Treaty gave explicit power to the European Council to set a date for its beginning. The Luxembourg proposals were also, in the spirit of the German Treaty, more explicit on the convergence criteria in terms of price stability, balanced public finances and the approximation of interest rates, and the French proposal to take account of the development of the role of the ECU was also included. All these new requirements (compared to the Commission's draft Treaty) for participation in the third stage were later given more detailed substance in the

Maastricht Treaty. The Luxembourg draft Treaty also gave somewhat more substance to the derogations for Member States which would not fully participate in the third stage, by indicating that their voting rights would be suspended in the area of monetary policy. This aspect was also worked out in much greater detail in the Maastricht Treaty.

Another way of looking at the progress under the Luxembourg Presidency is to compare the Luxembourg draft Treaty with the Maastricht Treaty. Such a comparison allows the identification *ex post* of the issues which were *de facto* agreed to a large extent at the time of the Luxembourg summit in June 1991. These issues are listed in panel A of Table 3, which aims to present the main issues ranked by degree of difficulty encountered, and are briefly discussed in the following.

1. Objectives and Principles of EMU (Articles 2 and 3a). Compared to the Luxembourg draft Treaty, the Maastricht Treaty did not change the objectives of the Community as stated in Article 2, signalling early agreement. These objectives are now more wide-ranging than in the Treaty of Rome and also more in line with the modifications to the Treaty introduced by the Single European Act. The establishment of EMU has been added – alongside that of the common market – as one of the objectives of the Community, the activities of Articles 3 and 3a are mentioned as the instruments and a number of new objectives are introduced, such as: sustainable and non-inflationary growth while respecting the environment, a high level of employment and social protection, economic and social cohesion, and solidarity among the Member States.

Article 3a lists the activities relating to EMU. These activities are not included in Article 3 since they relate to activities of the Community *and* of the Member States, contrary to Article 3 which lists the activities of the Community only. The first paragraph of Article 3a defines what is understood by the 'economic policy' of EMU (i.e. close coordination of national economic policies, the internal market and the definition of common objectives), and was hardly changed between the Luxembourg draft Treaty and the Maastricht Treaty. The second paragraph defines the 'Monetary Union' as consisting of the irrevocable fixing of exchange rates leading to the introduction of a single currency – the ECU, and the existence of a single monetary policy and exchange rate policy. The main changes between Luxembourg and Maastricht relate to the deletion of the mention that exchange rates will be irrevocably fixed 'between the currencies of the Member States' and the recognition of monetary policy and exchange rate policy as two separate policies. The former seems linked to the possibility that not all currencies would be irrevocably fixed (due to the possible exemptions for the United Kingdom and Denmark), while the latter emphasizes that the final

Table 3:
Main EMU Issues
(ranked by degree of difficulty encountered)

A 1. Objectives and principles of EMU
  2. Principle of free movement of capital and payments inside the Community

  3. Multilateral surveillance procedure including broad guidelines for economic policies
  4. Special measures appropriate to the economic situation
  5. Principle of prohibition on monetary financing
  6. Prohibition on privileged access
  7. No bail-out

  8. Primary objective of price stability
  9. Monetary policy tasks of the ESCB
  10. Consultative tasks of the ECB
  11. Set up of the ESCB
  12. Independence of the ESCB in the third stage

  13. Appointment of members of the Executive Board of the ECB
  14. Cross participation between the Council and the ECB
  15. Democratic accountability of the ESCB
  16. Monetary Committee – Economic and Financial Committee

  17. Start of stage two

B 1. Exceptions to free movement of capital inside or outside the Community:
     – place of residence/investment
     – measures preventing infringement of national law
     – existing derogations
  2. Capital movements to or from third countries
     – liberalization with standstill clause
     – safeguard measures
     – economic sanctions

  3. Financial assistance mechanism
  4. Prohibition on monetary financing (overdraft facility)
  5. Excessive deficit procedure
     – criteria (definition, reference values)
     – sanctions (financial)

  6. Role of ECB in issuing banknotes and coins

7. Role of ECB in prudential supervision
8. Financial provisions of the ESCB (transfer of foreign reserves, capital key)
9. External representation
10. Exchange rate policy and international monetary agreements

11. Content of stage two:
    - application of excessive deficit procedure
    - process of independence central banks
    - which monetary institution (ESCB/EMI)
    - strengthening of the ECU

12. The European Monetary Institute
    - external President
    - own resources
    - tasks (reserve management)

13. Institutional matters
    - voting rules
    - right of initiative
    - involvement of European Parliament
    - role of ECOFIN Council versus European Council
    - seat of EMI and ECB

14. Transition to the third stage
    - convergence criteria
    - role European Council versus ECOFIN
    - voting rules
    - critical mass
    - opting out
    - deadline/irreversibility
    - derogations (procedure, content)
    - introduction of single currency

15. Economic and social cohesion

---

responsibilities for the single monetary policy and exchange rate policy are not in the same hands, since the Council plays a specific role for exchange rate policy.

2. Principle of Free Movement of Capital and Payments inside the Community (Articles 73a and 73b). Both the Maastricht Treaty and the Luxembourg draft Treaty contain the provision in Article 73a that Articles 67 to 73 will be replaced on 1 January 1994, i.e. at the beginning of the second stage of EMU, by new articles. This implies that, from the second stage, the free movement of capital and payments would also be in the Treaty alongside the other freedoms on the movement of goods, services and persons. This is important since the free movement of capital and payments in the Treaty of Rome could only be established by means of secondary legislation such as the 1988 Directive on the liberalization of capital movements.[29] There are, however, important differences between the Maastricht and Luxembourg texts for Article 73b, which specifies the content of the liberalization. The Luxembourg text limits the liberalization of capital to that belonging to persons resident in the Member States, whereas the Maastricht text gives rights to persons residing outside the Community by also liberalizing capital movements between Member States and third countries. In other words, the Luxembourg draft Treaty liberalized capital movements only inside the Community, whereas the Maastricht Treaty not only liberalizes capital inside, but also outside the Community. On the other hand, the Luxembourg draft Treaty prohibits any discrimination on capital movements inside the Community based on the place of residence of the parties or the place where the capital is invested, whereas such distinctions according to national tax law are allowed in the Maastricht Treaty provided they are not arbitrary or a disguised restriction on the free movement of capital.[30] One may therefore conclude that the principle of liberalization of movement of capital and payments inside the Community was agreed at the time of the Luxembourg summit, but that liberalization with respect to third countries and exceptions to the principle still had to be agreed.

3.   Multilateral Surveillance Procedure including Broad Guidelines for Economic Policies (Articles 102a and 103). There is broad similarity between the Luxembourg and Maastricht texts regarding the multilateral surveillance procedure. The broad framework is defined in Article 102a, which gives Member States the obligation to conduct their economic policies with a view to contributing to the Community's objectives of Article 2 and in the context of broad guidelines. Article 103 next specifies how the objectives of Article 102a are to be accomplished. The first element is that Member States should coordinate their economic policies in the Council. As one of the goals for coordination, the Council defines broad guidelines for the economic policies of the Member States and the Community. The Luxembourg text contained two options as regards the decision procedure for the broad guidelines, one involving the European Council and the other involving the Council. In the Maastricht Treaty, however, there is a compromise formulation which gives the formal power of decision on the guidelines to the Council, after discussion in the European Council.

The multilateral surveillance procedure is designed to ensure the coordination of economic policies, by monitoring developments in the Member States and in the Community, by monitoring the consistency of economic policies with the guidelines, and by carrying out an overall assessment. In addition to the 'peer pressure' in the multilateral surveillance, the Council may also address recommendations to the Member States if their policies are not consistent with the broad guidelines or are jeopardizing the functioning of EMU more generally. The Maastricht Treaty specifies that such recommendations can be made public. This possibility was also present in the Luxembourg draft Treaty but was subject to the condition that there should have been an earlier, confidential recommendation. According to the Maastricht Treaty, therefore, the Council can issue directly public recommendations.

4.   *Special Measures Appropriate to the Economic Situation (Article 103a(1))*. In the Treaty of Rome, Article 103(2) gives the Council, acting by unanimity, the possibility to 'decide upon the measures appropriate to the situation'. This Article has been used in the past for the convergence decisions of 1974 and 1990, but also to set up an oil distribution scheme in times of shortage.[31] The latter was based, in addition, on Article 103(4) which specifies that the Council can also take measures if any difficulties should arise in the supply of certain products. The text of this Article in the Luxembourg draft Treaty is literally that of Article 103(2) of the Treaty of Rome. It was put into square brackets, however, adjacent to an Article (taken from the Commission's draft Treaty) describing the possibility for the Council to grant financial assistance in case of difficulties. Apparently, the general possibility for the Council to take measures appropriate to the situation was put on an equal footing with the financial assistance mechanism. In the Maastricht Treaty it appears to have been recognized that financial assistance is only one of the possibilities for the Council to take special measures, since both of the two possibilities have been retained. The formulation of Article 103a(1) of the Maastricht Treaty merges Articles 103(2) and 103(4) of the Treaty of Rome. The only change compared to the Luxembourg draft Treaty and the Treaty of Rome is that the measures should be appropriate to the *economic* situation, thus being somewhat more restrictive.

5.   *Principle of Prohibition on Monetary Financing (Article 104)*. Although the words 'monetary financing' do not appear in the Maastricht Treaty, it is clear that Article 104 relates to this aspect of the financing of government debt. The Maastricht Treaty contains several changes compared to the Luxembourg draft Treaty regarding monetary financing. In particular, the list of potential beneficiaries which are excluded from overdraft facilities with the

central banks or the direct purchase of debt instruments from them, is more extensive, and it is also made clear that publicly owned banks should not be treated differently from private banks in the context of the supply of reserves by central banks. Two other changes also stand out. On the one hand, whereas the Luxembourg draft Treaty only prohibited the *obligatory* purchase by central banks of public debt instruments, the Maastricht Treaty is more restrictive by prohibiting *all* direct purchases by central banks of such instruments. On the other hand, the Protocol which contains the so-called 'opting-out' provisions for the United Kingdom specifies that it may maintain its 'ways and means' facility with the Bank of England so long as the United Kingdom does not move to the third stage. The United Kingdom therefore has an exception to the prohibition on overdraft facilities until it joins the third stage.

6. Prohibition on Privileged Access (Article 104a). The wording of the prohibition on privileged access by public bodies to the financial institutions also appears to have been largely agreed at the time of the Luxembourg draft Treaty. The modifications contained in the Maastricht text only concern the introduction of an exception in the case of prudential considerations and the obligation for the Council to specify definitions for the application of the prohibition on privileged access before the start of the second stage. In particular, it may be expected that this legislation will address more precisely the meaning of the concept 'privileged access' and of the exception allowed in the case of prudential considerations.

7. No Bail-Out (Article 104b). The no bail-out rule as specified in the Luxembourg draft Treaty was made somewhat more explicit in the Maastricht Treaty with only one change of substance. According to the Luxembourg draft Treaty, Member States would not be liable for the commitments of Community institutions, whereas this prohibition is no longer present in the Maastricht Treaty. Given the fact that the Member States have to provide the Community's own resources such that the Community budget is in balance,[32] this seems a logical modification.

8. Primary Objective of Price Stability (Article 105(1)). In the Maastricht Treaty, Article 105 has been extended, compared to the Luxembourg draft Treaty, in order to state explicitly what was already implied by Article 3a of both Treaties, namely that the primary objective of the ESCB should be to maintain price stability and that, without prejudice to this objective, the ESCB should support the general economic policies in the Community. Agreement on this point was therefore already a fact under the Luxembourg Presidency. The Treaty does not, however, specify what is meant by price stability.

According to Duisenberg (1992), European central bank governors define this pragmatically 'as an inflation rate between nil and 2 per cent'.

9.   Monetary Policy Tasks of the ESCB (Articles 105(2) and (3)). Article 105(2) gives four basic tasks to the ESCB. The first of these, the task 'to define and implement the monetary policy of the Community' was also described in the Luxembourg draft Treaty and therefore could count on early agreement. The description of the second task, 'to conduct foreign exchange operations consistent with the provisions of Article 109', is a slightly modified wording in which the words 'in accordance with' were replaced by 'consistent with'. This seems to emphasize the fact that the Council can only formulate general orientations for exchange rate policy, thus leaving the ESCB the responsibility for exchange interventions. The third task, 'to hold and manage the official foreign reserves of the Member States', together with Article 105(3) which specifies that governments may hold and manage foreign exchange working balances, constitutes a compromise regarding the question already indicated in the Luxembourg draft Treaty, namely to what extent foreign reserves are to be transferred to the national central banks in those countries where these reserves have hitherto been held by government agencies. The fourth task, 'to promote the smooth operation of payment systems' gives somewhat less responsibility in this field to the ESCB than under the Luxembourg draft Treaty, which gave the ESCB the task of 'ensuring' the smooth operation of payment systems.

10. Consultative Tasks of the ECB (Article 105(4)). Both the Maastricht Treaty and the Luxembourg draft Treaty provided that the ECB should be consulted by the Council on proposals for Community acts and by Member States on national draft legislative provisions. The coverage of the consultation was extended in the Maastricht Treaty from 'monetary matters' to the 'fields of competence', whereas for national draft legislative provisions, the Council would in addition set the limits and the conditions for the consultation. Compared to the Luxembourg draft Treaty, these are only minor modifications.

11. Set-Up of the ESCB (Articles 106, 108a and 109a). Apart from the order of the different provisions, there are relatively few differences between the Maastricht Treaty and the Luxembourg draft Treaty regarding the set-up of the ESCB, confirming the early agreement reached on the major aspects of this part of the Treaty. The 'Council of the ECB' was renamed the 'Governing Council of the ECB' and the list of articles in the statute of the ESCB which could be modified through secondary legislation was changed somewhat, along with the voting procedures for their adoption. The number of members of the Executive Board of the ECB (President, Vice-President and four other members) and their term of office (8 years), which were still in square brackets in the Luxembourg draft Treaty, were confirmed in the Maastricht Treaty.

12. Independence of the ESCB in the Third Stage (Article 107). The text of the Article on independence of the ECB and the national central banks remained virtually unchanged from that of the Luxembourg draft Treaty, thereby indicating early agreement on this issue.

13. Appointment of Members of the Executive Board of the ECB (Article 109a(2)). The appointment procedure for the members of the Executive Board, i.e. by common accord of the governments of the Member States, was changed from 'meeting at European Council level' to 'at the level of Heads of State or Government', implying that the appointment does not require a real meeting and can be done through a written procedure.

14. Cross participation between the Council and the ECB (Articles 109b(1) and (2)). Coordination between monetary policy as defined and implemented by the ESCB on the one hand, and economic policy as coordinated in the Council on the other, is ensured through cross participation between the Council and the ECB. The President of the Council and a member of the Commission may participate in meetings of the Governing Council of the ECB, while the President of the ECB may participate in Council meetings relating to the objectives and tasks of the ESCB. The Treaty texts describing these participations remained virtually unchanged from those of the Luxembourg draft Treaty.

15. Democratic Accountability of the ESCB (Article 109b(3)). The democratic accountability of the ESCB, which is ensured through the obligation that the ECB submit an annual report to be presented to the Council and the European Parliament and through the possibility for the European Parliament to organize a general debate on this report or to organize hearings of members of the Executive Board, was hardly changed in the Maastricht Treaty as regards the Luxembourg draft Treaty, a sign of early agreement on this issue.

16. Monetary Committee – Economic and Financial Committee (Article 109c). Both the Maastricht Treaty and the Luxembourg draft Treaty contain the provision that the Monetary Committee should be replaced by an Economic and Financial Committee which would, as an additional task, contribute to the preparation of the work of the Council concerning EMU. The date of this replacement was shifted from 1 January 1996 in the Luxembourg draft Treaty to the start of the third stage in the Maastricht Treaty. On the other hand, the task of contributing to the preparation of the work of the Council concerning EMU was also attributed to the Monetary Committee. The Luxembourg draft Treaty specified that the Economic and Financial Committee would be composed of *representatives* from the Member States, the Commission and the ESCB, the precise composition to be decided by the Council. The Maastricht Treaty adds to this that there should be no more than two members per Member State, the Commission or the ECB and, further, deletes the reference to 'representatives', suggesting that the members are appointed in a personal capacity rather than as official representatives, as in the Committee of Permanent Representatives (Article 151 EEC Treaty).

17. Start of Stage Two (Article 109e(1) and (2)). The Luxembourg and Maastricht Treaties each stipulate: that the second stage starts on 1 January 1994; that before that date each Member State should have taken the measures necessary to comply with the provisions on the free movement of capital and payments, monetary financing and privileged access, and should adopt if necessary multiannual convergence programmes; and that the Council should assess progress regarding convergence.

Contrary to the Luxembourg draft Treaty, the Maastricht Treaty does not specify, however, that the convergence programmes should be adopted in the framework of the multilateral surveillance procedure, thus emphasizing each Member State's own responsibility for its convergence programme. Regarding the assessment by the Council, the Maastricht Treaty adds that the implementation of Community law concerning the internal market should be assessed, thus translating the Rome I obligation that, prior to the start of the second stage, the single market should have been achieved.

Results under the Dutch Presidency

When first meeting under the Dutch Presidency in September 1991, the Ministers of Finance discussed a non-paper containing provisions for the transition and content of stage two and the transition to the third stage.[33] As regards the content of stage two, the paper proposed that a European Monetary Institute should be set up with an external president and vice-president but without capital or the possibility of managing foreign exchange reserves on behalf of Member States. For strengthening the ECU, two possibilities were given: freezing the ECU basket or a non-devaluable ECU. For the transition to the third stage, several issues were still left open: whether to introduce convergence criteria into the Treaty, the role of the Council versus the European Council, and the minimum number of Member States needed to start stage three. Each Member State meeting the obligations for stage three (such as independence of the national central bank) and the convergence conditions would have to decide separately whether to participate in the third stage ('opting-in'). Member States which did not opt in or did not meet the conditions could ask to participate later, and the Council would have to decide on their participation. These issues were also discussed at the informal ECOFIN Council in Apeldoorn at the end of September 1991 and it was reported[34] that the idea of a European Monetary Institute was finding broad agreement as well as the broad outline of the procedure for the transition to the third stage, based on a Belgian compromise proposal. In particular, there was broad agreement that the decision on the start of the third stage would be taken on the basis of three principles (no veto, no coercion and no discrimination), and that Member States lagging behind would get derogations allowing them to catch up later on the basis of the same criteria.

Early in October, the ministers discussed the results of the preparatory work by the Monetary Committee on excessive deficits.[35] The result of this work was a procedure which would be triggered with considerable automaticity on the basis of three triggers: when the gross debt-to-GDP ratio exceeds 60%, when the deficit exceeds 3% of GDP, or if the deficit exceeds government investment expenditure. In addition, it should be possible for the procedure to be triggered by a Member State, the Council or the Commission. After being triggered, the Council would exercise its judgment in order to decide whether a Member State has an excessive deficit. If so, the Council could take a number of steps which could lead to sanctions; in particular fines or the suspension of payments from the Community budget. It was reported that several elements of this procedure were not agreed, in particular the criteria which should be less stringent according to some Member States, and the content of the sanctions.

After these ministerial discussions, the Dutch Presidency presented a complete formal treaty proposal on 28 October 1991, which included a number of protocols (e.g. for the ESCB, the EMI, the excessive deficit procedure) and declarations (e.g. on the role of the ECOFIN Council). In an accompanying letter,[36] Minister Kok indicated as remaining differences: the transition to the third stage, the no-coercion principle, the excessive-deficit procedure, the financial assistance mechanism, some institutional aspects of the EMI, the transitional provisions for the ECB (extra decision-making body for all governors of central banks), the subscription key and the seat of the ECB, the strengthening of the ECU, prudential supervision, the role of the European Parliament and the role of the Commission. After two further meetings in the course of November 1991, on 30 November 1991 the finance ministers started their last round of negotiations prior to the European Council meeting, with some 15 points outstanding. This marathon by the ministers of finance ended on 3 December 1991 with agreement on all but three issues: the procedure for the transition to the third stage, the exemption clauses requested by the United Kingdom and Denmark, and economic and social cohesion. These issues were finally agreed upon at the Maastricht European Council meeting.

Panel B of Table 3 lists the main issues which the Dutch negotiators had to solve during their Presidency. It is based on a comparison of the Maastricht Treaty with the Luxembourg text and with the Dutch proposals of 28 October 1991, and on press reports. Each of the issues will be briefly discussed.

1. Exceptions to Free Movement of Capital Inside or Outside the Community (Articles 73d and 73e). Compared with the Luxembourg draft Treaty, Article 73d of the Maastricht Treaty contains three additional exceptions which are allowed concerning the free movement of capital inside the Community. First, non-arbitrary tax discrimination is allowed on the basis of the place of residence of tax-payers or on the basis of the place where their capital is invested. This seems to allow for certain imputation systems or for tax exemptions on capital earnings for non-residents, for instance. Secondly, restrictions on the right of establishment compatible with the Treaty implying restrictions on the movement of capital (either inside or outside the Community) remain fully applicable. This is of importance because the 1988 Directive[37] on the free movement of capital allowed for exceptions to the free movement of capital with third countries concerning direct investment, which may be covered by legislation concerning the right of establishment, such as that contained in the second banking Directive.[38] Thirdly, measures taken on the grounds of public policy or public security are allowed, although these grounds for measures in the past have been interpreted rather strictly for the other three 'freedoms'.

Article 73e relates to the derogations granted until 31 December 1992 to four Member States in the 1988 Directive on capital movements. According to this Directive, two of these Member States, i.e. Greece and Portugal, are allowed to extend their derogations until 31 December 1995. Furthermore, the 1988 Directive also allowed Member States to take safeguard measures for a maximum of six months.

In the Maastricht version, the text of the Article was changed in two respects compared to the Luxembourg draft Treaty. First, if Greece and Portugal asked, on the basis of the 1988 Directive, for an extension of their derogations beyond 1 January 1994 (the date at which the new provisions on the free movement of capital and payments become applicable), the derogations would now be granted automatically, whereas this required prior Council approval according to the Luxembourg text. Secondly, safeguard measures taken in agreement with the 1988 Directive cannot be maintained beyond 1 January 1994, after which the unconditional liberalization of capital movements inside the Community will be established.

2. *Capital Movements to or from Third Countries (Articles 73b, 73c, 73f and 73g).* The 1988 Directive on capital movements only contains (in its Article 7) a 'best endeavours' clause as regards the liberalization of the movement of capital between Member States and third countries. In contrast to the Luxembourg draft Treaty, the Maastricht Treaty, according to its Article 73b, liberalizes these capital movements completely from 1 January 1994, as well as payments. This is an important step, given the fact that such capital movements can currently be restricted by Member States at their own discretion. It is therefore not surprising that the Maastricht text contains a number of exceptions to the principle of liberalization with regard to third countries. First, there is a standstill clause for restrictions with respect to third countries involving direct investment, establishment, the provision of financial services or the admission of securities to capital markets which exist on 31 December 1993. As of 1 January 1994, the Council may decide, by qualified majority, to liberalize such restrictions or, by unanimity, to introduce more restrictions. Further liberalization is thus made easier than the introduction of more restrictions. Second, in the case of difficulties for the operation of EMU, the Council is always allowed, by a qualified majority, to take safeguard measures on the movement of capital with respect to third countries for a period not exceeding six months. The voting rule used for the introduction of temporary restrictions is therefore less strict than the unanimity required for indefinite measures which would restrict such capital movements. Thirdly, even if capital movements do not cause difficulties for the operation of EMU, the Council is still allowed to take sanctions concerning capital movements with third countries, provided that a joint action for such sanctions has been decided upon under Title V of the Maastricht Treaty, in the framework of the common foreign and security policy. In the absence of such joint action, a Member State may itself introduce such sanctions, which may however be abrogated by the Council.

3. *Financial Assistance Mechanism (Article 103a(2)).* From the Luxembourg draft Treaty, which put this Article in square brackets, it was obvious that there would be no early agreement on the introduction of the possibility for financial assistance to Member States in difficulties. On the one hand, it would not be logical to exclude such assistance in obvious cases, such as natural disasters or nuclear fall-out. On the other hand, such assistance should, in view of the no bail-out clause, not be given unconditionally or without regard to the responsibility of each Member State for the results of its economic policy. The compromise obtained in the Maastricht Treaty is that financial assistance, which is granted under certain conditions, can be decided upon more easily in the case of natural disasters (by a qualified majority) than in other exceptional occurrences beyond the control of the Member State concerned, where it requires unanimity.

4. Prohibition on Monetary Financing (Overdraft Facility) (Article 104). As set out above, there was early agreement on the principle that monetary financing should be prohibited from the start of the second stage. In several Member States, the government still has an overdraft facility with the central bank allowing it to finance temporary cash shortages, in some cases without paying interest. As is clear from the Protocol for the United Kingdom annexed to the Maastricht Treaty, the United Kingdom had difficulties in accepting the prohibition on overdraft facilities in the second stage. This follows from the fact that Article 11 of the said Protocol allows the Government of the United Kingdom to maintain its 'ways and means' facility with the Bank of England if and so long as the United Kingdom does not move to the third stage.

5. Excessive Deficit Procedure (Article 104c and Protocol). The two main differences between the Maastricht Treaty and the Luxembourg draft Treaty as regards the excessive deficit procedure are the introduction of quantified criteria and of an explicit list of sanctions which the Council may take against a Member State which, despite earlier warnings by the Council, does not correct its excessive deficit. The Luxembourg draft Treaty already indicated that account would have to be taken of the development of the public debt-to-GDP ratio, the deficit-to-GDP ratio and the relationship between the deficit and public investment. The former two criteria are specified more precisely in the Treaty. The debt-to-GDP ratio should not exceed 60%, unless the ratio is sufficiently diminishing and approaching 60% at a satisfactory pace. This exception is very important for those Member States which now have ratios far greater than 60%: it gives them the opportunity, while not respecting the 60% threshold, to show that their efforts in reducing public debt are nevertheless sufficient to take part on that score in the third stage. The deficit-to-GDP ratio should not exceed 3%, unless the ratio has declined substantially and continuously and reached a level close to 3%, or unless the excess over 3% is exceptional and temporary and the ratio remains close to 3%. As for the debt-to-GDP ratio, the first of these exceptions is important for Member States which currently have a very high deficit-to-GDP ratio. If the requirements under one of the two criteria are not respected, the Commission is obliged to make a report which is to be discussed in the Monetary Committee, after which the Commission may recommend to the Council that a decision be taken, after an overall assessment, on whether the Member State concerned has an excessive deficit. The Commission's report has to take account of whether the government deficit exceeds government investment expenditure, thereby introducing the third element which already figured in the Luxembourg draft Treaty. It also stipulates that the Commission should take account of all relevant factors in its report, which it may also issue if the criteria are not violated but if the Commission considers that there is risk of an excessive deficit. From this procedure it is clear that the excessive deficit procedure is not a mechanistic procedure: the criteria or the judgement of the Commission are used to start a process which, after careful consideration of all relevant aspects, may lead to the judgement that a Member State has an excessive deficit. Given the fact that, according to economic theory, an excessive deficit is difficult to define on the basis of strict criteria alone, this seems a balanced compromise.

The procedure which follows once the Council decides that a Member State has an excessive deficit is largely that which was spelled out in the Luxembourg draft Treaty: confidential recommendations, public recommendations, a notification to take specific measures and finally sanctions. The latter were not specified in the Luxembourg draft Treaty, and comprise: the requirement that the Member State concerned publish additional information before issuing bonds and securities, inviting the European Investment Bank to reconsider its lending policy towards the Member State concerned, a non-interest bearing deposit or fines of an appropriate size. The first sanction should be seen in relation to the so-called Prospectus Directive[39] which specifies rules for the content of prospectuses to be offered to the public when offering transferable securities to the public, but which exempts governments. Another provision which was added compared to the Luxembourg draft Treaty is that the Council should abrogate its measures taken against a Member State to the extent that the excessive deficit has been corrected. For instance, a step in the right direction could result in the abrogation of a sanction, although the deficit would still be excessive.

Furthermore, the Maastricht Treaty stipulates that the decisions on such measures are taken by the Council by a qualified majority without the votes of the Member State concerned. Further provisions concerning the excessive deficit procedure, such as the definitions used for government, deficit and public debt are given in a Protocol. This Protocol also contains the reference values of 3% for the deficit criterion and 60% for the debt criterion. Since secondary legislation is foreseen which should replace the Protocol (to be adopted by unanimity), the reference values or other additional features of the procedure can be adapted if needed without re-convening a new Intergovernmental Conference.

6. *Role of ECB in Issuing Banknotes and Coins (Article 105a).* The Luxembourg draft Treaty stipulated that the ESCB should regulate the issue and circulation of notes and coins, which alone would be legal tender. The October 1991 Dutch draft Treaty proposals were more specific: the issue of *banknotes* was to be authorized exclusively by the ECB, and only the banknotes issued by the ECB and the national central banks would have legal tender status. This would imply that other banks could be authorized to issue

banknotes, but that such notes would never be given the status of legal tender. For *coins*, however, the power to regulate the issue of coins and the volume thereof within the Member States would be given to the Council, which could also harmonize the denominations and specifications of all circulating coins. The Dutch proposals for the regulation of the issue of banknotes were retained in the Maastricht Treaty, albeit with the requirement that the ECB must respect as far as possible existing practices regarding the issue and design of banknotes. For coins, the responsibilities were divided between the ECB and the Council: coins may be issued by Member States, but their volume, since this has an impact on the money supply, is subject to approval by the ECB, whereas their denominations and technical specifications may be harmonized by the Council to permit their smooth circulation within the Community. The latter is important in view of the practical use of coins by citizens throughout the Community.

7. *Role of ECB in Prudential Supervision (Articles 105(5) and (6))*. Currently, the prudential supervision of financial institutions takes place in Member States by different authorities, usually the central bank and/or the ministry for finance. Prudential supervision is important due to its role as a safeguard for the stability of the financial system. Giving responsibility in this area to the ECB would therefore have the advantage that the ECB could immediately take action in the prudential field if monetary stability were to be threatened.

On the other hand, the dual responsibility for price stability and the stability of the financial system could in some cases confront the ECB with conflicting objectives. It would also mean that some finance ministries would see their prudential powers transferred to the ECB. This presumably partly explains the difficulties in reaching agreement on the role of the ECB in the prudential area. Whereas the Luxembourg draft Treaty still foresaw that the ESCB would 'take part, as required, in the definition, coordination and execution of policies relating to prudential control and stability of the financial system', the Maastricht Treaty limits the tasks of the ESCB in the prudential field to its contribution to the smooth conduct of policies pursued by the competent authorities relating to the prudential supervision of credit institutions and the stability of the financial system. Specific tasks, which are moreover limited to financial institutions with the exception of insurance undertakings (therefore completely excluding financial markets), can only be assigned by the Council to the ECB by unanimity.

8. *Financial Provisions of the ESCB (Statute of the ESCB Articles 26 to 33)*. A comparison of the Maastricht Treaty with the October 1991 Dutch proposal allows some of the issues concerning the financial provisions of the ESCB to be identified. As regards auditing, the Maastricht Treaty provides, contrary to

the earlier proposal, for a role for the Court of Auditors, which is however limited to the operational efficiency of the ECB's management. As regards the capital of the ECB, the only noteworthy change between the two versions is that the key for capital subscription is fixed in the Treaty as being equal to 50% of a Member State's share of Community population and 50% of its GDP share. In the earlier version, these percentages were to be decided upon separately by the Council, and a third element depending on the relative share in extra-EC imports was also proposed. A new provision is that the resulting percentage for the key for capital subscription will be rounded up to the nearest multiple of 0.05 percentage points, implying that if no further adjustment to the key is made, the sum of these percentages can exceed 100% with a maximum of almost 0.5 percentage points.

The October 1991 Dutch proposal brought a solution to the question of whether governments of Member States should be allowed to keep part of their official foreign reserves, by specifying that this would only be allowed for foreign exchange working balances (Article 105 (3)). The implication is that all other official foreign reserves will have to be transferred to the national central bank. Articles 30 and 31 of the Statute specify that the ECB may, in its turn, call up such reserves from the latter. Transactions above a certain limit, either by the national central banks with their official foreign reserves, or by the governments of the Member States with their foreign exchange working balances, require the approval of the ECB.

9.   External Representation (Articles 109(4) and (5)). The EMU Treaty assigns the exclusive competence for monetary policy to the ESCB. The competence for economic policy remains mainly in the hands of the Member States, whereas the competence for exchange rate policy is shared between the Council and the ECB. This implies that *a priori* it is neither clear who determines the position of the Community on the international stage (e.g. in G-7 or IMF meetings) in matters regarding EMU, nor who should represent the Community. This presumably explains why the October 1991 Dutch proposals, following the earlier Luxembourg draft Treaty proposals, gave the Council the power to decide on this separately by a qualified majority on a proposal of the Commission and after consulting the ECB. The Maastricht Treaty amends this provision in two ways. First, the decision on the position of the Community was separated from that on its representation, the latter now being decided by unanimity. Secondly, a new paragraph 5 was introduced confirming the right of Member States to negotiate in international bodies and conclude international agreements subject to Community competences and agreements as regards EMU.

10. Exchange Rate Policy and International Monetary Agreements (Articles 109(1) to (3)). A comparison of the successive draft Treaties shows the difficulties that have been encountered in reaching an agreement on external monetary policy. The main origin of these difficulties is undoubtedly that exchange rate policy is a two-edged sword: it has a direct impact both on monetary policy and on economic policy. Given the different competences in these two areas for the ECB, the Council and the Member States, it is clear that a compromise needed to be found regarding the final responsibility. This has been done by sub-dividing exchange rate policy into three areas. Whereas the Commission's draft Treaty only talked about exchange rate policy, the Luxembourg draft Treaty added the notion of an exchange rate system, in particular the adoption, adjustment or abandoning of central rates *vis-à-vis* third currencies. In the Maastricht Treaty, this was further extended in the form of three different decision procedures.

The *first procedure* concerns the conclusion of so-called formal agreements on an exchange rate system for the ECU in relation to non-Community currencies. The agreements, for instance, on a fixed parity between the ECU and a third currency, seem to have been called 'formal' to distinguish them from 'informal' agreements such as the Plaza-Louvre agreements. The formal agreements are concluded by the Council by unanimity, after it has consulted the European Parliament and the ECB. The latter should be consulted 'in an endeavour to reach a consensus consistent with the objective of price stability', thus emphasizing the possible impact of such an exchange rate system on price stability but giving the final responsibility to the Council. The unanimity requirement also ensures that any Member State can block an agreement if it considers that the objective of price stability is endangered. The Council decides on a recommendation either from the Commission or from the ECB. The Commission therefore has to share its usual right of initiative with the ECB, but not with the Member States or the Council which can only make a request to the Commission to formulate a recommendation through Article 109d.

The *second procedure* concerns the adoption, adjustment or abandoning of the central rates for the ECU in any exchange rate system adopted according to the first procedure. This follows the same procedure as before, except that the European Parliament is now informed after the measures have been taken and that the Council decides by a qualified majority. Given the confidentiality which has to be observed for parity modifications in order to surprise exchange markets, it seems logical in this case for the European Parliament to be informed *ex post*.

The *third procedure* operates in the absence of a 'formal' agreement on an exchange rate system. It gives the Council, again on a recommendation from either the Commission or the ECB, the possibility to formulate by a qualified majority 'general orientations for exchange rate policy'. The ECB is obliged, according to Article 3 of the Statute of the ESCB, to carry out foreign exchange operations consistent with these orientations; it has however, according to Article 109(2), also the discretion to decide whether these orientations are prejudicing the primary objective of price stability, for which it is thus given the final responsibility.

The compromise found for exchange rate policy is therefore that the Council has the final responsibility to decide on 'formal' agreements on exchange rate systems and that the ECB, if it considers that the primary objective of price stability is prejudiced, may override the general orientations of the Council in 'informal' systems or in the absence of any system, such as a free float.

In addition to the three procedures in the field of exchange rate policy, the Maastricht Treaty also contains, in Article 109(3), a general provision for negotiating not only the foreign exchange regime, but also monetary matters more generally. This procedure derogates from the normal procedure of Article 228, according to which it is the Commission which is mandated to negotiate and the Council which concludes the agreements. Instead, the Council decides separately for each case by a qualified majority on a recommendation of the Commission on the arrangements for the negotiation and conclusion for such agreements, albeit the Community should express a single position and the Commission should be fully associated. The derogation from the standard procedure of Article 228 seems to have been introduced for this Article and for Article 109(1) due to the specific role of the ECB in monetary and foreign exchange matters, which would leave it outside the standard procedure.

11. Content of Stage Two (Articles 108, 109e(3) to (5), 109f(1) and 109g).
Given the fact that EMU is to be achieved in three stages, the logical question arises of when the different provisions of the Treaty become applicable. Four major problem areas can be identified.

First, there was the question of *when* the provisions of the chapter on economic policy would enter into force (Articles 103 to 104c). The Commission's draft Treaty already included a provision according to which any of the articles on economic policy could be implemented by the Council, after a separate decision, in the second stage. The Luxembourg draft Treaty went further by proposing that all the articles concerned would apply directly in the second stage. In the Maastricht Treaty, this proposal was taken over, with a few exceptions. The broad guidelines for economic policy and the multilateral surveillance procedure are now applicable upon *ratification* instead of from the start of the second stage. On the other hand, the binding elements of the excessive deficit procedure (the binding principle that they should be avoided, the possibility of notification and sanctions by the Council) become applicable from the start of the *third stage*. The binding principle of Article 104c(1), that excessive deficits should be avoided, is replaced in the second stage by the best endeavours clause of Article 109e(4).

A second aspect concerned the question of whether the *monetary institution* to be set up at the start of the second stage would be the ESCB or another institution. The October 1991 Dutch draft Treaty proposal did away with the earlier complicated Luxembourg proposal according to which at the start of the second stage there would be a Council of Governors as well as the ESCB, but that the latter would only start to operate later during the second stage. Instead, it was proposed that at the start of stage two only one institution be set up, the European Monetary Institute (EMI), whose the tasks would be taken over by the ESCB which would be established as soon as a date for the start of the third stage had been determined. This proposal was retained in the Maastricht Treaty, albeit the set up and tasks of the EMI proved to be another difficult hurdle (see below). Although this construction violated the interpretation of the Rome I conclusions, according to which it would be the ESCB which should have been set up at the beginning of the second stage, it is clear according to the formulation of the Maastricht Treaty that the EMI is virtually to be considered as the precursor of the ESCB.

A third aspect relates to the timing of the *independence of national central banks*. The Rome I conclusions spelled out that the second stage would start after 'a process has been set in train designed to ensure the independence of the new monetary institution at the latest when monetary powers have been transferred'. This had been translated in the Luxembourg draft Treaty by the provision that before 1 January 1994, Member States would have to start the process with a view to the independence of their central bank being achieved not later than at the date of the transition to the final stage of EMU. The October 1991 Dutch draft Treaty retained this provision, but added another Article specifying that the Member States should ensure, before the beginning of the third stage, that their national legislation including the statutes of the national central banks would be compatible with the Treaty. The implication of this Article would be that all Member States, including those with a derogation or even an exemption, would have to make their central banks independent. Since in the first Dutch proposals the third stage would not start irrevocably, this would oblige Member States to make their central banks independent even if the third stage did not start at all. The Maastricht Treaty solves this dilemma; first, by specifying in Article 108 that the independence should be achieved at the latest at the date of the establishment of the ESCB (at which date it is sure that the third stage will start) and second, by adding in Article 109e(5) that each Member State should, during the second stage, only start 'as appropriate' the process leading to the independence of their central bank. The 'as appropriate' implies, for instance, that as long as the United Kingdom does not ask to participate in the third stage, it does not have to make the Bank of England independent.

Fourthly, the question concerning the *strengthening of the ECU* in the second stage had to be solved. The October 1991 Dutch draft Treaty proposed that, from the start of the second stage, the currency composition of the ECU basket would be irrevocably fixed. Since the next five-yearly revision of the ECU basket is due in 1994, this would *de facto* imply a fixing of the current basket composition. This explains why the Maastricht Treaty specifies that the ECU basket composition will not be changed after ratification rather than after the start of the second stage, since this would amount to the same in practice.[40] The Maastricht Treaty also deleted that the fixing would be 'irrevocable'. Instead, it indicates that at the starting date of the third stage, the irrevocably fixed rate between the ECU (which then is no longer a basket currency) and the national currencies participating in the third stage will be adopted. This rate is not necessarily that implied by the fixed currency composition of the ECU basket, although it is specified that the external value of the ECU should not be modified by the irrevocably fixed conversion rate.

12. The European Monetary Institute (Article 109f and Protocol). Although, as noted above, it seemed to be accepted rather soon after the start of the Dutch Presidency that the EMI and not the ESCB would be established at the start of the second stage, the institutional set-up and tasks of this body remained the subject of controversy. A comparison of the Maastricht Treaty with the October 1991 Dutch draft Treaty shows four major changes.

The first major change concerns the *composition* of the Council of the EMI which will direct and manage the EMI. If this Council were to consist not only of the governors from the national central banks (as proposed in the Luxembourg draft Treaty) but also of one or more external persons, this would make it clear that the EMI would not simply be a continuation of the Committee of Governors of National Central Banks. The October 1991 text proposed that there would be an external president and vice-president for the Council of the EMI, both to be appointed by common accord of the governments of the Member States on a recommendation from the Council. The Maastricht text has changed this: the vice-president will not be external, but appointed (by the Council of the EMI) from among the governors of the national central banks; secondly, the external president will be appointed, not on a recommendation from the Council, but on a recommendation from the Council of the EMI.[41]

The second major change concerns the *financing* of the EMI. If it were endowed with its own capital, this would add to its independence. If this independence were identified with a transfer of powers in the monetary field before the introduction of a single monetary policy, an alternative would be to finance the EMI by means of annual contributions from the national central banks. It was this last solution which was contained in the October 1991 proposals. The Maastricht Treaty, however, shows a compromise between the two possibilities sketched above (Protocol on the EMI, Article 16): the EMI will be endowed with its 'own resources', the size of which should be sufficient to ensure adequate income to cover the administrative expenditure incurred by the EMI, and provided out of contributions from the national central banks which have to be paid by the date of establishment of the EMI. Rather than having a capital, the return on which should cover the EMI's running costs, it will get one lump sum at the time of its establishment which should guarantee sufficient income to cover its expenses during its lifetime, which will be until 1 January 1999 at the latest.

The third change relates to the question of to which extent the EMI is the *precursor* of the ESCB. If it were the true *precursor*, it should, in the context of the preparation of the third stage, already be given the possibility to take binding decisions concerning the tasks of the ECB. If it were considered that such decisions could only be taken by the ESCB itself and only with independent central banks of those Member States sharing in the single monetary policy, the role of the EMI would have to be purely consultative. The October 1991 text specified that the Council of the EMI could adopt guidelines, without binding force however, laying down the methods for the implementation of the conditions necessary for the ESCB to perform its functions in the third stage of EMU, to be submitted for decision to the ECB. The Maastricht Treaty added to this that the EMI should, by 31 December 1996 at the latest, specify the regulatory, organizational and logistical framework necessary for the ESCB to perform its tasks in the third stage, and that this framework should also be submitted for decision to the ECB at the date of its establishment. Without being given the possibility to take decisions which are binding on the ESCB, it is clear that the EMI has to prepare for the operation of the ESCB to the largest possible extent, therefore being its virtual precursor.

The fourth major change concerns the *tasks* of the EMI. The October 1991 text gave the EMI the task of undertaking functions with respect to the ECU clearing system and of overseeing and promoting the development of the ECU. In the Maastricht Treaty, these tasks have been weakened: the EMI should now 'facilitate the use of the ECU and oversee its development, including the smooth functioning of the ECU clearing system'. A factor that may have played a role in this change of formulation is that by undertaking functions with respect to the ECU clearing system, the EMI would have already performed some of the banking functions of the third stage. Also, promoting a basket currency whose value, through parity changes in the ERM, could decrease with respect to one or more of its constituent currencies may have played a role. On the other hand, the Maastricht Treaty added a task for the EMI which would give it experience in one of the functions to be performed by the ECB in the third stage, i.e. foreign exchange management, through the provision that the EMI is entitled to hold and manage foreign exchange reserves as an agent for and at the request of national central banks.

13. Institutional Matters. A comparison of the successive Treaties shows that the institutional matters must have been a major subject for negotiation: this is apparent from the numerous changes observed in the institutional aspects and from the diversity of procedures which eventually resulted (see the overview of procedures in Table 4). It is not difficult to find causes explaining these results. Firstly, the introduction of a new Community body in the form of the ESCB required a new institutional equilibrium. Secondly, the shared responsibilities in the field of economic policy between the Member States and the Community required specific solutions. Thirdly, the exclusion from voting in some cases had to be dealt with. Fourthly, the specific responsibility for the European Council and the ECOFIN Council regarding EMU had to be translated into operational terms. Finally, the creation of the EMI and the ECB added to the problem of the seats of the institutions.

Currently, after the Single European Act, the following *voting rules* exist for decisions taken by the Council:[42]

   – simple majority;

   – qualified majority: this requires a minimum of 54 out of a total of 76 weighted votes. For a vote which is not taken on a proposal from the Commission (e.g. on a recommendation from the Commission), at least eight Member States should vote in favour;

   – the cooperation procedure with the European Parliament: this is a mixture of qualified majority/unanimity voting;

   – unanimity.

The Council may *amend* the text on which it is invited to vote by the same majority as required for its adoption, except when the Council acts on a proposal from the Commission: unanimity is always required for an act constituting an amendment to a proposal from the Commission.[43]

In addition to the above voting rules, some decisions are taken by common accord of the governments of the Member States (e.g. on the seat of the institutions). Furthermore, the Single European Act institutionalized the European Council, but did not specify its voting rules. Normally, the European Council as a body does not take formal Community decisions,[44] but reaches conclusions by consensus,[45] on the basis of which formal decisions can be taken by the Council.

To these existing voting rules, the EMU part of the Maastricht Treaty adds several novelties. For instance, in the context of the excessive deficit procedure, qualified majority voting in the Council is introduced, defined as two-thirds of the weighted votes excluding those of the Member State with an excessive deficit.[46] If the votes of such a Member State were not excluded, Member States with a large number of votes could more easily obtain a blocking majority in cases where the Council is deciding on measures against them, such as sanctions. The same type of qualified majority voting is also introduced in a number of cases concerning voting by the Council on monetary policy or exchange rate matters, this time excluding the votes of the Member States which have not irrevocably fixed their exchange rate.[47] This exclusion also applies to unanimity voting in the same areas,[48] as well as to some decisions to be taken by common accord.[49]

The Maastricht Treaty also modifies the nature of the *decision-making bodies* in the Community. In the Treaties establishing the European Communities, there is only one Council, consisting of representatives of the Member States in the form of a member of each government. In other words, decisions to be adopted by the Council in a particular field, for instance agriculture, can be adopted by the so-called General Affairs Council consisting of ministers for foreign affairs because of the 'unicity' of the Council. This 'unicity' is affected in two ways in the EMU Treaty. First, for a number of decisions concerning the transition to the third stage,[50] the EMU Treaty specifies that they are adopted by the Council 'meeting in the composition of the Heads of State or Government'. This formulation ensures that such decisions can be taken formally at the highest political level by a qualified majority within the Community legal framework. Secondly, a declaration affirms that in the areas concerning EMU, the usual practice according to which the Council meets in the composition of economic and finance ministers will be continued. The introduction of the Heads of State or Government as the Council also appears for decisions to be taken by *common accord* of the governments of the Member States, in particular for the appointment of the President of the Council of the EMI, the members of the Executive Board of the ECB and the seat of the EMI and the ECB.[51] Finally, the role of the *European Council* was affected. The European Council was institutionalized by the Single European Act as consisting of the Heads of State or Government and the President of the European Commission, and assisted by the ministers for foreign affairs and by a member of the Commission. In the Treaties establishing the European Communities, however, no role was foreseen for the European Council. In the EC Treaty, as modified by the Maastricht Treaty, this changes: according to Article 103(2) the European Council is given a role since it has to discuss a conclusion on the broad guidelines of the economic policies of the Member States and the Community. In addition, a declaration specifies that the President of the European Council shall invite the economic and finance ministers to European Council meetings when matters concerning EMU are discussed. The difference between the appearance of the European Council in Article 103(2) and the 'Council meeting in the composition of Heads of State or Government' in Articles 109j and 109k is that in the former, no formal decisions are taken (the European Council has to 'discuss a conclusion') whereas, in the latter, formal decisions have to be taken by a qualified majority.

The traditional *right of initiative* of the Commission to make proposals to the Council has been affected in four ways in the EMU part of the Maastricht Treaty. First, in a number of cases, the Council decides on a recommendation rather than on a proposal from the Commission.[52] The implication is that no unanimity is required for the Council to amend the recommendation from the Commission. This type of initiative has been introduced mainly when the Council takes decisions which concern a particular Member State (recommendations, sanctions or balance-of-payments support) or when the right of initiative is shared with the ECB. If unanimity were required in the former case, the Member State concerned could block any amendment; in the latter case, the unanimity requirement would create the asymmetry that amendments to a recommendation from the ECB by the Council would be easier to make than amendments to a proposal from the Commission. A second impact concerns the fact that for decisions on exchange rate agreements and secondary legislation in the monetary field, the Commission shares the right of initiative with the ECB. This is a reflection of a new institutional balance. Thirdly, in decisions where the *Heads of State or Government* play a role as part of the European Council (economic policy guidelines), as Council (start of the third stage, granting of derogations), or as intergovernmental body (appointment of members of the Executive Board of the ECB), the Commission makes recommendations to the Council which then makes recommendations to the Heads of State or Government. Fourthly, in addition to the existing Article 152, which gives the Council the right to request that the Commission submit proposals to it, a new Article 109d extends this right to recommendations in a number of EMU areas, where *individual Member States* may now also make such a request.

The *European Parliament* is involved in several ways in the decisions regarding EMU: by giving its assent, through the 'cooperation' procedure of Article 189c, through consultation or by being informed of certain decisions by the Council. The former two procedures are used for 'legislative' acts of the Council, whereas the latter are mostly applied for 'executive' acts. In addition, there is the democratic accountability of the ECB: the annual report of the ECB is presented by the President of the ECB to the European Parliament which may hold a general debate on that basis; at its request, any member of the Executive Board, including the President, may be heard at any time.

The establishment of the EMI and the ECB added to the problem of the *seat* of the institutions of the Community. This problem was solved in 1967 through the Decision on the provisional location of certain institutions and departments of the Communities.[53] The Maastricht Treaty specifies imperatively, however, that the decision as to where the seat of the EMI and the ECB will be established has to be taken before the end of 1992.

14. Transition to the Third Stage (Articles 109j, 109k, 109l and 109m; Articles 43 to 49 of the Statute of the ESCB; Protocols). The transition to the third stage was one of the most difficult issues, as demonstrated by the fact that it was among the few outstanding problems on EMU which were discussed at the European Council meeting in Maastricht itself. These problems were based, on the one hand, on the position of the United Kingdom and Denmark which were unable to commit themselves irrevocably at an early stage to the advent of a single currency and, on the other hand, on an 'insider-outsider' problem due to the possibility of derogations. The ensuing issues to be solved can be grouped under the catch-words 'why, when, who and how?'.

The '*why*' issue resulted from the fact that the United Kingdom, and, in a later stage, also Denmark were unable to subscribe at the time of signing the Treaty to the single currency, and wanted a possibility before the start of the third stage for a separate decision on their participation. As early as the informal ECOFIN meeting in May 1991 in Luxembourg, it was reported in the press[54] that President Delors had proposed to meet the British objections of that time through a separate declaration by the British Government that it was not yet ready to subscribe to a single currency. This point had been left open in the Luxembourg draft Treaty and was first treated formally in the October 1991 Dutch draft Treaty, which proposed a so-called 'opting-out clause' whereby each Member State could notify the Council if its national parliament did not feel able to approve the irrevocable fixing of its currency. This general possibility to opt out before the start of the third stage was however not retained in the Maastricht Treaty. Denmark obtained a Protocol which would allow it to have an indefinite exemption with the same implications for participation in the third stage as those of a Member State with a derogation. The United Kingdom obtained a much more detailed Protocol which would also allow it to have an exemption. The latter would, however, differ in its content from a derogation in several respects, the most important being that the United Kingdom would not have to make the Bank of England independent and would not be subject to the principle that excessive deficits should be avoided. In exchange, as it were, Denmark and the United Kingdom joined the other Member States in signing a Protocol which states that 'no Member State shall prevent the entering into the third stage'. If one or both countries were to opt for an exemption, therefore, they should not obstruct the others from moving to the third stage, as they could, for instance, through their voting behaviour.

The *'when'* question for EMU was first discussed in the Delors report with the conclusion that there should not be fixed dates, either for the second stage or for the third stage. This was changed in the Rome I conclusions, where it was said that at the latest within three years from the start of the second phase, the decision concerning the passage to the third stage should be prepared, which should occur within a reasonable time. This did not set an absolute deadline, but gave at least the certainty that stage three would happen, and an approximate time frame. According to the Luxembourg draft Treaty, the European Council would have to set the date for the beginning of the third stage 'once it has ascertained that the conditions for transition to the final stage...are united', thus leaving open when or under which conditions the third stage would start. The October 1991 Dutch proposals were very explicit: if the European Council would not conclude on a date for the third stage the first time, the procedure would be repeated every two years. In the Maastricht Treaty, a completely new formula was introduced, according to which a first decision on the start of the third stage would have to be taken before the end of 1996. If negative, a positive decision on the start of the third stage could still be put off until the end of 1997. If, by that time, no date had been set, the third stage would begin automatically on 1 January 1999.

The discussion on the starting date was very much related to the *'who'* question: which countries would participate initially, should there be a minimum ('critical mass') and what would happen to the Member States being left behind? The October 1991 Dutch proposals were the first to impose explicitly the condition that there should be a minimum number of Member States without a derogation or an exemption in order to start the third stage, proposing that the minimum should be seven Member States. This proposal was also reflected by introducing simple majority voting which, with twelve Member States, would be tantamount to seven Member States voting in favour of the start of the third stage. In the Maastricht Treaty, the idea of a minimum number of Member States that should be ready was retained for the first batch of decisions: for any positive decision taken before the end of 1997, it is required that at least a majority of Member States fulfil the necessary conditions,[55] the decision being taken however by a qualified majority. Since the Council does not decide on a proposal from the Commission, this qualified majority requires a vote in favour cast by at least eight Member States. However, in accordance with the Protocol on the transition to the third stage of EMU, a Member State with a derogation is required to respect the will of the Community to enter swiftly into the third stage and may not prevent the others from entering into the third stage. In the case of an automatic start of the third stage on 1 January 1999, there is no minimum requirement: only

Member States fulfilling the necessary conditions will participate, even if they do not form a majority.

A further question concerned the integration, in a later stage, of Member States with a derogation or an exemption. According to the Luxembourg draft Treaty, a derogation would be of a specific duration, and it was left open whether, after its expiration, the derogation would be automatically suspended or not. According to the October 1991 proposals, each derogation or exemption would be of indefinite duration, with the possibility of being examined and abrogated at least once every two years. The procedure for this abrogation differed however from the earlier one for the start of the third stage. In the Maastricht Treaty the idea of an indefinite derogation with a review every two years was retained, with the addition however of the possibility for the Member State concerned to make, itself, a request for abrogation at any time and according to almost the same procedure as that used for the start of the third stage.

The '*how*' of the decisions on the transition to the third stage involved negotiations on a rather wide range of issues. The issue attracting most attention was undoubtedly that of the *convergence criteria*. The Rome I conclusions mentioned convergence as regards price stability and the restoration of sound public finances. In the Commission's draft Treaty proposal, there were references to the integration of markets and convergence of economic and monetary developments. The Luxembourg draft Treaty made it explicit, in addition, that the required degree of convergence concerned price stability, balancing of the budget and interest rates. In the October 1991 draft Treaty, this was worked out further, almost into its final form. For price stability, the criterion became an inflation rate not exceeding by more than 1.5% that of, at most, the three best performing countries (this formulation allows, in its most flexible interpretation, an inflation differential of 1.5% compared to the third best performing country). For public finance, an indirect criterion was chosen in the form of the absence of an excessive deficit according to the excessive deficit procedure. For interest rates, the criterion became a long-term interest rate differential of not more than 2% with respect to, at most, the three best performers in terms of price stability. Furthermore, a fourth criterion was added: the respect of the normal fluctuation margins of the ERM without a devaluation. The incentive provided by this criterion replaced the Rome I condition for the start of the second stage that the largest possible number of Member States should participate in the ERM. In addition, account would also have to be taken of the development of the ECU, the results of the integration of markets, the current account, unit labour costs and other price indices.

The *decision procedure* on the transition to the third stage created problems due to several factors. Without any further provisions, the voting rule would implicitly determine the critical mass. The Rome I conclusions indicated that somehow the European Council should have a major part in the decision-making process, the problem being its role as a body in the Community legal framework and the fact that it normally reaches its conclusions by consensus. Also, an equilibrium needed to be found as regards the weight to be given to the ECOFIN Council's conclusions on the fulfilment of the necessary conditions for the third stage. The link between voting rule and critical mass was solved by the provision in the Protocol on the transition to the third stage of EMU that a Member State with a derogation should not prevent the others from moving to the third stage. The problem of incorporating the European Council was solved by introducing the special composition of the Council with the Heads of State or Government ('Heads of State Council'). This allowed a voting rule to be specified other than unanimity (i.e. qualified majority) while still taking the decision at the highest political level and within the Community legal framework. A proper role for the ECOFIN Council was ensured by introducing a two-step decision-making procedure: the Commission and the EMI first report to the ECOFIN Council, which by a qualified majority assesses for each Member State whether it fulfils the conditions for the adoption of a single currency, and whether there is a majority of such countries. The reports of the Commission and of the EMI, the opinion of the European Parliament and the recommendations of the ECOFIN Council then go to the Heads of State Council which, on the basis of the recommendations of the ECOFIN Council, takes the formal decision by a qualified majority on whether a majority of the Member States fulfils the conditions and whether it is appropriate for the Community to enter the third stage. Only if both requirements are met does it set a date for the beginning of the third stage.[56] After a formal decision by the Council meeting in the composition of Heads of State or Government, either implicitly or explicitly, on which Member States fulfil the conditions, the formal decision by the ECOFIN Council on the derogations is straightforward. For the abrogation of derogations, the ECOFIN Council has more weight, however, since the Council meeting in the composition of Heads of State or Government is only given the role of discussing the Commission's recommendation to that effect, rather than taking the formal decision, which is left to the ECOFIN Council.

Although the principle of granting derogations was accepted early on in the negotiations, their actual *content* was only agreed upon in a later stage. The Commission and Luxembourg Draft Treaties only contained some general provisions concerning the exclusion from monetary and exchange rate policy decision-making, leaving open the possibility of further decisions by the Council. The October 1991 draft Treaty, however, contained a precise description of the implication of a derogation for a Member State, without giving the Council the possibility to decide on additional elements, for instance, country-specific. The derogations agreed upon in Maastricht provide for Member States to participate in many aspects of the third stage. For instance, they can benefit from the financial assistance mechanism, they have the obligation to avoid excessive deficits, they have to consult the ECB on their legislative proposals, specific tasks exercised by the ECB in the field of prudential supervision could apply to them, they have to subscribe to the primary objective of price stability and make their central banks independent (which then become part of the ESCB), and they are represented in the General Council of the ESCB which takes over the functions of the EMI and contributes to the work of the ECB. On the other hand, the Council cannot impose sanctions on them in the context of the excessive deficit procedure, and they do not participate in, nor have responsibility for the single monetary policy and exchange rate policy, nor do they take part in the appointment of the members of the Executive Board of the ECB.

A final issue linked to the start of the third stage concerned the moment at which the ECU will be introduced as a single currency. According to the Luxembourg draft Treaty, separate measures by the Council would be needed, after the fixing of the exchange rates between the currencies of the Member States at the start of the third stage, for the introduction of the ECU as a single currency. The October 1991 proposals specified that one of these separate measures, i.e. the rate at which the single currency would be substituted for the national currencies, would also have to be determined at the starting date of the third stage. The Maastricht Treaty added to this provision that it would make the ECU 'a currency in its own right', thus distinguishing it from the basket currency. Furthermore, it was added that, by fixing its rate to the national currencies, the external value of the (basket) ECU should not be modified.[57] Finally, the measures for the introduction of the ECU as the single currency would have to be taken 'rapidly'.

15. Economic and social cohesion (Articles 130a to 130e, Protocol on economic and social cohesion). The subject of economic and social cohesion was a horizontal issue between the EMU and EPU conference which also needed final negotiation in Maastricht. In the Luxembourg draft Treaty, the possibility was foreseen for the Council to set up, by unanimity, new structural funds. In the Maastricht Treaty, this provision was replaced by one saying that before 31 December 1993 a Cohesion Fund would have to be set up to provide a financial contribution to environmental projects and trans-European networks for transport infrastructure. Contrary to the other structural funds, the criterion for participation in this fund is one of *national* relative prosperity, viz. a national GNP per capita below 90% of the Community average. Moreover, a link with convergence was introduced through the requirement that eligible Member States have a 'convergence programme leading to the fulfilment of the conditions of economic convergence of Article 104c'. Without being specific, the Protocol on economic and social cohesion also stated that the level of Community participation in structural fund programmes and projects could be modulated, thereby alleviating the budgetary pressure imposed on Member States by the so-called 'additionality' requirement in the reformed structural funds.[58] The Protocol also declared that the system of own resources should take more account of the contributive capacity of Member States and that means should be examined for correcting, for the less prosperous Member States, existing regressive elements.

From Maastricht to the Third Stage

What are the remaining steps to be taken in the run-up to the third stage of EMU? First of all, the Treaty on European Union should be ratified by all Member States, after which it enters into force on 1 January 1993 or, failing that, as soon as all Member States have ratified it. Before the end of 1992, the seat of the EMI and the ECB will also have to be determined. In the meantime, Member States have already started presenting convergence programmes, as they should before the start of the second stage. The Committee of Governors of Central Banks has started the preparations for the EMI and even for some aspects of the operation of a single monetary policy in the third stage.[59] After ratification, the Council will have to adopt complementary legislation which has to be ready before the start of the second stage, such as complementary legislation for the excessive deficit procedure, the definition of 'privileged access', the multilateral surveillance procedure or the rules for consultation of EMI by the Member States for their legislative proposals. Table 4 lists in panel A the articles of the Treaty on the basis of which complementary legislation can or should be adopted. In addition, the Council should also adopt after ratification the broad guidelines for economic policies of the Member States and, before the end of 1993, appoint the first President of the Council of the EMI.

After the start of the second stage, the EMI will have three years to complete the preparation of the third stage. The Member States should further consolidate and extend their achievements in the field of convergence, helped thereby through the excessive deficit procedure. Moreover, some Member States would still need to enter into the narrow band of the ERM. The Council should adopt complementary legislation, in particular that concerning the statutes of the ESCB after the starting date of the third stage has been decided upon.

During the second stage, two events could change the background picture for EMU. The first is enlargement. The application for membership of EFTA

Table 4: Decision-Making Procedures Concerning EMU in the Maastricht Treaty

Article	Description	Voting rule	Involvement of:			When possible?
			Commission	EP	ECB/EMI/CoG/MC	
A:	**Complementary legislation adopted by the Council**					
73c(2)	Capital liberalization to or from third countries	QM[1]	prop. Com.	-	-	stage two
103(5)	Legislation surveillance procedure	Procedure of Article 189c (cooperation)			-	ratification
104a(2)	Legislation privileged access	Procedure of Article 189c (cooperation)			-	ratification
104b(2)	Legislation monetary financing + no bail-out	Procedure of Article 189c (cooperation)			-	ratification
104c(14)	Amendment protocol excessive deficits	UN	prop. Com.	cons. EP	cons. ECB**	ratification
	Legislation excessive deficit protocol	QM	prop. Com.	cons. EP	-	ratification
105(6)	Enabling clause prudential supervision ECB	UN	prop. Com.	assent EP	cons. ECB	stage three
105a(2)	Harmonization of coins	Procedure of Article 189c (cooperation)[2]		assent EP	cons. ECB	stage three
106(5)	Simplified amendment Statutes 1)	QM	cons. Com.	assent EP	rec. ECB	stage three
	or 2)	UN			cons. ECB**	
106(6)	Sec. legislation Statutes 1)	QM	prop. Com	assent EP	rec. ECB	if start stage three known
	or 2)	UN			cons. ECB**	
109c(3)	Composition of Ecofin Committee	QM	prop. Com.	info EP	cons. ECB** + MC	ratification
109f(6)	Framework for consultation of EMI	QM	prop. Com.	cons. EP	cons. EMI**	ratification
109f(7)	Enabling clause other tasks EMI in stage two	UN	prop. Com.	cons. EP	cons. EMI**	ratification
16.2[3]	Rules for key EMI contributions	QM	prop. Com.	cons. EP	cons. CoG + MC	ratification
109j(1)[4]	Amendment protocol criteria for stage three	UN	prop. Com.	cons. EP	cons. EMI/ECB** + MC	ratification

[1] For a step backwards as regards liberalization, unanimity is required.

[2] Excluding the votes from Member States with a derogation.

[3] Article 16.2 of the Protocol on the Statute of the European Monetary Institute.

[4] The legal basis is Article 6 of the Protocol on the convergence criteria referred to in Article 109j of the Treaty establishing the European Community.

Article	Description	Voting rule	Involvement of: Commission	EP	ECB/EMI/CoG/MC	When possible?
B:	**Other activities ('executive tasks')**					
73f	Safeguard clause capital movements	QM	prop. Com.	-	cons. ECB**	stage two
73g(1)	Sanctions capital movements with third countries	QM[5]	prop. Com.	-	-	stage two
73g(2)	Amendment/abolition national sanctions	QM	prop. Com.	info EP	-	stage two
103(2)	Broad guidelines economic policies					
	- report to European Council by Council:	QM	rec. Com.	-	-	ratification
	- adoption[6]:	QM	-	info EP	-	ratification
103(3)	Surveillance	-	reports Com.	info EP	-	ratification
103(4)	Confidential recommendations for surveillance	QM	rec. Com.*	-	-	ratification
103(4)	Public recommendations for surveillance	QM	prop. Com.*	Hearing EP	-	ratification
103a(1)	Enabling clause appropriate measures	UN	prop. Com.	-	-	ratification
103a(2)	Financial assistance (natural disasters)	QM	prop. Com.	info EP	-	stage three
103a(2)	Financial assistance (other exceptional occurrences)	UN	prop. Com.	info EP	-	stage three
104c(3)	Violation excessive deficit criteria or risk	-	report Com.	-	-	stage two
104c(5)	Excessive deficit exists or may occur	-	opinion Com.	-	-	stage two
104c(6)	Decision that excessive deficit exists	QM	rec. Com.*	-	-	stage two
104c(7)	Confidential recommendations excessive deficit	QM-	rec. Com.*	-	-	stage two
104c(8)	Public recommendations excessive deficit	QM-	rec. Com.*	-	-	stage two
104c(9)	Notification to reduce excessive deficit	QM-/QM--	rec. Com.*	-	-	stage three
104c(11)	Sanctions for excessive deficit	QM-/QM--	rec. Com.*	info EP	-	stage three
104c(12)	Abrogation excessive deficit	QM-	rec. Com.*	-	-	stage two
109(1)	Conclusion of agreements on exchange rate system	UN--	rec. Com.*	cons. EP	rec./cons. ECB[7]	stage three
109(1)	Modification central rates in exchange rate system	QM--	rec. Com.*	info EP	rec./cons. ECB[7]	stage three

---

[5] This decision has to follow the procedure of Article 228a.

[6] The adoption should take place on the basis of the conclusion of the European Council.

[7] The ECB and the Commission may each make recommendations. In either case, the ECB should be consulted in an endeavour to reach a consensus consistent with the objective of price stability.

Article	Description	Voting rule	Involvement of:			When possible?
			Commission	EP	ECB/EMI/CoG/MC	
109(2)	Broad exchange rate guideline　1)	QM--	rec. Com.*	-	cons. ECB	stage three
	or 2)	QM--	-	-	rec. ECB	Stage three
109(3)	Monetary/exchange agreements procedure	QM--	rec. Com.*	-	cons. ECB	stage three
109(4)	International position	QM--	prop. Com.*	-	cons. ECB	stage three
	External representation	UN--	prop. Com.*	-	cons. ECB	stage three
109a(2b)	Appointment members Executive Board ECB	CA/HSG[8]	-	cons. EP	cons. ECB	stage three
109b(1)	Motion President of the Council to ECB	not specified	-	-	-	stage three
109e(2)	Convergence assessment before stage two	-	report Com.	-	-	ratification
109f(1)	Appointment President EMI	CA/HSG[9]	-	cons. EP	rec. CoG/EMI Council	ratification
	Appointment Vice-President EMI	-	-	-	appointment by EMI Council	ratification[10]
109h(2)	Granting mutual assistance	QM	rec. Com.	-	cons. MC	stage two
109h(3)	Revoking/changing Commission authorization of protective measures	QM	-	-	-	ratification[10]
109i(3)	Modifying protective measures of Member States	QM	opinion Com.	-	cons. MC	ratification[10]
109j(2)	Assessment on the conditions for stage three + Recommendations to HSG Council	QM[11]	rec. Com.*	cons. EP	report EMI	stage two
109j(3)	Decisions HSG Council on start of stage three:		report Com.	opinion EP	report EMI	stage two[12]
	- decision if a majority meets the conditions	QM[13]				
	- decision on appropriateness move to stage three	QM				
	- set the starting date	QM				

8　The appointment takes place on a recommendation from the (Ecofin) Council and excluding the votes of the Member States with a derogation.

9　The appointment takes place also after consulting the (Ecofin) Council.

10　After stage three, this Article only applies to Member States with a derogation.

11　The recommendation of the (Ecofin) Council should be on the basis of the reports by the Commission and the EMI.

12　These decisions have to be taken before 31.12.1996.

13　This decision is taken on the basis of the recommendations from the (Ecofin) Council.

| Article | Description | Voting rule | Involvement of: | | | When possible? |
			Commission	EP	ECB/EMI/CoG/MC	
109j(4)	Decisions HSG Council if start of stage three in 1999: - assessment which Member States meet the conditions	QM¹³	report Com.	opinion EP	report EMI	1998 first semester
109k(1)	Derogations:					
	- if start stage three decided before 1998	QM¹³	rec. Com.*	-	-	stage two
	- if stage three starts on 1.1.1999	follows automatically from Art. 109j(4)				1998 first semester
109k(2)	Abrogation derogations	QM¹⁴	prop. Com.*	cons. EP	report ECB	if derogations exist
109l(1)	Nomination first members Executive Board ECB	CA/HSG⁸	-	cons. EP	cons. EMI	if start stage three known
109l(4)	Adoption conversion rates	UN--	prop. Com.*	-	cons. ECB	starting date stage three
109l(4)	Adoption measures single currency	UN--	prop. Com.*	-	cons. ECB	stage three
109l(5)	Conversion rate for Member States joining later	UN---	prop. Com.*	-	cons. ECB	stage three

Legend

QM = qualified majority
QM- = majority of two-thirds of weighted votes excluding the Member State concerned
QM-- = 1) qualified majority defined as majority of two thirds of weighted votes of Member States without a derogation
     2) amendment of proposal of Commission by unanimity of these Member States
UN = unanimity
UN-- = unanimity of Member States without a derogation
CA = common accord
CA/HSG = common accord of governments at the level of Heads of State or Government
MC = Monetary Committee (before stage three)/Economic and financial committee (in stage three)
EP = European Parliament
HSG Council = Council meeting in the composition of Heads of State or Government
* = Article 109d applies (Member State or the Council may request the Commission to make a proposal/recommendation)
** = consultative role taken over by EMI before establishment of the ECB or Committee of Governors before 1.1.1994

prop. = proposal
cons. = consultation
rec. = recommendation
info = information
CoG = Committee of Governors
Com. = Commission

¹⁴ After the submission of reports by the Commission and the ECB, this decision is taken by the (Ecofin) Council after a discussion in the HSG Council.

countries such as Austria, Finland, Sweden and Switzerland could lead to their accession before the start of the third stage. Since these countries are highly developed and in most cases respect the convergence criteria, their membership of the Community will facilitate the start of the third stage. Secondly, the Treaty on European Union specifies[60] that a new Inter-governmental Conference will be convened in 1996 '...with the aim of ensuring the effectiveness of the mechanisms and the institutions of the Community'. This could also have an impact on the functioning of EMU, especially in the institutional field.

In addition to these events, others could arise which could be either beneficial to the EMU process or delay it. It is clear that German unification and the process of political and economic reform in Central and Eastern Europe and the former Soviet Union has had an impact on economic convergence and the thinking about the constitution of Europe. The recession which descended on the industrialized world in 1991 may hamper the convergence process, especially in the field of budgetary consolidation. However, after ratification of the Treaty, none of these challenges will prevent, on 1 January 1999 at the latest, exchange rates being irrevocably fixed between a large number of Member States of the European Community. As this paper has demonstrated, it took a long time, with difficult negotiations, to get there. Sometimes there is a tendency, amidst all the problems, to forget that EMU should bring net benefits, economically and politically. This objective should not be lost from sight.

NOTES

1. See Council/Commission of the EC (1992).
2. For the purpose of this chapter, Articles 2, 3a, 73a to 73h, 102a to 109m, the Protocols 3 to 13 (numbered as in the Final Act) and the declarations 3 to 8, 10 (partly) and 33 (also as numbered in the Final Act) will be considered as the EMU part of the Treaty establishing the European Community as modified by the Treaty on European Union and will be called the 'EMU Treaty'. Article 2, describing the objectives of the Community, is a general article but has been included because of its importance for EMU.
3. Committee for the Study of Economic and Monetary Union (1989).
4. The texts on which the discussion in this chapter is based were either published officially or widely distributed. For references, see the footnotes to Table 2.
5. See Hasse (1990) or Ungerer et al. (1990).
6. Report to the Council and the Commission on the realization by stages of Economic and Monetary Union in the Community (Werner Report), Bulletin of the European Communities (11/1970), Supplement.
7. Resolution of the Council and of the Representatives of the Governments of the Member States of 22 March 1971 on the attainment by stages of Economic and Monetary Union in the Community, reprinted in Monetary Committee (1989).
8. See Hasse (1990).
9. The final communiqué of the Conference of Heads of State or Government of Member States and future members of the European Communities (Paris, 19-21 October 1972) is reprinted in Monetary Committee (1989).
10. Council Regulation (EEC) no. 907/73 of 3 April 1973 establishing a European Monetary Cooperation Fund, OJ no. L 89, 5 April 1973, p. 2.
11. Council Decision of 18 February 1974 on the attainment of a high degree of convergence of the economic policies of the Member States of the European Economic Community (74/120/EEC), OJ no. L 63, 5 March 1974, p. 16.
12. Agreement of 13 March 1979 between the Central Banks of the Member States of the European Economic Community laying down the operating procedures for the European Monetary System, reprinted in Monetary Committee (1989).
13. See Ludlow (1982) for an account of the making of the EMS.
14. In the period 1979-1983, realignments in the ERM, on average, compensated almost completely for accumulated price differentials relative to Germany. Thereafter, this compensation only amounted to some 50%, see Emerson et al. (1992).
15. Completing the Internal Market, White Paper from the Commission to the European Council (Milan, 28-29 June 1985), COM(85) 310 final.
16. Council Regulation (EEC) no. 4064/89 of 21 December 1989 on the control of concentrations between undertakings, OJ no. L 395, 30 December 1989, pp. 1-12.
17. The initiative for Political Union was taken in April 1990 in a letter from Chancellor Kohl and President Mitterrand.

18. Council Decision of 12 March 1990 on the attainment of progressive convergence of economic policies and performance during stage one of Economic and Monetary Union (90/141/EEC) OJ no. L 78, 24 March 1990, pp. 23-24.

19. Council Decision of 12 March 1990 amending Council Decision 64/300/EEC on cooperation between the Central Banks of the Member States of the European Community (90/142/EEC) OJ no. L 78, 24 March 1990, pp. 25-26.

20. See Monetary Committee (1990).

21. In Articles 130r, 130s and 130t.

22. Europe Documents, no. 5325, 10-11 September 1990.

23. The Committee of Governors drafted the missing parts at a later stage after receiving political guidance. On the same basis, it drafted the Statutes of the European Monetary Institute.

24. A first version of the multilateral surveillance procedure had already been adopted as part of the preparation for the first stage of EMU. See Council Decision of 12 March 1990 on the attainment of progressive convergence of economic policies and performance during stage one of Economic and Monetary Union (90/141/EEC) OJ no. L 78, 24 March 1990, pp. 23-24.

25. Contrary to the existing medium-term financial assistance facility, this financial assistance mechanism could not only provide loans, but also grants ('budgetary interventions'). See Council Regulation (EEC) no. 1969/88 of 24 June 1988 establishing a single facility providing medium-term financial assistance for Member States' balances of payments, OJ no. L 178, 8 July 1988, pp. 1-4.

26. H.M. Treasury (1991).

27. H.M. Treasury (1989).

28. Europe Documents, no. 1688, 1 February 1991.

29. Council Directive of 24 June 1988 for the implementation of Article 67 of the Treaty (88/361/EEC), OJ no. L 178, 8 July 1988, pp. 5-18.

30. According to Declaration no. 7 adopted at the signing of the Maastricht Treaty, this only applies to provisions which exist at the end of 1993. However, this standstill clause is restricted to capital movements and payments between Member States.

31. Council Directive of 24 July 1973 on measures to mitigate the effects of difficulties in the supply of crude oil and petroleum products (73/238/EEC), OJ no. L 228, 16 August 73, pp. 1-3.

32. Cf. Council Decision of 7 May 1985 on the Communities' system of own resources, OJ no. L 128, 14 May 1985, pp. 15-17.

33. Europe Documents, no. 1731, 6 September 1991.

34. Europe Documents, no. 5573, 23-24 September 1991.

35. Europe Documents, no. 5584, 9 October 1991.

36. Europe Documents, no. 5599, 30 October 1991.

37. Council Directive of 24 June 1988 on the implementation of Article 67 of the Treaty (88/361/EEC), OJ no. L 178, 8 July 1988, pp. 5-18.

38. Second Council Directive of 15 December 1989 on the coordination of laws, regulations and administrative provisions relating to the taking up and pursuit of the business of credit institutions and amending Directive 77/780/EEC, OJ

no. L 386, 30 December 1989, pp. 1-13.

39. Council Directive of 17 April 1989 coordinating the requirements for the drawing up, scrutiny and distribution of the prospectus to be published when transferable securities are offered to the public (89/298/EEC), OJ no. L 124, 5 May 1989, pp. 8-15.

40. With the exception of the possibility foreseen in the EMS agreements to modify the composition of the basket if the weight of any currency has changed by 25%. See the text of the EMS agreement as reprinted in Monetary Committee (1989).

41. The first appointment would be on a recommendation from the Committee of Governors of the National Central Banks, since the Council of the EMI would not yet exist.

42. See Articles 148 and 149 of the EEC Treaty.

43. See Article 149 of the EEC Treaty.

44. At its meeting in Madrid (June 1989), the European Council *decided* that the first stage of EMU would start on 1 July 1990.

45. According to the Solemn Declaration on European Union (also known as the 'Stuttgart Declaration', see Bulletin of the European Communities, no. 6-1983), the European Council could, in matters concerning the European Communities, act as the Council in the sense of the Treaties.

46. This concerns Articles 104c(7) to (12).

47. This concerns Articles 104c(9) and (11), 105a(2), 109(1) to (4).

48. This concerns Articles 109(1), 109l(4) and (5).

49. This concerns Articles 109a(2b) and 109l(1).

50. This concerns Articles 109j(2), 109j(3), 109j(4) and 109k(2).

51. For these decisions, the expression 'meeting in the composition' has been replaced by 'at the level', suggesting that an actual meeting is not needed, and a written procedure could suffice.

52. The possibility for the Council to decide on a recommendation rather than a proposal of the Commission exists already in the present Articles 108 and 109 of the EEC Treaty.

53. Decision of the representatives of the governments of the Member States on the provisional location of certain institutions and departments of the Communities (67/446/EEC), OJ no. L 152, 13 July 1967, pp. 18-20.

54. Europe Documents, no. 5490, 13-14 May 1991.

55. If the United Kingdom or Denmark do not wish to participate, they are not included 'among the majority of Member States which fulfil the necessary conditions'.

56. The separate decision on the 'appropriateness' to move to the third stage is a relic from the October 1991 proposals where it was still the European Council which had to assess (as opposed to decide on) this appropriateness in the light of the formal decisions to be taken thereafter by the ECOFIN Council on derogations and possibly by Member States on exemptions. Despite the fact that the possible exemptions for the United Kingdom and Denmark will now be known beforehand and that the Heads of State Council itself takes the formal decision, the provision on the appropriateness may be of some use, for instance in the situation where one or more of the large Member States did not yet meet the necessary

conditions.

57. This formulation also appears, in the context of basket revisions, in the European Council Resolution of 5 December 1978 on the establishment of the EMS and related matters.

58. According to this requirement, the annual increase in the appropriations for the structural funds should result in at least an equivalent increase in the total volume of official or similar aid in each Member State concerned. See Commission of the EC (1989).

59. See Committee of Governors of the Central Banks of the European Community (1992).

60. See Articles B and N.

REFERENCES

Balladur, E., Mémorandum sur la construction monétaire européenne, *ECU Newsletter*, no. 3, March 1980.

Commission of the EC, *Guide to the Reform of the Community's Structural Funds* (Luxembourg: Office for Official Publications of the European Communities, 1989).

Commission of the EC, Economic and Monetary Union, Luxembourg: *Communication of the Commission*, 21 August 1990.

Committee for the Study of Economic and Monetary Union, *Report on Economic and Monetary Union in Europe*, 1989.

Committee of Governors of the Central Banks of the Member States of the European Economic Community, *Annual Report (July 1990-December 1991)*, April 1992.

Council/Commission of the EC, *Treaty on European Union* (Luxembourg: Office for Official Publications of the European Communities, 1992).

Duisenberg, W., *Financial and Monetary Policy in a Europe ohne frontières*, Address at the XXXIInd Annual Eurofinas Conference, 19 May 1992.

Emerson, M., et al, *One Market, One Money* (Cambridge: Cambridge University Press, 1992).

Genscher, H.-D., 'Memorandum für die Schaffung eines europäischen Währungsraumes und einer Europäischen Zentralbank', *Auszüge aus Presseartikeln*, Deutsche Bundesbank, 1 March 1988.

Hasse, R.H., *The European Central Bank: Perspectives for the Further Development of the European Monetary System* (Gütersloh: Bertelsmann Foundation, 1990).

H.M. Treasury, *An Evolutionary Approach to Economic and Monetary Union* (London: H.M. Treasury, 1990).

H.M. Treasury, *Economic and Monetary Union – Beyond Stage I: Possible Treaty Provisions and Statute for a European Monetary Fund* (London: H.M. Treasury, January 1991).

Jenkins, R., *Europe's Present Challenge and Future Opportunity*, Florence: The First Jean Monnet Lecture, 27 October 1977.

Ludlow, P., *The Making of the European Monetary System* (London: Butterworth Scientific, 1982).

Monetary Committee, *Compendium of Community Monetary Texts* (Luxembourg: Office for Official Publications of the European Communities, 1989).

Monetary Committee, *Economic and Monetary Union Beyond Stage 1; Orientations for the Preparation of the Intergovernmental Conference*, published as annex to a letter from the Dutch Minister of Finance, Tweede

Kamer der Staten-Generaal, vergaderjaar 1990-1991, kamerstuk 21501/07, no. 12.

Ungerer, H., et al., 'The European Monetary System: Developments and Perspectives', *Occasional Paper* no. 73 (Washington: IMF, November 1990).

INSIDER OR OUTSIDER?
THE CASE OF AUSTRIA

Alexander Dörfel, Barbara Eggl, Aurel Schubert

Introduction

It is not surprising that the development of the internal market into an Economic and Monetary Union (EMU) is, for three main reasons, of crucial importance for Austria. Firstly, because of the monetary policy the Austrian National Bank (ANB) has followed for more than two decades (tying the schilling informally to the *Deutsche mark*), developments in the Community have immediate repercussions on Austrian monetary policy, although Austria is not an EC member. Secondly, Austria hopes to join the Community during stage two of EMU, giving it the chance to actively participate in the preparation for the final stage of EMU from its very beginning and to be in the first group of full EMU members. Thirdly, economic changes in EC countries directly influence Austria's economic environment because of the close economic links between Austria and the EC.

Meanwhile, the Austrian monetary authorities conduct policy as if Austria were already an EC member. As an example of this one could cite the fact that Austria has decided to abolish all capital controls and thus fully meets the requirements for stage one of EMU. In addition, it fulfils all the criteria for stage three.

The following paper is divided into three parts, starting with a description of Austrian monetary policy since World War II, followed by an analysis of Austria's approach to the European Monetary System (EMS) and concluding with an outline of the likely consequences of EMU for Austria.

The Austrian Exchange Rate Policy after World War II

According to the Austrian constitution, monetary policy matters are the domain of the federal authorities, but important aspects of monetary and exchange rate policy have been delegated to the Austrian National Bank.[1]

K. Gretschmann (ed.), Economic and Monetary Union: Implications for National Policy-Makers, 115–146.
© 1993 European Institute of Public Administration. Printed in the Netherlands.

The guiding star for the exchange rate policy of the Austrian National Bank has been the very clear and unambiguous legal obligation laid down in Article 2 (3) of the National Bank Act:

'It shall ensure with all the means at its disposal that the value of the Austrian currency is maintained with regard to its domestic purchasing power and to its relationship with stable foreign currencies.'

This maintenance of the relationship with stable foreign currencies has been interpreted as keeping the *nominal* exchange rate of the Austrian schilling tied to the stable currencies in Europe.

The long-standing preference for low inflation and a hard currency cannot be understood independently of Austria's monetary history in the last seventy years. Austria had to go through a traumatic hyperinflation between 1920 and 1922, a currency crisis in 1931 and turbulent times directly after World War II.[2] These events have formed the monetary policy consensus on which the Austrian National Bank and its policies are built to this day.

For more than 20 years Austria has been successfully – however not always with the approval of the international financial institutions – following the hard-currency option. A strong schilling should serve to import stability from abroad, thus complementing and reinforcing the domestic stabilization efforts.

With the closing of the gold-window by President Nixon in August 1971 and the consequent collapse of the post-war international monetary order, the Bretton-Woods system, Austria did not share the general enthusiasm for freely floating exchange rates that was promoted by many economists at that time. For the Austrian monetary policy-makers, it was clear from the very beginning that for such a small and open economy as the Austrian one, a system of (relatively) fixed exchange rates – at least with respect to its main trading partners – would be far superior to freely floating rates. Austria was the first country to apply the concept of linking its currency to a basket of currencies. In order to best fulfil the legal obligation of maintaining a fixed relationship to 'stable currencies', the Austrian National Bank built its own reference basket consisting of the (weighted) currencies of the main trading partners.

However, the initial composition of the basket did not last very long, as individual currencies started to develop in undesirable ways. In order to avoid the repercussions of such unwanted changes, some reference currencies were successively dropped from the basket. One currency after another was eliminated until only the *Deutsche mark* remained as a sensible and useful reference anchor, due to both the very close economic links between Austria and Germany and the role of the *Deutsche mark* as the stability anchor in Europe. One has to keep in mind that about 39% of Austrian exports go to Germany and 43% of its imports originate from there, also about 65% of the tourists visiting Austria come from

Germany. Therefore the choice of this peg was a natural one and consistent with the ANB's legal duty to maintain the value of the schilling.

With the creation of the European Monetary System in 1979 the link to the *Deutsche mark* received an extra dimension; it became a link to the zone of monetary stability in Europe. With two thirds of Austrian trade occurring with the EC countries, this exchange rate target allows a very large part of trade to occur with no, or only very minimal, exchange rate risk, reducing uncertainty and eliminating the need for exchange rate hedging for importers as well as exporters. This boosted the foreign competitiveness of the Austrian tradeable sector.[3]

In the Austrian view the best monetary strategy consists of combining the central bank's key goal – stabilization of the value of the currency – with a maximum degree of stabilized expectations.[4]

Tying one's currency permanently to a very stable or even the most stable currency in Europe is not just a matter of announcement, as the recent experiences of not only Finland but also Sweden have shown quite dramatically.[5] The present Austrian exchange rate policy requires – like any credible fixed exchange rate commitment – that the fundamental macroeconomic variables, like inflation, unit labour cost, current account and economic growth or budget deficit, have to concur with the respective variables in the anchor country over the medium term. As far as Austria is concerned, this economic link has been accepted by all relevant policy-makers and has influenced the fiscal and income policies pursued. A very important precondition for the general acceptance and the success of the stability-oriented monetary policy in Austria has been the institutional involvement of the social partners in the decision-making process. The major social groups in Austrian society, like trade unions, federal chamber of commerce, agriculture, cooperatives and commercial banks are among the shareholders of the Austrian National Bank and have seats on the policy-making body and the Governing Board.[6]

As the stability of the exchange rate between the schilling and the *Deutsche mark* shows, Austria managed to keep its fundamentals sufficiently in line with those of Germany to maintain the confidence of the markets. This confidence has reached such a high level that the historical positive (long-term) interest rate spread between Austria and Germany completely disappeared by early 1990 and even turned negative at times.

The exchange target implies a very limited autonomy in setting Austrian interest rates as Austria imports the money supply target from Germany and no major differences in the development of money demand exist between the two countries. However, institutional and structural peculiarities might lead to temporary deviations, especially in short-term interest rates, like the more pronounced fluctuations in Austrian call money rates in relation to those in Germany, mainly due to tight domestic market conditions.[7] Any attempts to undercut the interest rate policy followed in the anchor country would very quickly result in large capital outflows, reducing domestic liquidity and driving up domestic interest rates (or putting pressure on the exchange rate). Therefore, Austria does not follow a money supply targeting policy. It is actually importing the money supply target from the anchor country. The crucial factor is therefore money demand. The use of monetary policy instruments is directed at maintaining an adequate interest differential with respect to Germany, using either the domestic or the foreign source component (active participation in the foreign exchange markets).[8]

Two more points are worth noting with respect to this exchange rate policy. First, that it has been embarked on and pursued without a safety net. Austria does not have access to either interventions by partner countries and credit facilities like those for EMS members, nor can it fall back on bilateral swap arrangements like those of the central bank of Norway (*Norges Bank*) with the different EC central banks. Second, it has been supplemented by a gradual but determined liberalization of capital movements between Austria and the rest of the world. This process, which remained without any negative repercussions due to the underlying credibility of the exchange rate policy, culminated in the abolition of the last exchange restrictions in November 1991. On that date Austria joined the very exclusive club of countries that have fully liberalized, a club that still has to wait a few years before being able to count all the EC countries among its members.

The success of the Austrian monetary policy is in the meantime regularly acknowledged by international financial institutions, like the International Monetary Fund (IMF) or the Organization for Economic Cooperation and Development (OECD), two institutions that used to pass a rather cautionary or even critical judgement in the early days of the hard currency policy. However, the persistence of the Austrian National Bank and the results achieved have convinced even the most sceptical analysts.

It was an especially great pleasure and very satisfactory for Austria that the EC Commission, in its opinion on the Austrian membership application, stated quite clearly that from an economic point of view Austria was uniquely qualified to become a member of the Community. Among the assets, the report explicitly noted 'Austria's long experience of monetary stability and the special relationship between the schilling and the German mark, and through it with the other EMS currencies'.[9] Along the same lines, the Commission made it very clear what role it expects Austria to play on the path toward further monetary integration in Europe. The Community would benefit from the accession of Austria, 'which would widen the circle of countries whose economic, monetary and budgetary performance will speed EMU on its way'.

The long-standing contribution of Austria to the zone of monetary stability in Europe has also been noted by the Committee of Governors of the Central

Banks of the Member States of the European Economic Community in its first annual report.[10]

For the past one-and-a-half decades Austria has pursued a monetary and exchange rate policy that can only be judged as fully compatible with the present and future monetary policy goals of the European Community. This policy was always geared towards integration, be it either integration into the world economy in general (during the Bretton-Woods system) or into the European zone of monetary stability in particular (after the collapse of the Bretton-Woods system). The approach followed was never a dogmatic one, but rather an eclectic one, firmly based, however, on the legal obligation of the Austrian National Bank to secure stability and on the application of the optimum-currency-area theory.

The planned evolution of the European Monetary System into a genuine EMU confronts the Austrian monetary policy and its decision-makers with new challenges. The track record gives us confidence that Austria is well prepared to meet these new challenges successfully. It is with good reason that the EC Commission report concludes that Austria's application for accession to the Community '...is in a quite different category from those of previous applicants'.

Austria and the European Monetary System

Despite the intense factual ties between Austria and the EMS, there are only a few formal links. To date, all Austrian efforts to link itself officially to the EMS have been rebuffed by the EC. The most probable explanation for this attitude of the EC is that it is not willing to create a precedent at a time when it has not yet decided how to deal with the problem of enlarging its membership while preserving its goals and efficiency.

In this chapter we will examine the steps taken to date by Austria towards the EMS and the benefits and costs of potential alternative monetary arrangements.

AUSTRIA APPROACHES THE EMS

Participation in the Daily Concertations. On 9 September 1986 the EC central bank governors approved the Austrian National Bank's request for inclusion in the foreign exchange concertation procedure. This procedure consists of three regular daily telephone conference calls between the EC central banks as well as the Federal Reserve Bank of New York and the central banks of Japan, Canada, Norway, Finland, Sweden, Switzerland and Austria. Each central bank informs the others about the intra-day movements of its currency compared to the previous day, the key short-term interest rates of the country and the degree of currency intervention on that day. Once a week a general concertation is held between senior central bank officials at which opinions are exchanged concerning the foreign exchange markets in each country. Apart from these routine contacts, *ad hoc* concertations are called when specific situations arise in the financial markets requiring the immediate attention of the central banks. A sophisticated telephone system linking all the central banks has been created specifically for this purpose. The Concertation Group also meets monthly (at the Bank for International Settlements) to monitor developments in the foreign exchange markets globally and to assess actions taken by various authorities in response to those developments.

The continuous exchange of information allows the central banks to react immediately to developments in the markets in a concerted way. Indeed, the concertation mechanism is one of the key factors in the functioning of the EMS. Currently, the Austrian central bank cannot play an active role concerning EMS decisions, it only provides and receives information. However, the regular dialogue with the EC central banks has given it an insight into their decision-making processes and has proven to be very valuable.

Official Quotation of the ECU at the Vienna Currency Exchange. Since 1 January 1986 the Austrian National Bank has been determining an official daily rate for the private ECU during the daily fixing which is then quoted at the Vienna Currency Exchange. In their dealings with retail customers, commercial banks can choose to use this official rate, however, they are not obliged to.

The rationale behind the decision by the Austrian National Bank to provide an official ECU quotation was due to complaints by tourists when they presented travellers' cheques denominated in ECU. Since no official rate for private ECU was available prior to 1986, banks quoted widely divergent rates according to their particular ECU supply and demand. By quoting an official rate for private ECU these problems were alleviated and, at the same time, Austria was able to demonstrate a clear sign of its readiness to integrate the ECU into its financial markets.

Regular Contacts with the EC Monetary Committee. The EC Monetary Committee is an advisory body that was established according to Art. 105 (2) of the Treaty of Rome. It has a number of important responsibilities that deal mainly with enhancing cooperation between EC member countries in monetary policy matters. It achieves this by monitoring the monetary and financial developments in member countries and reporting regularly to the EC Council and the Commission. The Council and the Commission are obliged to consult it whenever questions arise concerning:
- the liberalization of capital movements,
- monetary and exchange rate policy in the framework of the EMS,
- payments systems, and

- balance of payments crises.

Each Member State appoints a representative from the central bank and the ministry for finance, and the EC Commission appoints two high-level members. The Committee usually meets once a month, however meetings can occur more or less often. Due to the extensive responsibilities that have been assigned to the Monetary Committee by the EC, it plays an important role in the Community's decision-making process concerning economic and monetary policy and also in the mutual surveillance procedure.[11]

For all these reasons the Austrian National Bank considers it critical to maintain close contact with the Committee. It approached the Committee in 1987 with a request for a regular exchange of information similar to that already established by the central bank of Norway (*Norges Bank*). The aim of these regular contacts was and is to further cooperation in the field of monetary policy and to contribute to healthy and stable international relations in this area. These contacts have taken various forms. Once a year representatives of the Austrian monetary authorities meet with the Chairman of the Monetary Committee to exchange information and opinions concerning subjects of mutual interest. Furthermore, there are continuous contacts between the Austrian National Bank and the Secretary of the Committee. Finally, the Chairman of the Committee can invite representatives of the Austrian monetary authorities to informal discussions with members of the Committee. The Committee has stressed that while these contacts have been regularized they remain informal and do not establish a precedent for other non-member countries.

The Austrian Position versus the ECU.
(1) Official ECUs. Official ECUs are created by the European Monetary Cooperation Fund (EMCF) through the contribution of at least 20% of the participating central banks' gold holdings and of their gross dollar reserves.[12]

Since 1985, the EMCF can grant central banks of non-member countries and international monetary institutions the right to hold and use official ECUs. These so-called 'Other Holders' can acquire official ECUs through swaps or purchases with a sell-back obligation from EC central banks or other authorized ECU holders against any other currency.[13] Official ECUs can be used only for these specific transactions. The Austrian National Bank was granted the status of 'Other Holder' on 11 July 1989.

This status, however, is largely symbolic since it does not provide access to additional information concerning the EMS or any other crucial developments. The rationale for the Austrian National Bank to maintain this status is essentially a political one. Holding a small part of the exchange reserves in official ECUs, the Austrian National Bank demonstrates the Austrian interest to link itself more closely to the EC and the EMS and the underlying commitment to support the development of the ECU into a fully fledged currency.

(2) The Use of Private ECUs by the Public Sector. The ECU Eurobond market has been used regularly by Austrian public issuers since the mid-1980s. After fairly low volumes until 1987 (around or under ECU 100 million per year) the Republic of Austria started to issue ECU bonds more actively, since this market segment offered very favourable financing opportunities through swap arrangements into other target currencies. As a consequence, gross ECU issues jumped to over ECU 500 million. During the following two years issues by public entities (Republic of Austria, *Oesterreichische Kontrollbank*) continued at approximately this level (1989: ECU 450 million, 1990: ECU 600 Million).[14] In 1991, interest by borrowers (especially by the Republic of Austria) in ECU issues was subdued, the only issue being one by the *Oesterreichische Kontrollbank* of ECU 150 Million. However, in 1992 issue volume has recovered reaching ECU 200 Million in the first two months.

The Austrian National Bank has for many years held private ECU in its foreign currency reserves in addition to the official ECU mentioned before.

(3) The Use of Private ECUs by the Private Sector. In recent years Austrian banks have considerably increased their ECU business, both on the asset and liability sides of their balance sheet. ECU liabilities especially have shown continued strong growth since 1988 (foreign currency liabilities rose from ECU 500 million or 1% at end 1987 to ECU 2 billion or 4% by the third quarter of 1991). The principal reason for this expansion was the public ECU bond issues discussed above. Asset growth has been slower (stagnation in 1990 and the first quarter of 1991), but nevertheless still considerable. Between the end of 1987 and the third quarter of 1991, the banks' ECU assets more than doubled to far over ECU 1 billion. According to Austrian National Bank statistics, ECU bonds accounted for about ECU 150 million of asset holdings by September 1991, the remainder being most probably ECU denominated loans. Compared to countries of similar size, Austrian banks' ECU business lies well ahead of even some EC countries (Denmark, Ireland) and other EFTA countries (Finland), but significantly lags behind countries like Switzerland or Sweden. Both for ECU assets and liabilities, interbank transactions are more prevalent in Austria with transactions with non-banks accounting for only one eighth and one seventh of assets and liabilities, respectively.

During the last three years Austrian investors have increasingly purchased ECU bonds. By October 1991, ECU bond-holdings (over ECU 600 million) accounted for between 9% and 10% of Austrian non-banks' total foreign currency bond portfolios, expanding from only ECU 150 million or 4% three years earlier.

(4) Considering an ECU Peg. Due to the peg to the *Deutsche mark* that the Austrian monetary authorities have successfully followed for the last two

decades, the schilling has indirectly and unofficially formed part of the EMS (see graphs 1, 2 and 3). The schilling's movements in relation to the ECU consequently correspond to the *Deutsche mark*'s movements. Thus, though the schilling is not officially and directly linked to the ECU, its exchange rate development over the last years was far more closely correlated with the ECU than that of any other of the new ECU peggers (such as Sweden, Finland and Norway).

This indirect relationship has led to arguments for a formal linking of the schilling to the ECU.[15] An analysis of the exchange rate developments since 1979 demonstrates that the schilling has significantly appreciated *vis-à-vis* the ECU due to the *Deutsche mark* peg (see graph 4). The nominal effective exchange rate index of the *Wirtschaftsforschungsinstitut* suggests a nominal appreciation of 42.6% from 1978 to 1988, and the real effective exchange rate index an appreciation of 5% for the same period.[16]

Compared to the ECU central rate, the *Deutsche mark* has appreciated the most among all EMS currencies during the first ten years of the EMS (22%). Using a fictitious ECU/schilling central rate, the schilling has appreciated even more, namely by 26.4%. Thus, if the schilling had been in the EMS for this period, it would have qualified as the 'strongest' EMS currency. While this performance is partly due to the fact that the schilling was significantly undervalued relative to the *Deutsche mark* in 1979,[17] the success of the *Deutsche mark* pegging strategy is clear.

Judging from past experience, it would seem that a change in the Austrian exchange rate policy from a *Deutsche mark* peg to an ECU peg, would not by itself enhance the external stability of the schilling. Indeed, such a policy change might endanger the credibility of the Bank's commitment to exchange rate stability since the ECU has been and most likely will be 'softer' in the long-term perspective than the *Deutsche mark*.[18] International financial markets could conceivably interpret this move as a loosening of the Bank's monetary policy stance which could in turn lead to a destabilization of expectations.

SCENARIOS FOR THE FUTURE

In this section three alternative scenarios will be examined. These scenarios depict Austria's possible policy choices relative to the EMS.
The scenarios include:
  – maintaining the *status quo*;
  – actively pursuing association;
  – entering the EMS as a full member (albeit with full membership of the EC or prior to it).

Graph 1(a):
ATS vs DEM in EMS Band
from March 1979 to December 1983

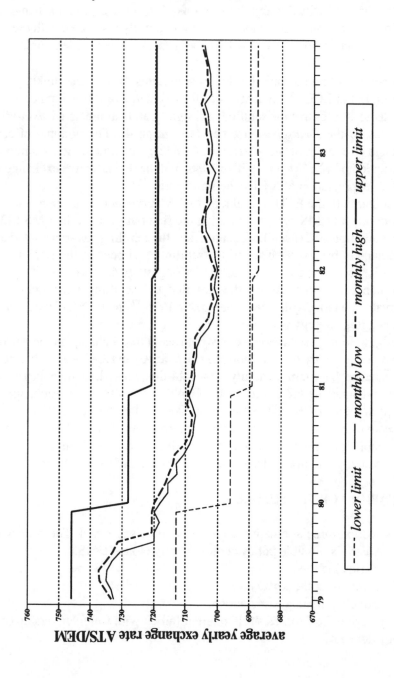

Graph 1(b):
ATS vs DEM in EMS Band
from January 1984 to December 1988

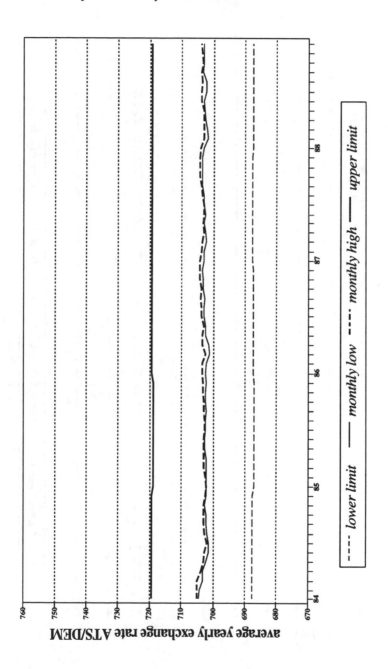

Graph 1(c):
ATS vs DEM in EMS Band
from January 1989 to December 1991

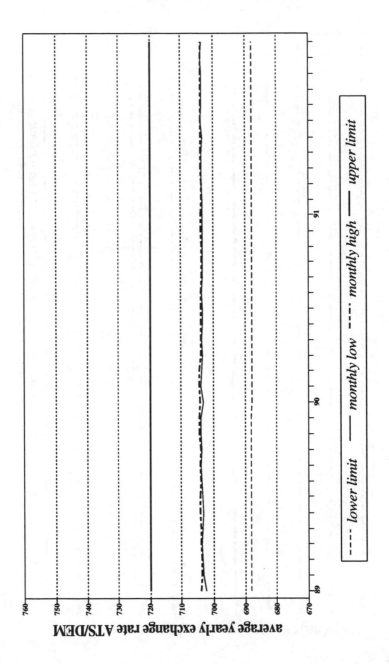

Graph 2(a):
ATS vs FRF in EMS Band
from March 1979 to December 1983

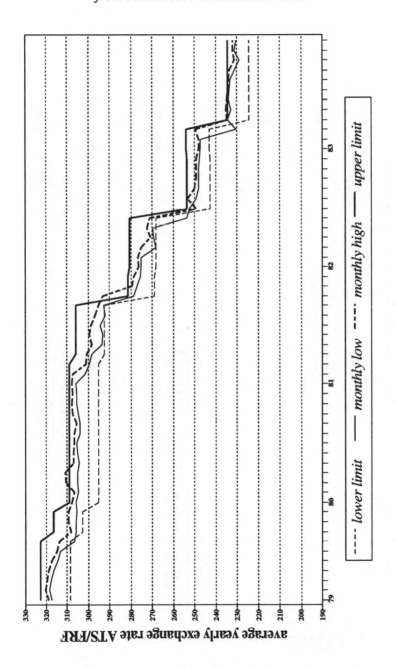

Graph 2(b):
ATS vs FRF in EMS Band
from January 1984 to December 1988

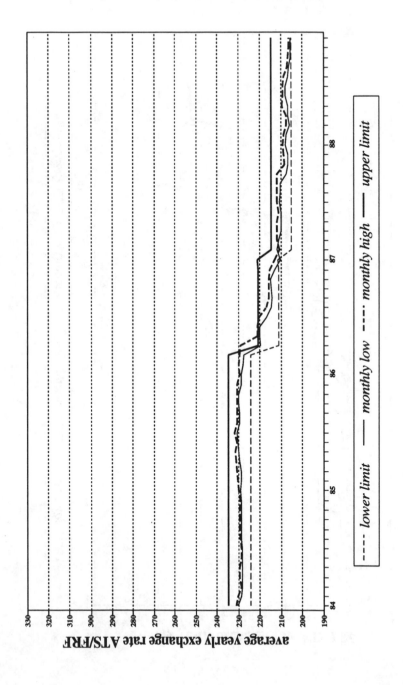

Graph 2(c):
ATS vs FRF in EMS Band
from January 1989 to December 1991

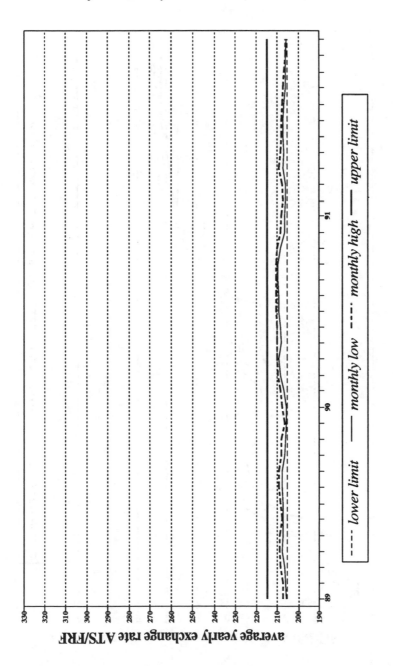

Graph 3(a):
ATS vs DKK in EMS Band
from March 1979 to December 1983

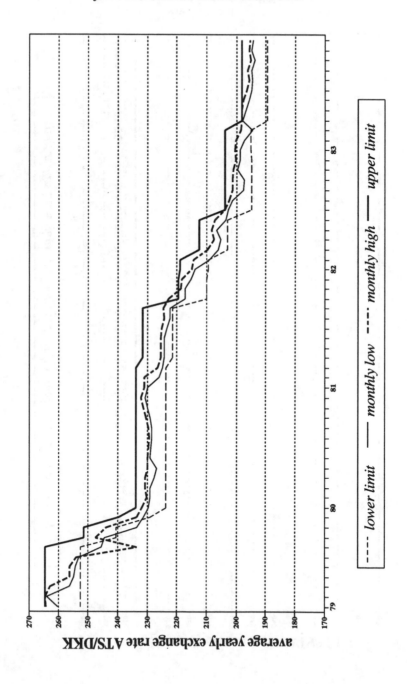

Graph 3(b):
ATS vs DKK in EMS Band
from January 1984 to December 1988

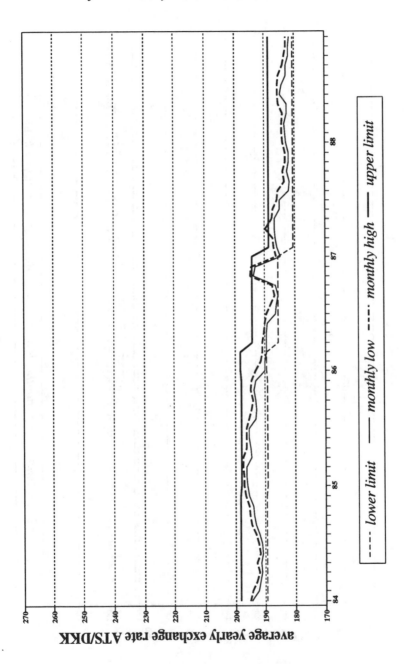

Graph 3(c):
ATS vs DKK in EMS Band
from January 1989 to December 1991

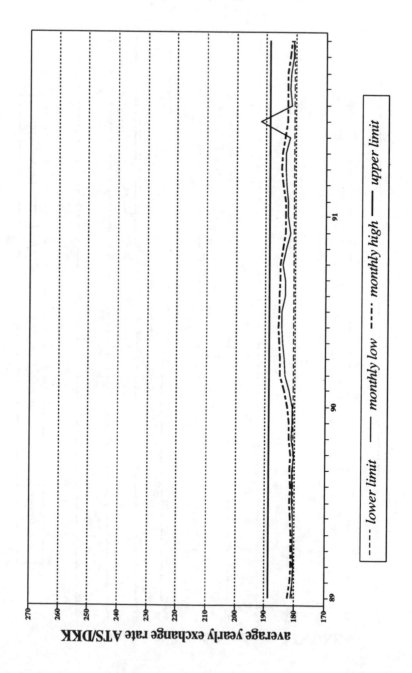

Graph 4:
Exchange Rate ECU in ATS

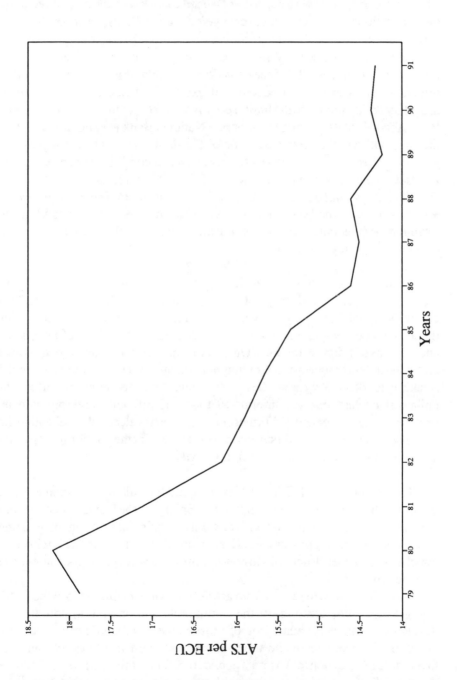

Maintaining the Status Quo (until Austria joins the EC). The *status quo* is currently characterized by the Austrian National Bank's commitment to pursue a hard currency policy via a peg to the *Deutsche mark* with the goal of reducing the fluctuations of the schilling exchange rate to the *Deutsche mark* almost to zero. This, in turn, implies a virtual loss of autonomy concerning the Bank's interest rate policy since any significant divergence in interest rates between Austria and Germany will induce considerable capital flows in one or the other direction.[19] However, the freedom still exists to change the orientation of monetary policy subject to the limits set by Article 2 (3) of the Austrian National Bank Act of 1955 (requiring the Austrian National Bank to explicitly maintain the 'internal' and the 'external' value of the schilling). Such a change is not justified under present circumstances. However, if conditions change, e.g. the *Deutsche mark* ceases to be the anchor of stability that it has been so far, the Bank's strategy for monetary policy could be reconsidered. Therefore, the *status quo* is to maintain the *Deutsche mark* peg, which has been so successful, while retaining the freedom of choice as to the means with which to achieve the goals of monetary policy in the future.

(1) Benefits and Disadvantages for Austria. The current situation allows Austria to choose its monetary policy subject to the principles of Article 2 (3) of the National Bank Act. However, it remains to be tested whether this theoretical autonomy in monetary matters still exists in a world of liberalized and interlinked financial markets. On the other hand, the autonomy to formulate an 'independent' monetary policy might endanger Austria's credibility in the financial markets. Recent studies have shown that the credibility effects of unilateral declarations are inferior to those of officially entering into an exchange rate agreement.[20] Furthermore, if Austria decided to abandon its courting of the EMS, it would surrender to a large extent the possibility of having an input into the formation of the future EMU.

(2) The Position of the EC. The EC is currently formulating a comprehensive policy for the admission of new applicants. Enlarging the Community by more than three or four members will certainly require adaptation of existing structures. During this process of reflection and discussion, the EC is relatively reluctant to consider closer links to non-member countries until procedures have been determined.

If Austria chooses to refrain from actively seeking membership in the EMS, it might take some pressure off the Community and provide it more time to develop procedures for admission of prospective members. It can be argued, however, that because of the timetable agreed upon in Maastricht and the favourable EC reaction to Austria's application for membership, the EC cannot delay indefinitely coming to terms with the admission of new members.[21]

If Austria maintains the *status quo* the Community has little to lose, since the Austrian authorities will continue their commitment to the hard currency policy for the foreseeable future. Then, at an appropriate point, the EC could reconsider its position.

Association with the EMS.
(1) Definition and Problems. According to Art. 5 (2) of the EMS Treaty, countries characterized by particularly close economic and financial ties with the EC can participate in the exchange rate and intervention mechanism of the EMS. The basis for such an association are agreements between the EC central banks and the central bank of the associated member. In addition, the EC Council of Ministers and the EC Commission must be informed of such an agreement.

This definition of an association is somewhat vague regarding its preconditions, its form and extent as well as the exact legal mechanism governing the agreement. There is no concise clarification regarding which countries would be suitable as associated members. Concerning the form of the agreement, some parties believe it should be a set of parallel bilateral agreements between the associated country's central bank and *each* EC central bank. Others feel that a multilateral agreement between all the EC central banks as a group and the associated country's central bank corresponds better with the spirit of the Article. Another critical and unclear issue relates to the extent to which EC bodies would have to become involved if an association agreement were to fundamentally alter EMS principles. However, these issues have not yet been resolved and have confounded the admission of associated members.

(2) The Dalgaard Report of 1990.[22] A panel of EC central bank experts met under the chairmanship of Mr Dalgaard and attempted to address these and other ambiguities. At the conclusion of the proceedings they presented some alternative solutions. This report stressed that the question of association is essentially a *political* one. The EC has to determine whether an EMS association of third countries would endanger the process of EMU or maybe even support it. There are certainly only few technical problems in integrating additional (associate or full) members into the EMS mechanism as the Austrian example demonstrates clearly (see previous sub-section on 'Maintaining the *Status Quo*').

On closer inspection, the provisions of Art. 5(2) of the EMS Treaty are too vague for the selection of potential candidates for association. In order to minimize the risk to the EMS as a whole, the Dalgaard Report suggests that only those countries should be considered as candidates for association:
  - whose economy is healthy;
  - which follow a responsible, stability-oriented economic policy; and
  - which have abolished all restrictions hindering the free movement of

capital.[23]

The EC would still have to decide in each specific case if it indeed wants to strengthen ties with a certain country. A typical case would be a country that has been accepted as a member but has not yet completed the accession procedure. This is certainly an indication for close ties with the EC.

The Dalgaard Report examined these issues and proposed two different approaches regarding the extent of association that should be considered. They are:

– the *minimalist* approach, where the associate member would only participate in the exchange rate and intervention mechanism (somewhat similar to the 'Snake'), and;

– the *maximalist* solution, which would give the associated member the opportunity to be involved in additional policies of the EMS (concertation, creation of ECU, etc.).

In both cases – according to the Report – a rigid form of association seems to be preferable with the narrow band of ± 2.25% and participation in realignments, but with only partial integration into the decision-making process of the EMS. Associated members would have to commit themselves to the EMS consensus (financing of intramarginal interventions by short-term financing, observation of economic indicators, etc.).

The decision for one or the other approach would have to be made according to *political* preferences since both of them have their advantages and shortcomings. Under the minimalist approach the EMS wins more influence simply because it has more members. The EC, however, cannot subject such an associated member to the same obligations and controls as a full member. This might endanger the credibility and stability of the whole system.

A stronger involvement, as planned under the maximalist approach, might strengthen the system even more. The associated members, however, would demand more information and influence concerning decision-making, which the EC is currently reluctant to grant to non-EC member countries.

An alternative strategy might be to allow different associated members to follow different approaches to membership. In addition, the association could be tightened after a trial period based upon the minimalist approach.

Another issue is the development of EMU. Until the end of 1993 (stage one), it will be relatively simple from an organizational point of view to integrate associated members into the EMS, since the whole structure is still relatively open and a great number of countries are already unilaterally aligned to the ECU. After that date, EC cooperation will be raised to a different level and so become much more complex (creation of the European Monetary Institute (EMI), preparations for a single European currency, etc.) and therefore less open to those seeking association.

(3) Advantages and Disadvantages for Austria of an Associated Membership. Austria is clearly a country that has close economic and financial ties with the EC. Furthermore, it has over the years strengthened and intensified its contacts with the EMS (see Introduction). It has a healthy economy, follows a stability-oriented policy and has just recently abolished all capital controls. Moreover, it applied for membership of the EC in 1989 – as the first of the EFTA countries seeking membership of the EC. The relevant Opinion of the EC Commission cited Austria as a prime example of a country ready for membership.[24] Austria has therefore contemplated associated membership of the EMS according to the maximalist approach of the Dalgaard Report.

It is already an informal EMS member by its link to the *Deutsche mark*. However, it does not receive relevant information concerning EMS decisions, EC monetary policy and international monetary policy as far as the G7 is concerned. Thereby, it has no part in the EMS decision-making and nor does it play any role in the conception of EMU in which it will participate after its entry into the Community. Its monetary policy has attained a high level of credibility but still lacks the final confirmation of a legally binding agreement, such as an EMS association.

Such an association would make it easier to fulfil the convergence criteria which states that a country has to have operated within the EMS narrow fluctuation band of ± 2.25%, without problems, for at least two years prior to the 'examination' of convergence. Since candidates for the EC membership cannot even join the EMS until they are members of the Community, a very narrow interpretation of the Maastricht accord might argue that such countries would therefore not be able to enter into stage three of EMU, should it begin in 1997, unless they are EC members by mid-1994 – a rather unlikely scenario. Such an interpretation might not have been the intent of those formulating the convergence criteria but the letter of the agreement might be applied literally for political reasons. An EMS association prior to membership should, however, satisfy even the strictest interpretation of the Maastricht agreement.

From the Austrian point of view doubts still remain concerning the additional benefits of an EMS association. These doubts derive from the asymmetric nature of a proposed association structure and from the success of the Austrian monetary policy so far. An association could result in a significant change in Austrian monetary policy. The composition of the ECU under EMU has not been fully determined yet. As a result it is hard to predict the future development of the ECU and therefore the financial markets might interpret a change in Austrian monetary policy as a softening of the hard currency policy.[25] It is obvious that a change in monetary policy could lead to heightened insecurity and consequently higher costs for the economy until credibility is established again. Furthermore, there might be additional obligations to intervene in the foreign exchange markets that have to be followed regardless of domestic considerations. Both approaches discussed above do not grant equal participation in decision-making to the associated member that is not sufficiently integrated into the EMS organizational structure (particularly concerning realignments). This could be compensated by a chance to participate in the preparations for EMU (e.g. membership of the EMI). Association would result in a loss of autonomy, forcing Austria to conform with the obligations of the EMS Treaty without being granted the rights of a full EMS member. In addition, an associated membership could be wrongly interpreted as substitute for a speedy entry into the Community.

(4) The Position of the EC. Over the last years more of a consensus seems to have developed in the EC regarding the structure of an association agreement. Specifically, points such as which major provisions would have to be taken and to what extent an associated member might expect to obtain information and participate in the decision-making process have been clarified. The crucial point, not yet clarified, is whether the acceptance of associated members could in any way endanger the process of EMU. Since these considerations are almost exclusively political, the EC has been reluctant to voice any official comments.

From the EC point of view there are definite advantages to be cited for EMS association by qualified countries: first of all, the zone of exchange rate stability would be enlarged which, in turn, would probably lead to more economic convergence and stability in a greater part of Europe. This effect would be most pronounced if it required a fundamental move towards monetary stability on the part of the newly associated member (this is not the case for Austria since it has followed stable policies for two decades). Secondly, to accept a country that is committed to economic stability like Austria would enhance the economic policy credibility of the Community and, finally, association would strengthen the influence of the Community because intervention policies of associated members would have to conform with EMS rules.

However, some negative points need to be considered: associated members could cause realignments which might lead to higher instability for the system as a whole (this seems highly unlikely in Austria's case). EMS countries might have to defend the exchange rate of an associated member whose economic policy they cannot sufficiently influence and, most critically, the EC would have to share its autonomy in decision-making.

Full EMS Membership. To date there have been only informal discussions, initiated by Sweden, concerning the question of very close cooperation with the EMS by a non-EC country.[26] Sweden's arguments in favour of such a move include: its decision to officially peg its currency to the ECU, its formal application for membership of the EC and its fulfilment (according to Swedish calculations) of the convergence criteria agreed upon in Maastricht. The EC has not yet officially reacted to the Swedish proposal but will consider the technical consequences of such an approach for the development of EMU as well as procedural questions concerning participation in committees and policy-making. The Swedish approach is being considered carefully by Austria since circumstances are quite similar in both countries (although Austria applied almost two years earlier for membership and its currency has been tied successfully to the EMS since its inception).

Legally, only an EC Member State can also be an EMS member. This can be derived from the relevant articles of the EEC Treaty concerning the coordination of economic and monetary policy (Art. 105), exchange rates (Art. 107) and the duties and responsibilities of the EC Council (Art. 145). Furthermore, EC institutions such as the EC Council, the Monetary Committee and the Committee of Central Bank Governors, play crucial roles in the EMS decision-making process. Thus the full EMS membership of a non-EC member country could only be a *de facto* one, tolerated and supported by the EC.

(1) Austrian Considerations Concerning Full EMS Membership. Most of the disadvantages mentioned earlier resulting from the asymmetry of an association status would not be present for Austria in the case of full membership of the EMS. The loss of autonomy would be balanced by the right to participate in EMS decisions and receive full information about EC monetary policy. In all probability, being a full EMS member would hasten the entry of Austria into the Community. There remains only a possible adverse market reaction, assuming that Austrian monetary policy would undergo a softening by entering into the EMS.

(2) The Position of the EC. There is great reluctance on the part of the EC to open its structures to non-EC countries. Firstly, according to those who advocate deepening, the EC needs primarily to adapt its inner organization to be able to accommodate the entry of new members, and this should also be true for all separate structures, like the EMS.

Secondly, EMS membership itself poses legal and technical problems concerning the integration of a non-EC member into EC structures since such a member would not have to commit itself to the EC Treaties and would still have all rights under the EMS agreement. Possibly of more concern is that if a country that is a full EMS – but not an EC – member failed to fulfil EMS rules, this would hurt the credibility of its own economic policy and thus endanger the EMS as a whole.

One could cite as advantages to the EC of admitting non-EC countries as full *(de facto)* EMS members that potential EC members would have to follow a disciplined monetary policy under the rules of the EMS. This would prepare them efficiently for entry into the Community and the Community would even be able to influence non-members which would further economic convergence in Europe.

As we have shown in the Introduction, Austria has made overtures to the EMS and prepared for even closer cooperation by following a successful and stability-oriented monetary policy. The arguments presented in the first part of this chapter make it clear that such a cooperation would bring certain advantages for Austria. A closer link between Austria and the EMS would be certainly beneficial for Austria and the EC, particularly in the light of further development of EMU.

European Monetary Union and its Repercussions for Austria

As we mentioned before, Austria was the first (July 1989) of the EFTA states to apply for membership of the European Community. The Austrian authorities have always made it very clear that they intended to start participating in the EMS Exchange Rate Mechanism, at the latest concurrently with entry into the EC.

The same approach applies also to EMU. Austria is not only willing but also well prepared to participate fully and from the very beginning in EMU. It is already fulfilling all the entrance criteria set by the Treaty of Maastricht, the so-called convergence criteria[27] – something that only a few of the twelve present EC members can claim.

The potential gains for Austria from participation in EMU are manifold, despite the fact that due to the successful adherence to the hard-currency policy, many of the advantages of adherence to a stable currency area already exist in Austria. But a further widening of the zone of monetary and exchange rate stability in Europe can only be welcomed by a country that is so highly dependent on foreign trade. The remaining exchange rate risks *vis-à-vis* some of the EC countries would finally disappear, improving further the international business environment for the Austrian economy. In addition, the dynamic effects of EMU will most likely be much more important than the static ones, but those will be accruing predominantly to those countries participating fully in EMU.

The main pillars of the future ECB policies are very similar to, if not the same as, those of the Austrian National Bank, namely orientation toward price stability, independence and prohibition of budget financing. In addition, the statutes of the ESCB rest on another principle that is rather new for the European Community but has a long tradition in Austria, the principle of subsidiarity.[28]

Therefore, participation in EMU will not change the fundamentals of Austrian monetary policy. What will change, however, is the way in which monetary policy decisions are made and (possibly) the way in which they will be implemented. There will no longer be an *Austrian* monetary policy, but a European one. Decision-making with regard to that European policy will be shared by all national central banks participating fully in the ESCB. The decision-making rule for the ECB Board, namely 'one country, one vote', will allow the Austrian National Bank to have the same voice in European monetary matters as any other of the EC central banks. The real influence on policy, however, will depend on the quality of the arguments presented by the Austrian National Bank. In order to succeed in this 'market for the best arguments', the ANB will have to join the club well prepared. This will be especially important since it will have to overcome its handicap of not having participated in a considerable part of the preparatory phases of EMU. It will have to enter the competition without the training-camp experience of the 'old' EC central banks.

This was recognized early on by the present management of the ANB and, as a result, the preconditions for becoming 'fit for Europe' are already being created. Nevertheless, it will be important for Austria to be able to participate as soon as possible in the preparation of EMU and the ESCB, preferably even before the formal end of the accession process.

Conclusions

Let us return to the introduction: Austria finds itself presently in the waiting room of the EC. It has adopted, to a large extent, the EMS rules-of-the-game, has furthermore liberalized its financial system and, as already mentioned, fulfils at this point all the convergence criteria required for entry into the final stage of EMU.

We hope to have shown in this chapter that even though Austria is not yet a formal member of the EMS and is therefore unable to formally satisfy one of the EMU convergence criteria (to have kept its currency without strain for two years in the narrow band of the EMS), it fulfils the requirement of monetary stability, in some respects even better than some EMS member countries. Therefore, we are of the opinion that Austria is fully prepared for EMU. Furthermore, we are convinced that Austria could significantly strengthen EMU by its firm and long-standing commitment to stability.

A last brief excursion into history shows that Austria has already some advantage over the EC concerning the extremely sensitive area of 'monetary psychology': during the time of the Austro-Hungarian Empire, the front of the banknotes in circulation showed the denomination not only in German, but in as many as eight other official languages, whereas the text on the reverse was entirely in Hungarian. Considering the heated discussions following the Maastricht agreement about the introduction of a single European currency and the abolition of the cherished national currencies, Austria certainly has experiences

that it is keen to share and they might prove quite valuable for all the EC
countries.

NOTES

1. See Hochreiter and Schubert (1991), p. 137.
2. For a detailed account of the 1931 currency crisis, see Schubert (1991).
3. The year 1979 has also taught Austrian monetary policy-makers a very important message about the lack of room for independent national monetary policy. The attempt to 'dive through' an international surge in interest rates resulted in a considerable capital outflow and a concurrent loss of foreign exchange reserves, forcing policy-makers to respect the (self-imposed) constraints of a fixed exchange rate policy.
4. See Pech and Weninger (1990).
5. In May and June 1991, respectively, Sweden and Finland pegged their currencies unilaterally to the ECU. However, after only five months Finland had to devalue the *markka* relative to the ECU by 14%. At the same time, Sweden had to face a first market test of its peg. Greater uncertainty about the *krona* created exchange market pressures and the *Riksbank* had to make a clear declaration of the firmness of the new Swedish exchange rate policy. In defence of the fixed ECU peg, it was forced to raise the marginal overnight rate in two steps from 10.5% to 17.5%. With the help of this rather drastic interest rate move, it managed to overcome this confidence crisis. During the weeks preceding the French referendum on the Maastricht Treaty both the *markka* and the *krona* came under immense pressure: the Bank of Finland thus decided to end the *markka*'s link to the ECU. The *Riksbank* reacted by raising its short-term lending rates to unprecedented highs.
6. The representatives of the social partners hold 50% of the shares of the ANB, while the other 50% are held by the Federal Republic.
7. See Pech and Weninger (1990).
8. See Hochreiter and Schubert (1991), p. 138.
9. See Commission of the European Communities (1991).
10. See Committee of Governors (1992).
11. See Cwik (1991), p. 393.
12. Entschließung des Europäischen Rates vom 5 Dezember 1978 über die Errichtung des EWS und damit zusammenhängende Fragen, Section A., paragraph 3.8.
13. However, the 'Other Holder' cannot participate in the *creation* of official ECU through the EMCF.
14. See Monthly Statistics of the Austrian National Bank, Table 10.3.
15. This would allow for more fluctuation against the *Deutsche mark* than at present, e.g. for Sweden an ECU peg of 1.5% on either side of the ECU central rate means that the maximum margin for fluctuations with the *Deutsche mark* is much higher at ± 3.79% (see Bank of Sweden, Annual Report 1991).
16. See Mooslechner (1989), p. 652.
17. See Mooslechner (1989), p. 653.
18. See Duchatczek and Schubert (1992).
19. See Branson (1991), p. 7.
20. See OECD (1992), p. 33.
21. It has to be noted that, in the present discussion about widening versus deepening,

there is also quite an important party of supporters of the *widening-first-in-order-to-achieve-deepening* school who are very much in favour of admitting new members into the Community as soon as possible. These issues were discussed in depth during a Colloquium, organized by the College of Europe, Bruges in June 1991 'The European Community in the 1990s: Widening Versus Deepening', in which it was concluded that the admission of new members will be inevitable, but only after a period of inner consolidation for the EC.

22. Ausschuß der Präsidenten der Zentralbanken der Mitgliedstaaten der Europäischen Wirtschaftsgemeinschaft, Expertengruppe unter dem Vorsitz von Herrn Dalgaard (1990), Fragen im Zusammenhang mit einer eventuellen Assoziierung von Drittländern mit dem Europäischen Währungssystem (Dalgaard Report).

23. See Dalgaard Report (1990), p. 5.

24. See EC Commission (1991), p. 29.

25. It could in any case be necessary and recommendable to follow the Dutch approach and keep the direct link of the schilling to the *Deutsche mark*, even within the EMS. In this case the markets could be convinced that *no* fundamental change in policy has occurred.

26. Officially, the *Riksbank* stated that opportunities of creating firmer cooperation between Sweden and the EMS by means of association should be taken as soon as they arise (see Bank of Sweden, Annual Report 1991).

27. See Pauer (1992).

28. The Director-General of the European Institute of Public Administration, Spyros Pappas, even went as far as to state that in most countries of the European Community the word '*subsidiarity* is not widely known', see foreword to Proceedings of the Jacques Delors Colloquium, EIPA, 1991.

    Subsidiarity forms one of the main pillars of the political programme of the second largest party and junior partner in the Austrian Government, the *Österreichische Volkspartei*. It has its Austrian roots in the *Katholische Soziallehre* (Catholic Social Doctrine) which puts the human individual in the centre of attention and distrusts large centralistic bureaucracies with their disregard for the strengths of human individuality.

REFERENCES

Ausschuß der Präsidenten der Zentralbanken der Mitgliedstaaten der Europäischen Wirtschaftsgemeinschaft, Expertengruppe unter dem Vorsitz von Herrn Dalgaard, *Fragen im Zusammenhang mit einer eventuellen Assoziierung von Drittländern mit dem Europäischen Währungssystem* (Brussels: Dalgaard Report 1990).

Bank of Sweden, *Annual Report 1991* (Stockholm: 1992).

Branson, W.H., *Exchange Rate Policy for the EFTA Countries in the 1990s,* Geneva: EFTA Occasional Paper no. 35, 1991.

Commission of the European Communities, *Austria's Application for Membership, Commission Opinion* (Brussels, 1991).

Committee of Governors of the Central Banks of the Member States of the European Economic Community, *Annual Report,* April 1992.

Cwik, M., 'Auf dem Weg zur Wirtschafts- und Währungsunion – steigende wirtschaftliche Abhängigkeiten und die Währungsintegration', in M. Röttinger and C. Weyringer (eds), *Handbuch der Europäischen Integration,* (Vienna: Manzsche Verlags- und Universitätsbuchhandlung, 1991) pp. 389-437.

Duchatczek, W. and Schubert A., 'Die Zukunft der österreichischen Währung im Zusammenhang mit der Europäischen Währungsunion', *Schriftenreihe des österreichischen Institutes für Sparkassenwesen,* 4/91 (Vienna: 1992).

European Institute of Public Administration, *Subsidiarity: The Challenge of Change,* Proceedings of the Jacques Delors Colloquium 1991, (Maastricht: EIPA, 1991).

Hochreiter, E. and Schubert A., 'National Economic Policies in Other Major OECD Countries: Austria, Sweden, Canada, and Australia', in D. Salvatore (ed.), *National Economic Policies,* (New York: Greenwood Press, 1991) pp. 133-168.

Klier, R., 'Das Europäische Zentralbanksystem und die Rolle nationaler Notenbanken', in H. Kienzl (ed.), *Österreichs Wirtschafts- und Währungspolitik auf dem Weg nach Europa,* (Vienna: 1991) pp. 73-90.

Mooslechner, P., 'Dollar, Dinar, EWS: Ein Kurzporträt von zehn Jahren Wechselkursentwicklung des Schillings', *Monthly Reports of the Austrian Institute of Economic Research* 11/89 (Vienna: 1989).

OECD Secretariat, *Adjustment Under Fixed Exchange Rates,* Note for Working Party No.1 of the Economic Policy Committee (Paris: 1992).

Pauer, F., 'Fulfilment of Convergence Criteria by the EC-Member Countries and the EC-Applicants Sweden and Austria', *Reports and Summaries,* 1/1992 (Vienna: Austrian National Bank, 1992).

Pech, H. and Weninger F., 'Comments on the Policy Instruments of the Austrian National Bank', *Reports and Summaries,* 3/1990 (Vienna: Austrian

National Bank, 1990).

Schubert, A., *The Credit-Anstalt Crisis of 1931* (Cambridge: Cambridge University Press, 1991).

SECTION 2:

CENTRAL BANK POLICY IN A NEW INSTITUTIONAL FRAMEWORK

THE EUROPEAN CENTRAL BANK AND THE ROLE OF NATIONAL CENTRAL BANKS IN ECONOMIC AND MONETARY UNION

Ian Harden

Introduction

Political stability, price stability, and the stable growth of employment and prosperity together form a virtuous circle. The provisions for Economic and Monetary Union (EMU) in the Maastricht Treaty on European Union are a further stage in the process of trying to create this virtuous circle on a Community-wide basis. Their full implementation will involve not just a change of economic system (Emerson *et al*, 1992), but significant constitutional changes for the Community, for its Member States and for the citizens of the European Union.[1] Clear institutional rules are needed at the Community level, as well as corresponding adaptations of the rules and structures of the Member States (Tietmeyer, 1992: 20).

The third stage of EMU – the irrevocable fixing of exchange rates between the currencies of Member States, followed by the rapid introduction of the ECU as the single currency – will begin, at the latest, on 1 January 1999. Under certain conditions, it could begin earlier.[2] The third stage will bring into operation the European Central Bank (ECB) and the European System of Central Banks (ESCB), the latter comprising the ECB and the central banks of the Member States.

This chapter will first consider the principles that are to govern EMU and the problems of designing institutions to give effect to them. It will then examine the structure and functions of the ECB and ESCB and the future role of national central banks, to see how successfully the problems have been tackled in the drafting of the Treaty and its Protocols.

K. Gretschmann (ed.), Economic and Monetary Union: Implications for National Policy-Makers, 149–167.

EMU: Principles and Problems of Institutional Design

PRICE STABILITY

The primary objective of the ESCB is to be the maintenance of price stability.[3] The commitment to price stability, binding on the Community as a whole,[4] is based on the view that acceptance of higher inflation cannot lead to a sustainably improved performance in respect of other economic objectives, such as growth or employment.

Despite committing themselves to this objective in the Treaty, governments may nonetheless be subject to electoral and other pressures to abandon it in practice. Price stability is more likely to be promoted by an independent central bank. The Treaty therefore contains provisions intended to ensure the independence of the ECB, from both the governments of Member States and Community institutions and bodies.

The requirement that the ESCB pursue price stability as its primary objective provides a legitimate basis for the ECB to resist pressures to inflate. However, it is not a rule which tells the ECB what to do. It is a principle to guide it in deciding what to do. Furthermore, it is a vague principle. 'Price stability' is not defined, either in quantitative or qualitative terms. It could mean zero inflation, though some economists have argued that a 1-2% annual rate of price increases is appropriate to reflect secular improvements in the quality of goods and services. A low and non-accelerating rate of inflation might also be described as 'price stability', especially if the costs of further reducing it are believed to outweigh the benefits (cf. Aiyagara 1990). The ECB will thus have discretion in interpreting the meaning of price stability as well as in deciding how to achieve it.

THE CONSTITUTIONAL FRAMEWORK OF MACROECONOMIC POLICY

Monetary policy involves the use of a variety of instruments to affect interest rates and credit creation. Taken together, monetary policy, budgetary policy (spending, revenue-raising and the difference between them) and external exchange rate policy, comprise macroeconomic policy.

In practice, the different elements of macroeconomic policy overlap, both in the instruments used and in terms of mutual interaction and dependence. Interest rates, for example, are at one and the same time an aspect of both domestic monetary policy and external exchange rate policy. They also have a fiscal impact by affecting the cost of servicing the public debt. To take another example, the financing of public debt by borrowing from the central bank has a direct impact on monetary policy.

At present, macroeconomic policy remains constitutionally the responsibility of Member States, albeit subject to obligations of cooperation at Community level. The Union Treaty confirms that the principle of subsidiarity is to govern the actions of the Community in areas which are not within its exclusive jurisdiction.[5] Application of this principle is complicated by the overlap between different elements of economic policy referred to above. However, the exchange rate of a single currency *vis-à-vis* other world currencies must obviously be a matter for the Community.

A single currency also necessarily involves a single Community monetary policy and hence the complete transfer of responsibility for such policy from Member States to the Community. This transfer has a somewhat different political and constitutional significance for Germany, whose monetary policy is already determined by the independent *Bundesbank*, than for States such as France, Italy and the United Kingdom, whose central banks are not independent (Louis, 1989; Toniolo, 1988) and whose governments are therefore responsible for monetary policy.

For Germany, the central question is whether its existing 'virtuous circle' of prosperity, price stability and political stability can be re-created successfully at Community level. For the other countries, EMU will involve going beyond the *de facto* sacrifice of autonomous monetary policy involved in benefiting from the low-inflation anchor role of the German mark in the European Monetary System (EMS). Instead of this voluntary (and, in principle, revocable) trade-off, there will have to be permanent constitutional constraints on government authority, both as regards the national central bank and in respect of budgetary policy.

Governments will remain responsible for national budgets and thus, for the foreseeable future, for the bulk of public expenditure in the Community. However, it is doubtful whether monetary policy can do more than postpone inflation in the face of undisciplined fiscal policy (Sargent and Wallace, 1981). Requirements of sound public finance are therefore to be imposed on Member States. The monetization of government debt (i.e. direct borrowing from the central bank) is to be prohibited.[6] There will also be monitoring of compliance with budgetary discipline, as regards the ratio of total government debt to Gross Domestic Product (GDP) and the budget deficit as a proportion of GDP. Gross errors will be identified through a procedure which may ultimately lead to the Community imposing sanctions on Member States, including fines.[7]

THE THIRD STAGE: DESIGN AND TRANSITION

To put EMU into effect it was necessary to design an institutional and constitutional framework for the operation of the third stage that would ensure the economic and political stability of the system. This involves not only determining the extent to which economic policy responsibilities are to be transferred from Member States to the Community, but also how those responsibilities are to be allocated between different Community bodies and institutions. The interconnection between monetary, budgetary and exchange rate policies complicates the latter question as much as the former.

There is also a two-fold problem of transition. Member States begin from different economic and constitutional starting points. Furthermore, the expectations of private economic actors are a key element in establishing and maintaining price stability at the least cost in terms of the other objectives of economic policy.

Fundamental to the Treaty's approach to both issues are two clear principles. First, before the beginning of the third stage, responsibility for monetary policy remains with the Member States. When stage two begins on the 1 January 1994, the European Monetary Institute (EMI) will take over the functions of the Committee of Governors of the Central Banks, together with administration of the European Monetary Cooperation Fund and associated responsibilities for the EMS and the exchange rate mechanism. The EMI will also have an important role in preparing for the third stage. However, it will not itself have any responsibility for monetary policy.

Second, whilst the Community will move irrevocably to the third stage no later than 1999, individual Member States must earn their 'entry ticket' to EMU. The only Member States to participate in the third stage will be those that fulfil the necessary conditions. These include criteria of sustainable economic convergence[8] and requirements concerning the compatibility of national legislation with the Treaty and with the Statutes of the ECB/ESCB. Member States which do not fulfil the conditions will have derogations and will not immediately take part in the irrevocable fixing of exchange rates and subsequently the single currency.[9]

The Treaty also contains Protocols which allow the UK and Denmark to opt out of the third stage. The effects of the Protocols are examined further below.

The Structure of the ECB/ESCB

The ESCB will consist of the ECB and the national central banks. The relationship between the two elements is determined by the need for a single Community monetary policy. The Statute of the ECB/ESCB lays down the general principle that the ESCB shall be governed by the decision-making bodies of the ECB. It also states that the national central banks are an integral part of the ESCB and shall act in accordance with the guidelines and instructions of the ECB.[10]

The national central banks will also be allowed to perform functions other than those specified in the Statute, unless the Governing Council finds by a two-thirds majority of the votes cast that these interfere with the objectives and tasks of the ESCB.[11] Although non-ESCB functions are to be carried out on the national central banks' own responsibility and liability, the banks will remain an integral part of the ESCB. The ECB will therefore be competent to issue binding guidelines and instructions in respect of the national central banks' non-ESCB activities.

The Community's monetary policy is to be formulated by the Governing Council of the ECB and implemented by its Executive Board, in accordance with the guidelines and decisions of the Governing Council. The formulation and implementation of monetary policy are thus clearly matters within the exclusive jurisdiction of the Community. Only its actual execution is to be governed by the principle of subsidiarity. To the extent deemed possible and appropriate, the ECB is to have recourse to the national central banks to carry out operations which form part of the tasks of the ESCB.[12] Since the issue involved is one of implementation, it will be for the Executive Board to deem what is possible and appropriate.

Subject to the authorization of the Governing Council of the ECB, the national central banks will be able to issue bank notes. As far as possible, existing practices regarding the issue and design of notes are to be respected,[13] thus allowing for the continued use of national symbols and emblems.

INDEPENDENCE OF THE ECB

The ECB's independence is to be ensured by appropriate provisions – many of them modelled on those which apply to the *Bundesbank* – concerning its personnel, its institutional status and the performance of its functions. The ECB is not to be subject to control and direction by any democratically accountable political authority. The ECB itself and members of its decision-making bodies will be prohibited from seeking or taking instructions from Community institutions or bodies, from any government of a Member State, or from any other body.[14]

The ECB is required to 'support the general economic policies in the Community', but this obligation is 'without prejudice to the objective of price stability'.[15] Since it is for the ECB itself to determine what price stability is and how best to exercise its powers so as to achieve it, the duty to support general economic policies does not provide any basis for other public authorities to seek to limit the ECB's discretion. In fact, the ECB is to be protected by a rather more tightly-drafted version of the provisions which apply to the *Bundesbank*.[16]

The President of the ECOFIN Council[17] and a member of the Commission are entitled to participate in meetings of the ECB's Governing Council. Whilst this means that they may contribute to the formulation of monetary policy through discussion, they have no right to vote.[18] The position of the ECB in this respect also will be analogous to that of the *Bundesbank*. Members of the German Federal Government may participate in meetings of the Central Council of the *Bundesbank* and may propose motions, but without voting rights. The President of the ECB may similarly submit motions for deliberation to the Governing Council. The ECB President is also to be invited to participate in ECOFIN meetings at which matters relating to the ESCB's tasks and objectives are under discussion, as the President of the *Bundesbank* is to meetings of the Federal Government where monetary policy is discussed.[19]

Members of the Executive Board of the ECB are to be appointed for a non-renewable eight-year term which can be terminated prematurely only by death or compulsory retirement by the Court of Justice. There are appropriate arrangements for determining the salaries and other terms of employment of members of the Executive Board.[20] Like most national central banks, the ECB's expenditure will be exempt from normal budgetary processes.

Unlike the US Federal Reserve System (FRS), and more clearly and unambiguously than the *Bundesbank*, the ECB's independence will have constitutional protection. Although the ECOFIN Council will have power to amend parts of the Statute, this will not apply to the independence or principal objectives of the ECB/ESCB.[21] These can be altered only by an amendment to the Treaty itself.

INDEPENDENCE OF THE NATIONAL CENTRAL BANKS

The national central banks are also required to be independent. Like the ECB, the banks as institutions and the members of their decision-making bodies will be forbidden to seek or accept instructions from governments.[22] This provision is not restricted to the performance of specific ESCB functions but applies whenever the national central banks are 'exercising the powers and carrying out the tasks and duties conferred upon them by the Treaty and the Statute'. For example, the Statute specifically empowers both the ECB and the national central banks to act as fiscal agents for the governments of Member States and other public sector entities.[23] This provision will permit those central banks which sell and manage government debt to continue to do so. However, the relationship involved must be consistent with the requirement of independence.[24]

There are no specific provisions relating to the appointment of Governors, though national laws must be consistent with the general principle of independence. However, the statutes of each national central bank must provide for the Governor's term of office to be no less than five years and a Governor may be relieved from office only if he no longer fulfils the conditions required for the performance of his duties or for serious misconduct. A decision to remove a Governor may be referred to the Court of Justice, either by the Governor concerned, or by the Governing Council of the ECB.[25]

During the second stage (i.e. from the beginning of 1994), each Member State is required, as appropriate, to start the process leading to the independence of its central bank, in accordance with Article 108.[26] The latter Article requires each Member State to ensure that its national legislation, including the statutes of its central bank, is compatible with the Treaty and the Statute of the ESCB/ECB. This must be achieved by no later than the date of establishment of the ESCB, which will take place once the date for the beginning of the third stage has been determined.[27]

The requirement for national central banks to be independent has a dual significance. First, it is obvious that they can function effectively as part of the ESCB only if they are independent of national governments. The second aspect of independence relates to the position of such Member States as are unable to meet the convergence criteria at the beginning of the third stage and which therefore require derogations. A State with a derogation would continue to have its own currency and hence its own monetary policy until such time as it did meet the criteria.

However, a derogation would not exempt a Member State from compliance with the constitutional requirement that its central bank be independent. Independence is to be achieved before the third stage begins and the relevant Articles are not subsequently excluded from application to a State with a derogation. It is for this reason that the Statute provides that '*central banks* of Member States with a derogation...shall retain their powers in the field of monetary policy according to national law'.[28]

The State's monetary policy would thus be determined by its independent central bank, not by its Government. Furthermore, the central bank would be part of the ESCB and so bound to make price stability its primary objective, with a view also to promoting fulfilment of the convergence criteria and making possible abrogation of the Member State's derogation.[29] The central bank would also be subject to the jurisdiction of the Court of Justice in cases where the ECB considered that it had failed to fulfil its obligations under the Statute.[30]

The only potential exception to the requirement that all national central banks shall be independent once the ESCB is established is provided by the UK opt-out Protocol. If this were to be exercised, the UK Government would be able to maintain the present position, in which the Bank of England is subject to directions from the Treasury and monetary policy is determined by government. Hence, in contrast to the position for States with a derogation, the Protocol provides that in the event of an opt-out 'the *United Kingdom* shall retain its powers in the field of monetary policy according to national law'.[31]

The Protocol also gives the United Kingdom a special position as regards overdraft facilities with the Bank of England. From the beginning of the second stage, the direct purchase of government debt instruments by national central banks will be prohibited. The same will apply to overdraft facilities.[32] However, the Protocol, whilst noting the practice of the UK Government to fund its borrowing requirement by the sale of debt to the private sector, allows it to maintain its 'Ways and Means' (i.e. overdraft) facility with the Bank of England, unless and until the UK moves to the third stage.

Subject to the UK Protocol therefore, governments will progressively lose the power to use national central banks as policy instruments. Monetary financing of debt must be abandoned at the beginning of the second stage. By the time the ESCB is established, all national central banks must be independent. The central banks of Member States without a derogation at the beginning of the third stage will become an integral part of the ESCB and must act in accordance with guidelines and instructions from the ECB. The central bank of a Member State with a derogation would retain responsibility for national monetary policy, but within the context of the objectives of the ESCB and independent of the government of the Member State.

THE ORGANS OF THE ECB

The ECB is to have two main organs: the Governing Council and the Executive Board. In case there are Member States with derogations, the Statute of the ECB/ESCB also provides for a General Council, whose voting membership will consist of the President and Vice-President of the ECB and the Governors of all the national central banks. The principal function envisaged for the General Council is to take over those tasks of the EMI which still have to be performed in the third stage because one or more Member States have derogations.

Although described in the Statute as a 'decision-making body of the ECB', the General Council is not to be one of the bodies which governs the ESCB, nor are any specific decision-making powers included in its list of responsibilities.[33] It is to have no role in the formulation or implementation of the Community's monetary policy. Apart from the General Council, Member States with derogations and the Governors of their central banks will be excluded from participation in the appointment and functioning of the ECB's decision-making bodies.[34]

The Governing Council is to consist of the Governors of the national central banks of States without derogations, together with the members of the Executive Board; that is: the President and Vice-President of the ECB and up to four others. The members of the Executive Board are to be appointed by common accord of the governments of Member States without a derogation, at the level of Heads of State and Government. If there are Member States with a derogation, the Executive Board may consist of less than six members, but there must be at least four.[35]

The Governing Council is expressly given the task of formulating the monetary policy of the Community, including decisions relating to intermediate monetary objectives, key interest rates and the supply of reserves in the ESCB. It is also to formulate guidelines for implementing these decisions. Voting for these purposes is to be by simple majority, without weighting. The Executive Board is to implement monetary policy in accordance with the Governing Council's guidelines and decisions and give the necessary instructions to national central banks.[36]

The constitution of the ECB contains a number of checks and balances. Although they will be legally independent, national central banks and their Governors can be expected to ensure that differences in the economic situations of the Member States are taken into account in the formulation of monetary policy. Hence the composition of the Governing Council means that the ESCB will resemble the US Federal Reserve System and the German *Bundesbank* in terms of the representation of regional interests in its structure.

Unless the third stage begins with fewer than five States participating (and a majority of Member States must participate if the third stage is to begin before 1999),[37] the Governors of national central banks will constitute a majority on the Governing Council. Since voting on monetary policy matters is to be by simple, unweighted, majority, a bloc of Governors that was sufficiently large could, in theory, dominate formulation of the Community's monetary policy.

However, giving instructions to the national central banks – and deciding which tasks to delegate to them – are responsibilities of the Executive Board. Moreover, although further powers may be delegated to it by the Governing Council, the Executive Board's fundamental task of implementing monetary policy is given to it directly by the Statute itself. Thus neither the Governing Council nor the Executive Board is ultimately answerable to the other for the performance of its functions. In implementing the Community's monetary policy, the Executive Board must interpret the meaning of what the Governing Council has decided. In doing this, it must be guided by the primacy of the objective of price stability.

Exchange Rate Policy

As with monetary policy, the laws and constitutions of Member States are not uniform in respect of the degree of control over exchange rate policy exercised by governments. There is general agreement that governments – and only governments – have authority to conclude international agreements on fixed exchange rates. However, the breakdown of the Bretton Woods system in the early 1970s meant that rates floated. That is, instead of political decisions to devalue or revalue currencies, changes in exchange rates are determined by markets.

Central banks intervene on a discretionary basis by buying and selling in the markets. As with the setting of interest rates (which are an instrument of both monetary and exchange rate policy), some central banks exercise their own judgment about intervention in the foreign exchange markets (and such interventions may also have an impact on domestic monetary policy). Others simply carry out the instructions of government.

The European Monetary System and its exchange rate mechanism have developed into a system of fixed rates, with limited bands of variation, between the currencies of the Member States of the Community. Once the transition to a single currency takes place, there will no longer be any exchange rates within the Community, except for the currencies of Member States with a derogation. The fundamental issue of Community exchange rate policy will therefore be the position of the ECU *vis-à-vis* non-Community currencies.

Since exchange rate policy and domestic monetary policy are interdependent (insofar as they are distinguishable at all), price stability is dependent on both. One commentator, writing before the Maastricht agreement was concluded, described exchange rate policy as 'the area where greatest risk to the ESCB's autonomy and orientation towards price stability lies' (Thygesen, 1991: 479). This warning seems to have been heeded, for the provisions of the Treaty are designed to minimize any such risk. Whilst recognizing the ultimately political nature of decisions about, and under, fixed exchange rate regimes, the Treaty constrains the authority of ECOFIN and maximizes the effective power of the ECB in order to protect the objective of price stability.

The ECOFIN Council will have power to conclude a formal agreement on an exchange rate system in relation to non-Community currencies. However, it can do so only by unanimity. The recommendation to act must come either from the ECB, or from the Commission. In the latter case, the ECB must be consulted in an endeavour to reach a consensus consistent with the objective of price stability. The same procedure will apply to the adoption, abandonment or adjustment of central rates for the ECU within the exchange rate system, though here the Council may act by qualified majority.[38]

The exchange rate policy to be pursued under a regime of floating rates will in practice be a matter for the ECB. The ECOFIN Council will have power, by qualified majority, to formulate 'general orientations' for exchange rate policy. This term is not defined, but implies something much less concrete than 'guidelines'. It would not justify any numerically expressed targets or ranges. In any event, if 'general orientations' are formulated, they must be without prejudice to the primary objective of the ESCB to maintain price stability. A general orientation could not, therefore, put the ECB under an obligation to act in a way which it judged to be inconsistent with the price stability objective.

FOREIGN RESERVE ASSETS

The basic tasks of the ESCB include conducting foreign exchange operations and holding and managing the official foreign reserves of the Member States.[39] The foreign reserves of all Member States, with or without a derogation, will therefore have to be held and managed by their national central banks. The only exception is for 'working balances', which governments may retain under their own control.[40]

Within the ESCB, the ECB itself is to be empowered to hold, manage and deal in precious metals and foreign exchange assets. Initially, the national central banks of Member States without derogations are to make available to the ECB up to 50,000 million ECU worth of such assets. Further calls beyond this limit may be authorized by the ECOFIN Council.[41]

With the foreign reserve assets which they retain, national central banks are to be permitted to perform transactions in fulfilment of their obligations to international organizations. Other operations, above a limit to be established in guidelines issued by the Governing Council, will be subject to approval by the ECB. The same requirement will also apply to transactions involving governments' 'working balances'.[42]

Banking Supervision

At the heart of monetary policy is the provision by the central bank of liquidity to the banking system. Some central banks also have responsibility for prudential supervision (i.e. seeking to ensure that banks and other commercial credit institutions adopt prudent lending policies, so as to avoid the risk of failure). Prudential supervision also involves a more general responsibility for the health of the financial system. These different roles may involve using the same instruments, or performing the same functions, for different purposes and with different ends in view. For example, in a crisis – either for the financial system as a whole, or for a particular institution – the central bank may become the 'lender of last resort' in more than a technical sense by providing credit to rescue the institution or system from failure.

Concern that a central bank may temper its pursuit of price stability with concern for the stability and liquidity requirements of commercial undertakings suggests that it may be preferable to give responsibility for prudential supervision to a separate institution. In Germany, for example, prudential supervision is the responsibility of the *Bundesaufsichtamt für das Kreditwesen*, in cooperation with the *Bundesbank*. In France, liquidity and solvency ratios are laid down by the *Comité de la réglementation bancaire* and applied by the *Commission bancaire*, in cooperation with the *Banque de France* (Louis, 1989: 164-166).

The original draft of the Statute of the ESCB and ECB, prepared by the Committee of Governors of the Central Banks, included as a fifth basic task of the ESCB:

to participate as necessary in the formulation, coordination and execution of polices relating to prudential supervision and the stability of the financial system.

However, this does not appear in the Treaty as finally agreed. Instead, the ESCB is:

to contribute to the smooth conduct of policies pursued by the competent authorities relating to the prudential supervision of credit institutions and the stability of the financial system.[43]

The Statute makes specific provision for the ECB to advise and be consulted by ECOFIN, the Commission and national authorities on the scope and implementation of Community legislation relating to prudential supervision and the stability of the financial system.[44]

Prudential supervision *per se* is not therefore an ESCB function, but national central banks which have that responsibility (such as the Bank of England and *Banca d'Italia*) may continue to exercise it, within the framework of Articles 18 and 14.4 of the Statute. Article 18 empowers the ECB and the national central banks to conduct credit operations with credit institutions and other market participants, with lending being based on adequate collateral. General principles for such operations are to be established by the ECB, including the announcement of conditions under which it, or the national central banks, stand ready to enter into such transactions.

The ECB could itself use the power to conduct credit operations to supply liquidity to the banking system (Bank of England, 1992: 65). Rescue operations consisting of lending by national central banks would also fall within Article 18 and thus will be matters in respect of which a national central bank must act independently of government.[45] Furthermore, in addition to acting in accordance with the ECB's general principles for credit operations, national central banks would have to adhere to any guidelines or instructions from the ECB concerning such lending.[46]

The ECB thus has ample powers to ensure that things done by a national central bank in the exercise of responsibilities for prudential supervision and the health of the financial system, do not compromise the monetary policy of the Community. Direct credit operations by a national central bank are subject to ECB regulation and instructions. If necessary, the ECB also has a reserve power to require national central banks to be divested of responsibilities under national legislation for prudential supervision and the health of the financial system.[47]

The Treaty gives the ESCB itself only a limited role in prudential supervision. However, the integration of financial markets (which the Treaty itself will further promote) may lead to the development of multinational financial institutions which are beyond the effective supervisory reach of national authorities. To deal with this eventuality, there is provision for the ECOFIN Council to extend the ECB's own functions. By a decision reached unanimously, ECOFIN may confer upon the ECB specific tasks concerning polices relating to the prudential supervision of credit institutions and other (non-insurance) financial institutions.[48] If such a decision is made, the ECB will acquire power to make regulations and decisions in pursuance of the specific tasks conferred upon it and to impose fines or periodic penalty payments on undertakings.[49]

Accountability

From its position of constitutionally protected independence, the ECB will exercise extremely important economic policy powers. Not only will it control monetary policy but – as long as the world does not return to a Bretton Woods-style system of fixed exchange rates, which it shows no signs of doing – the ECB will also *de facto* determine the Community's exchange rate policy for the ECU.

In using these powers the ECB will have a very large measure of discretionary authority, both to determine what the goal of price stability means and in deciding how to pursue that goal (and how to fulfil its subsidiary task of supporting the general economic policies in the Community) through the instruments which are available to it. It will have to account for the use of its discretion through an annual report on the activities of the ESCB and on the monetary policy of both the previous and current year. The report is to be addressed to the European Parliament, ECOFIN, the Commission and the European Council. It is to be presented to ECOFIN and to Parliament by the President of the ECB and the Parliament may hold a general debate.[50]

There is also a delicately-worded provision for oral hearings:

> The President of the ECB and the other members of the Executive Board, may at the request of the European Parliament or on their own initiative, be heard by the competent Committees of the European Parliament.

The effect of this appears to be that a hearing may be requested, either by the Executive Board, or by Parliament, but the Executive Board cannot insist on being heard and Parliament cannot compel them to appear.

These reporting requirements appear somewhat limited when compared, for example, with those applicable to the Board of Governors of the US Federal

Reserve System. The Board of Governors of the FRS must submit independent written reports to Congress in February and July each year. These reports must review and analyze recent developments affecting economic trends, including an analysis of the impact of the dollar exchange rate. They must also set out the objectives and plans of the Board of Governors and the Federal Open Market Committee with respect to monetary and credit aggregates in the current calendar year. The July report must also state objective and plans for the aggregates in the following calendar year. The Board must also consult the relevant committees of the Senate and House of Representatives and must explain the reasons for any revision to, or deviation from, the objectives and plans contained in its reports.[51]

In comparing these provisions with those governing the ECB, however, it must be remembered that Congressional insistence on strict oversight of the FRS is partly based on the suspicion that it might otherwise be over-influenced by the executive branch of government. It thus reflects the FRS's specific and somewhat peculiar position in the constitutional separation of powers, as well as a more general American predilection for using procedural devices to confine and structure the discretionary powers of public authorities (Harden, 1990a).

The question of accountability to national parliaments was identified as an issue that would need to be addressed in the inter-governmental conferences that preceded Maastricht (Leigh-Pemberton, 1991). In the event, neither the Treaty nor the Statute deals with the matter expressly. Some national parliaments currently expect the attendance of the central bank Governor at appropriate committee hearings. This is true in the United Kingdom, for example, though the British Parliament is not in any significant sense 'sovereign' over monetary policy (Harden, 1990b). This expectation will no doubt continue when the banks become an integral part of the ESCB.

The ECB and Political Union

The independence of the ECB and the provisions for its accountability are constitutionally appropriate ways of combining procedural legitimacy with a commitment to price stability as a substantive objective. The institutional design of the third stage is in line with the recommendations made by the Central Council of the *Bundesbank* (*Deutsche Bundesbank*, 1992: 53-54) and is in no small degree modelled on the legal framework of the *Bundesbank* itself.

A suitable constitutional structure for the ESCB is a necessary condition for achievement of the virtuous circle of price stability, political stability, and stable growth of employment and prosperity. However, it is not a sufficient condition. The impact of fiscal and monetary policy on the economy is a joint impact and the fiscal and monetary authorities must act together to secure the economic elements of the virtuous circle.

In addition to the 'entry ticket' requirements and the excessive deficit procedure, the Treaty also strengthens the provisions for coordination of the economic policies of the Member States through ECOFIN.[52] However, as the need for an excessive deficit procedure in the third stage demonstrates, coordination has its limits. It may be instrumentally sufficient as a way of aligning fiscal policy with monetary and exchange rate policies, but it can ensure neither that there is the political will to do so, nor that there is political accountability for the policies agreed.

ECOFIN is not itself a body with democratic legitimacy. Such as it has, it derives indirectly from the governments of the Member States. In the overall constitutional structure of economic policy responsibilities that emerges from the Treaty, the ECB stands alone as a Community-level body. ECOFIN will not be constitutionally responsible for a Community fiscal policy. Instead, governments of the Member States will be separately responsible, to their own electorates, for their individual fiscal policies.

This presents two interlocking dangers. First, the ECB will visibly be there as a Community institution. The name of its President will be known to millions in a way the name of the President for the time being of ECOFIN will never be. Second, fiscal policy will be the only macroeconomic instrument available to governments of Member States with which to respond to the political pressures created by the economic expectations of their citizens. The excessive deficit procedure and tax competition in the single market will constrain their real room for manoeuvre. They may be expected to guard jealously, and to use for their own purposes, that which remains.

As a result, the ECB may find itself regarded as, in effect, the economic government of the Community; in potential policy conflict with the governments of Member States, rather than cooperating with a Community-level 'fiscal partner'. This is a burden which the ECB will have neither the powers, nor the appropriate form of accountability, to discharge. Progress towards political union is thus not an optional extra to EMU, but an integral part of ensuring its success and stability (Tietmeyer, 1992, *Deutsche Bundesbank*, 1992).

NOTES

NB: where a provision of the Treaty is reproduced in identical terms in the Statute of the ESCB and ECB (hereafter 'Statute') only the Treaty reference is given.

1. The term 'constitutional' is used in this chapter to refer to the allocation of decision-making authority (i) within Member States, (ii) between Member States and the Community and (iii) between Community bodies and institutions, insofar as the allocation cannot legitimately be altered by ordinary legislative processes.
2. See Treaty, Article 109 j.
3. Treaty, Article 105 (1); Statute, Article 2.
4. See Treaty, Article 3 a.
5. Article 3 b, second indent:
    In the areas which do not fall within its exclusive jurisdiction, the Community shall take action, in accordance with the principle of subsidiarity, only if and insofar as the objectives of the proposed action cannot be sufficiently achieved by the Member States and can therefore, by reason of the scale or effects of proposed action, be better achieved by the Community.
6. Treaty, Article 104 (1).
7. Treaty, Article 104 c.
8. Treaty, Article 109 j (1) and Protocol on the Convergence Criteria.
    To be eligible to move to the third stage a state must:
    –   have had, for the previous year, an average rate of inflation no more than 1.5% higher than, at most, the three Member States with lowest inflation rates;
    –   not be the subject of a Council decision under Article 104 c (6) that it has an excessive budget deficit;
    –   have respected the normal fluctuation margins for its currency in the Exchange Rate Mechanism of the European Monetary System for the previous two years, without severe tensions and without any devaluation initiated by the state itself;
    –   have had, for the previous year, average nominal long-term interest rates on government securities no more than 2% above that of, at most, the three Member States with lowest inflation.
9. If and when they do meet the criteria, their derogations will be abrogated by decision of the Council, acting in the composition of Heads of State and Government and by qualified majority: Treaty, Article 109 k (2).
10. Statute, Articles 8, 14.3.
11. Statute, Article 14.4.
12. Statute, Article 12.1.
13. Treaty, Article 105 a; Statute, Article 16.
14. Treaty, Article 107.
15. Treaty, Article 105 (1).
16. The *Bundesbankgesetz* of 1957 provides that:

Without prejudice to the performance of its functions, the *Deutsche Bundesbank* shall be required to support the general economic policies of the Federal Government. In exercising the powers conferred on it by this Act it shall be independent of instructions from the Federal Government.

17. One of the Declarations appended to the Treaty of Maastricht affirms that, for the purpose of applying the provisions on (*inter alia*) economic and monetary policy, the usual practice according to which the Council meets in the composition of Economic and Finance Ministers shall be continued.
18. Treaty, Article 109 b (1).
19. *Bundesbankgesetz*, para. 13 sec. 2 and 3:
    Treaty, Article 109 b (1) and (2).
20. Statute, Article 14.3, 14.4.
21. Treaty, Article 106 (5).
22. Treaty Article 107.
23. Statute, Article 21.2.
24. The proposed Directive on the award of public service contracts excludes contracts concerning primary issues of government bonds and other activities in the area of public debt management. The preliminary recitals expressly base this exclusion on their connection with monetary policy. Once the ESCB is responsible for monetary policy, will there be any good reason why the relationship between government and a central bank acting as fiscal agent on its behalf should not be (a) contractual and (b) subject to the award procedures in the Directive?
25. Statute, Article 14.2.
26. Treaty Article 109 e (5).
27. Treaty, Article 109 l (1).
    The Italian Government has already taken a step towards greater independence for the *Banca d'Italia*, even before the start of stage two. *Legge 7 febbraio 1992 n. 82* empowers the Governor to decide changes in the discount rate and to set the interest rate on ordinary and fixed-term advances.
28. Article 43.2 (italics added for emphasis).
29. This is not set out explicitly, but is to be implied from the provisions of Article 2 of the Statute, combined with Articles 2 and 3 a of the Treaty.
30. Statute, Article 35.6.
31. Protocol on Certain Provisions Relating to the United Kingdom of Great Britain and Northern Ireland, Article 4 (italics added for emphasis).
    The Protocol on Certain Provisions Relating to Denmark provides for Denmark to have an 'exemption' if it decides not to proceed to the third stage. Save only as regards the procedure for its abrogation, an exemption would be equivalent to a derogation.
32. Treaty, Article 104.
    Historically (especially during wartime) the 'Ways and Means' facility has been used as the vehicle to monetize British Government debt.
33. Treaty Article 106 (3); Statute, Articles 45.1 and 47.
34. See Treaty, Article 109 k (3) (4) (5); Statute, Article 43.
35. Treaty, Article 109 l (1).

36. Statute, Article 12.
37. Treaty, Article 109 j.
38. Treaty, Article 109.
39. Treaty, Article 105 (2).
40. Treaty, Article 105 (3).
41. Statute, Article 30.
42. Statute, Article 31.
43. Treaty, Article 105 (5).
44. Statute, Article 25.1
45. Treaty, Article 107.
46. Statute, Article 14.3
47. Statute, Article 14.4.
48. Treaty, Article 105 (6).
49. Treaty, Article 108 a.
50. Treaty, Article 109 b (3).
51. 12 United States Code Annotated § 225 a.
52. Treaty, Articles 102 a, 103.

REFERENCES

Aiyagara, S. Rao, 'Deflating the Case for Zero Inflation', *Federal Reserve Bank of Minneapolis Quarterly Bulletin*, 14 (summer 1990), pp. 2-11.

Bank of England, 'The Maastricht Agreement on Economic and Monetary Union', *Bank of England Quarterly Bulletin*, 32 (1)(1992), pp. 64-68.

Driffill, John and Beber, Massimo, *A Currency for Europe. The Currency as an Element of Division or of Union of Europe* (London: Lothian Foundation Press, 1991).

Deutsche Bundesbank, 'Die Beschlüsse von Maastricht zur Europäischen Wirtschafts- und Währungsunion', *Monatsbericht der Deutschen Bundesbank* (February 1992), pp. 45-54.

Emerson, Michael (et al), *One Market, One Money. An Evaluation of the Potential Costs and Benefits of Forming an Economic and Monetary Union* (Oxford: Oxford University Press, 1992).

Harden, Ian, 'EuroFed or "Monster Bank"', *National Westminster Bank Quarterly Review* (1990a), pp. 2-13.

Harden, Ian, 'Sovereignty and the EuroFed', *Political Quarterly*, 61 (1990b), pp. 402-414.

Leigh-Pemberton, Robin, 'European Monetary Arrangements: Convergence and Other Issues', *Bank of England Quarterly Bulletin* (November 1991), pp. 516-520.

Louis, Jean-Victor (ed.), *Vers Un Système Européen de Banques Centrales* (Brussels: Editions de l'université de Bruxelles, 1989).

Sargent, Thomas J. and Wallace, Neil, 'Some Unpleasant Monetarist Arithmatic', *Federal Reserve Bank of Minneapolis Quarterly Bulletin*, 5 (fall, 1981), pp. 1-17.

Thygesen, Niels, 'Monetary Management in a Monetary Union', *European Economic Review*, 35 (1991), pp. 474-483.

Tietmeyer, Hans, 'Währungsunion – ein Weg ohne Umkehr', *Integration*, 1/92 (1992), pp. 17-24.

Toniolo, Gianni (ed.), *Central Banks' Independence in Historical Perspective* (Berlin/New York: Walter de Gruyter, 1988).

CONVERGENCE OF MONETARY POLICIES IN EUROPE – CONCEPTS, TARGETS AND INSTRUMENTS

Sylvester Eijffinger*

Introduction

In July 1978 the European Council of the Heads of State and Government meeting in Bremen agreed to establish the European Monetary System (EMS). The EMS went into operation on 13 March 1979 and replaced the 'snake arrangement' for the exchange rates of some Member States of the European Community. The then Member States of the European Community – Belgium, Denmark, France, Germany, Ireland, Italy, Luxembourg, The Netherlands and the United Kingdom – agreed to participate in the EMS and, except for the United Kingdom, in its Exchange Rate Mechanism (ERM). Of the more recent EMS-members, Spain joined the Exchange Rate Mechanism on 16 June 1989. After prolonged abstinence, the United Kingdom entered the Exchange Rate Mechanism and so did Portugal just recently. The EMS Exchange Rate Mechanism has succeeded in creating a zone of increasing monetary stability, at the same time gradually relaxing capital controls, and has improved monetary policy coordination between central banks of member countries. However, the fiscal policy coordination between the Ministers of Finance lagged behind. As stated in the Delors Report, the EMS has benefited from the role played by the *Deutsche mark* as an 'anchor' for participants' monetary and intervention policies.[1] This resulted in the asymmetrical functioning of the EMS, in that Germany focuses on a target for money growth and the other participants on a target for their currency's exchange rate *vis-à-vis* the *Deutsche mark*.

As a consequence of the Single European Act, at Hanover in June 1988 the Member States confirmed their intention to progressively establish an Economic and Monetary Union (EMU). The European Council, meeting at Madrid in June 1989, agreed to begin stage one of EMU from 1 July 1990. In June 1990, formerPresident Pöhl of the *Deutsche Bundesbank* proposed a two-speed EMU

* The author would like to thank Carel van den Berg, Henk van Gemert, Lex Hoogduin and the editor for their valuable comments on an earlier version of this chapter. Of course, the usual disclaimer applies.

169

K. Gretschmann (ed.), Economic and Monetary Union: Implications for National Policy-Makers, 169–193.

with France, Germany and the Benelux countries moving ahead and the other countries – including Italy, Spain and the United Kingdom – following later.[2] Of course, there were strong objections to this proposal by the 'following' countries. Nevertheless, the arguments in support of the two-speed approach are strong. The budget deficits in Greece, Portugal, Spain and Italy are (very) high and persistent and will to a large extent burden the convergence of monetary policy. Moreover, the lack of wage flexibility and labour mobility within the Community undermines competitiveness, especially in the countries mentioned, and huge regional and structural funds will be required to financially assist these countries.

In both a one-speed and a two-speed approach towards EMU, the convergence of monetary policy between France, Germany and the United Kingdom will be decisive. The purpose of this article is to investigate the degree of monetary policy convergence which has already been achieved in these three countries. First, we will discuss convergence in monetary policy implementation during the eighties: policy goals, monetary targets, monetary instruments and exchange and money market policy. Second, we will analyze the convergence of monetary policy performance during the last decade: inflation rates, real exchange rates, real capital and money market rates. The conclusion of the article will be that the convergence of monetary policy between Germany and France has accelerated since 1986 and is now at a high level. The reverse side of this convergence is the strong dependence of French monetary policy on that of Germany. On the other hand, the convergence of monetary policy between the United Kingdom and the continent lagged behind, because of the exceptional British position during the eighties, but could have been enhanced as a consequence of the pound joining the Exchange Rate Mechanism on 8 October 1990. However, speculative pressures on the pound and the Italian lira forced both currencies to leave the mechanism on 16 September 1992 and to float again.

Policy Goals

The policy goals of the *Deutsche Bundesbank* were legally established in the *Gesetz über die Deutsche Bundesbank* of 26 July 1957. The task of the *Bundesbank* is embedded in section 3 of the *Bundesbank* Act.[3]

Die Deutsche Bundesbank regelt mit Hilfe der währungspolitischen Befügnisse, die ihr nach diesem Gesetz zustehen, den Geldumlauf und die Kreditversorgung der Wirtschaft mit dem Ziel, die Währung zu sichern, und sorgt für die bankmässige Abwicklung des Zahlungsverkehrs im Inland und mit dem Ausland.

The Act emphasizes the responsibility of the *Bundesbank* for monetary stability, which means the stability of the value of the *Deutsche mark*. The central bank should consult the Federal Government and other economic policy-makers on general economic developments and the role of monetary policy. However, the primary task of the *Bundesbank* is to function as the guardian of the currency. As a consequence, section 12 of the Act made the central bank independent of instructions from the Federal Government in stabilizing both the internal and external value of the currency. The internal value corresponds with the domestic price level and may be considered as the main policy goal of the *Bundesbank*. It aims at price stability by controlling the growth of the money stock, at present measured by M3. The external value is regarded by the central bank as the purchasing power of the *Deutsche mark vis-à-vis* other currencies and thus as the effective real exchange rate of the *Deutsche mark*, i.e. the (effective) nominal exchange rate, corrected for inflation differences between Germany and other countries. In Germany, the objective of exchange rate stability has been subordinated to that of domestic price stability. This implies that the *Bundesbank* is only concerned with the consequences of exchange rate development for the domestic price level and not so much with competitiveness.

The policy goals of the *Banque de France* are provided for in Article 1 and 4 of *Les Statuts de la Banque de France* of 3 January 1973.[4]

> *La Banque de France est l'institution qui, dans le cadre de la politique économique et financière de la nation, reçoit de l'Etat la mission générale de veiller sur la monnaie et le crédit...,*

and

> *...elle contribue à la préparation et participe à la mise en oeuvre de la politique monétaire arrêtée par le Gouvernement et, avec le concours, dans le cadre de sa compétence, du Conseil National du Crédit....*

Both articles reflect the responsibility of the *Banque de France* for monetary policy and its relation with the government. The central bank is the guardian of currency and credit and functions as adviser to the government. Nevertheless, the government determines economic and financial policy to which monetary policy has been subordinated. The *Banque de France* contributes towards the preparation and participates in the implementation of monetary policy by the government in cooperation with the *Conseil National du Crédit*. Although the central bank is not independent of instructions from the government according to the statutory mandate, in practice its Governor decides monetary policy in consultation with the Minister of Finance. In that respect, the Governor focuses on the stability of the value of the French franc. In addition, the *Banque de France* tries to stabilize the internal currency value, corresponding with the domestic price level, by controlling the growth of monetary aggregates such as

M2 and M3. Stabilizing the external value implies the stability of the French franc's nominal exchange rate *vis-à-vis* the *Deutsche mark* as an 'anchor' for monetary stability, and may be considered the rule of conduct for the monetary authorities. In France, the objective of control of money supply has been subordinated to that exchange rate stability. Since 1987 the *Banque de France* has aimed at stability of the nominal French franc/*Deutsche mark* rate by its exchange and money market policy. It is trying to reduce the difference between the French and German money market rates.

The policy goals of the Bank of England are embedded in the Banking Act of 1979 (revised in 1987). The first task of the Bank of England is the prudential supervision of the banking system, while

> ...other Bank activities, governed by statute, include its note-issuing powers, its management of the Exchange Equalisation Account on behalf of the Treasury, and its duties as banker to the Government and as the Government's agent in managing the National Debt.[5]

Nevertheless, monetary policy is regarded as a component of economic policy and is therefore conducted by the government with the advice of the central bank. The Bank of England's advice is made available to the government both in day-to-day contacts between Bank and Treasury officials and by regular contacts between the Governor and the Chancellor of the Exchequer (Minister of Finance). The monetary authorities are trying to stabilize the internal value of the British pound, i.e. the domestic price level, by controlling the growth of monetary aggregates such as £M3 and M0. From March 1987 to March 1988 they tried to stabilize the external value by 'shadowing the *Deutsche mark*'. This experiment ended with the resignation of Chancellor Lawson. In October 1990, after the twilight of the Thatcher government, the monetary authorities decided to choose for external stability by entering the EMS Exchange Rate Mechanism. For the time being, they chose to maintain the pound within the broad band of ±6% as a cushion for speculative movements. Nevertheless, the Danish rejection of the Maastricht Treaty in June 1992 and the announcement of a French referendum on the Maastricht Treaty on 20 September 1992 increased tensions within the Exchange Rate Mechanism. Despite massive exchange market interventions and modest rises in the British base rate, speculation against the pound continued. On 16 September, the pound, together with the lira, was forced to leave the mechanism and float again.

Of course, in the long run the internal and external objectives are generally in line with each other. However, in the short run there is always the possibility of conflicting objectives. With the abolition of direct credit controls – in France only since 1986 – central banks are left exclusively with indirect credit control for internal stability. Thus, the control of monetary aggregates is implemented by money market policy. Besides exchange market interventions, central banks use money market policy to influence exchange rates for external stability, e.g. within the framework of the EMS Exchange Rate Mechanism. An increase (decrease) in the domestic money market rate or – in the United Kingdom – base rate is expected to result in an appreciation (depreciation) of the respective currency *vis-à-vis* the other currencies. Therefore, central banks may be confronted with conflicts between their internal and external objective and have to give priority to one or the other. In recent years the *Bundesbank* chose for internal stability and the *Banque de France* and the Bank of England for external stability.

Table 1:
Conflicts Between Internal and External Stability

External Stability / Internal Stability	*appreciation* of own currency by increase of money market or base rate	*depreciation* of own currency by decrease of money market or base rate
restriction of money growth by increase of money market or base rate	*no* conflict because internal and external objective in line	*conflict* of objectives Germany: 1986, 1987 France: 1987, 1988 United Kingdom: 1985, 1986
expansion of money growth by decrease of money market or base rate	*conflict* of objectives Germany: - France: - United Kingdom: -	*no* conflict because internal and external objective in line

Monetary Targets

At the end of 1974 the *Deutsche Bundesbank* was the first central bank to announce publicly a monetary target, i.e. a desired rate of growth for a monetary aggregate on an annual base. The *Bundesbank* decided to target the central bank money stock (*Zentralbankgeldmenge* – ZBG), a kind of weighted M3, because this aggregate takes into account the degree of liquidity of the various liquid assets and, in practice, appears to be strongly correlated with total domestic expenditures.[6] Since 1979 the flexibility regarding the external and cyclical circumstances has been given formal expression by the introduction of a target zone (*Zielkorridor*) for ZBG growth. Until 1985 the actual ZBG growth met the target zones on an annual base because of the flexible, but restrictive policy of the *Bundesbank*. Nevertheless, its credibility was somewhat undermined by the substantial overshooting of the target zones at the end of 1986 and 1987. This resulted from the large growth in currency and banknotes, which by definition has considerable influence – more than 50% – on the ZBG, and distorted monetary development. From 1988, the *Bundesbank* turned to a target zone for the 'unweighted' aggregate M3, which behaved, in the medium term, more or less the same as ZBG and which had been monitored next to ZBG since 1979. The reasons for this transition are the false interpretation of ZBG by the public as a monetary base concept and the higher sensitivity of ZBG to large fluctuations of domestic money market rates and *Deutsche mark* exchange rates, especially *vis-à-vis* the US dollar. This phenomenon can be explained by the strong preference of residents for currency and banknotes and the currency hoarding of the *Deutsche mark* by non-residents.

The lower sensitivity of M3 to interest and exchange rate fluctuations implies also a more limited effect of money market policy as compared to ZBG and therefore requires the central bank to have a longer policy horizon. While the actual M3 growth exceeded the target zone in 1988 and 1991 only slightly, it did meet the objectives for 1989 and 1990.

In December 1977, the *Banque de France* publicly announced for the first time a target for the growth of aggregate M2 on an annual base.[7] In France, for most years up to 1985, the actual M2 growth exceeded the target (zone) which, in the beginning, was considerably higher than in Germany.

After a temporary switch to a target zone for the growth of M2R (M2 with residents) in 1984 and 1985, and M3 in 1986 and 1987, the *Banque de France* has returned to an M2 target zone since 1987. The central bank motivated the announcement of target zones, not only as bench marks for the formation of inflationary expectations, but also by stressing its own responsibility for monetary stability and the *zone franc*.[8] According to the *Banque de France*, the objective of exchange rate stability alone is not sufficient for a large open economy such as France. The choice of M2 as a target variable is based on the simplicity, clarity and controllability of this aggregate. It is a familiar concept to the public and consists of assets which bear either no or only a fixed interest. On the other hand, the rise of new financial instruments such as CDs, CPs and *sociétes d'investissement à capital variable* (SICAVs) induced a transfer of liquidity from M2 to M3 and L. This transfer has been empirically confirmed by the contrary development of the income velocities of M2 and M3 after 1986. Since then, the velocity of M2 increases and that of M3 gradually decreases.[9] Therefore, it is no surprise that the actual M2-growth after 1987 developed within or even under its target zone, while in 1987 the actual M3-growth exceeded its target zone substantially. Furthermore, with the introduction of a plan for tax-deductible pension savings (*plan d'épargne populaire* or PEP) in February 1990, very large amounts were withdrawn from savings accounts (*comptes sur Livret*). Because of its very long maturity the PEP is not a component of M2, M3 or even L. This undermines the meaning of M2 for policy purposes. As a consequence, since 1991 the *Banque de France* has turned to a broader monetary aggregate, i.e. M3R, which also comprises the *Organismes de Placement Collectif en Valeurs Mobilières* (OPVCMs).

Table 2:
Monetary Targets and Rates of Growth[*)]

	Germany		France		United Kingdom[****)]	
Year	ZBG	M3	M2[**)]	M3[***)]	£M3	M0
1982	4-7 (6.1)		12½-13½ (11.9)		8-12 (11.2)	
1983	4-7 (7.0)		9 (13.5)		7-11 (9.9)	
1984	4-6 (4.7)		5½-6½ (9.6)		6-10 (12.3)	4-8
1985	3-5 (4.5)		4-6 (5.9)		5-9 (17.3)	3-7
1986	3½-5½ (7.7)			3-5 (4.5)	11-15 (22.9)	2-6 (4.7)
1987	3-6 (8.0)		4-6 (3.8)	3-5 (9.0)		2-6 (6.3)
1988		3-6 (6.8)	4-6 (3.9)			1-5 (5.8)
1989		ca. 5 (4.9)	4-6 (4.3)			1-5 (7.3)
1990		4-6 (5.6)	3½-5½ (-1.2)			1-5 (1.6)
1991		3-5 (5.2)		5-7 (4.5)		0.4 (2.8)
1992		3½-5½		4-6		

*)   Actual rates of growth between parentheses
**)   For 1984 and 1985: M2R = M2 with residents
***)   For 1991 and 1992: M3R = M3 plus Organismes de Placement Collectif en Valeurs Mobilières (OPVCMs)
****) For 1982 and 1983 also targets of 8-12% and 7-11% for M1 and PSL2 respectively.

Sources: *Deutsche Bundesbank, Banque de France*, and Bank of England.

In December 1976 the Bank of England publicly announced a target zone for the growth of £M3 on an annual base.[10] The targeting of £M3 was motivated by the relation between this aggregate and its three sources, namely the unfunded Public Sector Borrowing Requirement (PSBR), sterling lending to the private sector and external influences from the balance of payments. After additional target zones for the growth of M1 and Private Sector Liquidity 2 (PSL2) (a very wide aggregate) for the financial years 1982/83 and 1983/84, the Bank of England also announced a target zone for the growth of M0, the wide monetary base, as of the financial year 1984/85. Until 1983/84 the actual £M3-growth was gradually reduced but rose again from 1984/85 and was eventually abandoned as a target in March 1987 due to its unpredictable behaviour as a consequence of the financial innovations in the United Kingdom. From 1987/88 on, the central bank has only targeted the growth of M0, reducing its target zones and actual growth little by little. However, it should be noticed that the aggregate M0, being a base money concept, is more suited as an indicator than as a target for monetary policy. Since the summer of 1989, building societies – like Abbey National – have become banks, making M4 in the United Kingdom the most comparable concept with the broad monetary aggregates in Germany (M3) and France (M3R). The aggregate M4 also includes deposits and CDs with building societies. Nevertheless, up till now the Bank of England has not set up a target zone for M4-growth, perhaps because of its decreasing income velocity. Given the convergence towards broad money concepts in the Community, particularly in the larger countries, it is conceivable that the British monetary authorities may eventually decide to control M4.

Monetary Instruments

The monetary instruments of the *Deutsche Bundesbank* can be divided into temporary and permanent instruments.[11] The temporary instruments *(Feinsteuerung)* have a (very) short policy horizon and are intended to smooth short-term interferences. Among the temporary instruments are the exchange market interventions, including swaps, and the important repurchase agreements *(Wertpapierpensiongeschäfte)* of which the rate *(Pensionsatz)* has become directive for the interbank money market rate in recent years. The permanent instruments *(Grobsteuerung)* have a medium policy horizon and are used to counter longer-term disturbances. Permanent instruments are the official credit facilities and the cash reserve requirements for the banks. The official credit facilities can be subdivided into the regular discount facilities *(Rediskont-Kontingente)*, for which the central bank charges the discount rate *(Diskontsatz)*, and the additional Lombard facilities *(Lombardkredite)*, which are overnight advances by the central bank against the Lombard rate *(Lombardsatz)*. The discount rate was formerly the lower limit or floor for the interbank money market rate, but nowadays – from February 1985 – the Treasury bill rate *(Schatzwechsel-Abgabesatz)* acts as such. Treasury bills are issued by the Federal Government and sold by the *Bundesbank* at a rate which is, on average, half a point higher than the discount rate. The Lombard rate lies, in general, 1.5 to 2 points above the discount rate and may be seen as the upper limit or ceiling for the interbank money market rate, in Germany represented by the call money rate *(Tagesgeldsatz)*.

Before 1976 the cash reserve ratios *(Mindestreserven)* were regularly changed by the *Bundesbank*, but after that this was done less and less because of the lengthy time needed by the banks to adjust their cash reserves. However, the cash reserve ratios remained on a relatively high level because these requirements function as an 'automatic break' to monetary expansion and are therefore indispensable for the *Bundesbank*.

Since December 1986 the monetary instruments of the *Banque de France* have consisted of the exchange market policy and the money market policy.[12] Exchange market interventions not only directly influence the exchange market, but also indirectly the money market, insofar as they are not sterilized by the central bank. The money market policy comprises those instruments which operate through the interbank money market *(marché interbancaire)*: the official credit facilities, the money market operations and the cash reserve requirements of the *Banque de France*.

The first official credit facility is the 'calls for tender' *(appels d'offres)*, with a maturity of up to three weeks, which the central bank places at the disposal of the banks according to the expected money market volume. Its rate *(taux des appels d'offres)* acts as a 'hard' lower limit for the interbank money market rate. The second official credit facility is the 'five-to-ten-day repurchase agreements' *(pensions de 5 à 10 jours)* which the banks may use daily on their own initiative. Its rate *(taux des pensions de 5 à 10 jours)* is determined by the central bank and can be considered as a 'soft' upper limit for the interbank money market rate, in France also represented by the call money rate *(taux du jour le jour)*. Since the end of 1986 the spread between both official rates has varied from half to one point. In addition, in more specific circumstances, the *Banque de France* can carry out money market operations at the market rate for fine tuning. The money market operations may be subdivided into direct interventions in the interbank market *(pension à moins de 5 jours)* for one or two days and open-market operations *(concours/reprises de liquidité)* by purchases/sales of Treasury bills against cash, to influence the interbank market through the open market. While the direct interventions in the interbank market are very effective in directing the money market rate in the short term, the effectiveness of open-market operations is limited because of the small volume of the open market in France. From 1985 the cash reserve requirements *(système des réserves obligatoires)* have played an important role despite the fact that the cash reserve ratios are internationally quite low. With this instrument the *Banque de France* pursues three objectives. Firstly, it has to provide for a structural money market deficit to make the money market operations sufficiently effective. Secondly, the cash reserves have to act as an 'automatic break' on monetary expansion, just as in Germany. Thirdly, the *Banque de France* wants to use the cash reserve ratios as an 'active' instrument to control the growth of the monetary aggregates in the short term.

Table 3:
The Transmission Mechanism of Monetary Policy*

Transmission mechanism	Germany (since January 1988)	France (since December 1986)	United Kingdom (from October 1990 to September 1992)
Monetary instruments	Official rates Money market operations Cash reserve ratios (passive) Exchange market interventions	Official rates Money market operations Cash reserve ratios (active) Exchange market interventions	Dealing rates Money market operations Exchange market interventions
Monetary indicators	Interbank money market rate (Call and one month money rate)	Interbank money market rates (Call money rate)	Base rates of clearing banks
Monetary targets	Main target: M3 Additional target: Real $/DEM exchange rate	Main target: Nominal French FRF/DEM exchange rate Additional target: M2 respectively M3R	Main target: Relative position of £ within EMS-band (Nominal £/DEM exchange rate) Additional target: MO
Policy goals	Domestic price level (legally based)	Domestic price level (not legally based)	Domestic price level (not legally based)

*   For the theoretical analysis of the transmission mechanism of monetary policy, see: S.C.W. Eijffinger (1986: 85-95).

The monetary instruments of the Bank of England differ considerably nowadays from those of the above central banks as a consequence of the high degree of market orientation in UK monetary policy.[13] First of all, the Bank of England does not use official rates for its credit facilities as a lower (and upper) limit for the money market nor as a base rate in the medium and long run. In August 1981 the Minimum Lending Rate was replaced by an 'unpublished band for very short-term interest rates' in order to strengthen the influence of market forces on money market and base rates. The central bank uses these 'dealing rates' for purchasing eligible bills with a maturity of up to one month, e.g. Treasury Bills and Commercial Bills, from discount houses ('club-like system'). The discount houses supply liquidity to other financial institutions and must always set two-way prices (bid/offer rates) for them. By signalling dealing rates for 'band 1' (1-14 days) and 'band 2' (15-33 days), the Bank of England gives a floor for the base rate and, indirectly, for the money market rate in the very short run. This price policy is supplemented by its money market operations (outright purchases and repurchase agreements) with Treasury Bills. Secondly, the Bank of England does not use cash reserve requirements (ratios) as an instrument for monetary control. In June 1980 it abolished the Supplementary Special Deposit Scheme ('the corset'), which was acting effectively as a credit ceiling, and in August 1981 it also abolished the Reserve Asset Scheme because of the inverted effects on money growth (£M3). Cash reserve ratios are seen as a tax burden on the banking system, impeding the competitive power of the City. The banks also hold voluntary cash reserves by means of the Treasury Bill tender which is intended to provide for a deficit in the structural money market. Thus, the Bank of England does not have the effective cash reserve requirements to act as an 'automatic break' on monetary expansion, as in Germany and France. The lack of this instrument was, in my opinion, partly responsible for the instability of the income velocities of money aggregates. The other (external) cause was the high pace of financial innovation in the United Kingdom.

Exchange and Money Market Policy

The exchange and money market policies of the *Deutsche Bundesbank* are aimed at different targets, while those of the *Banque de France* and the Bank of England are directed at the same target, i.e. the stability of the French franc and the British pound nominal exchange rates, respectively, *vis-à-vis* the D-mark.

In Germany, the exchange market interventions by the central bank are less frequent than in France and the United Kingdom. This can be explained by the difference between the *Bundesbank* on the one hand and the *Banque de France* and the Bank of England on the other, regarding their independence from the Minister of Finance in exchange market policy. At present there is an important discrepancy between these central banks in the frequency and thus the effectiveness of exchange market interventions. Since influencing exchange rate expectations of market participants is empirically the main objective of exchange market policy nowadays, (very) frequent interventions in this market generally imply less effective interventions.[14] Furthermore, the short-term objectives of the exchange market policy in Germany and in the UK and in France differ as a consequence of the asymmetry within the EMS. While the *Bundesbank* mostly tries to smooth fluctuations of the D-mark/US dollar rate, the *Banque de France* and the Bank of England focus more on the *Deutsche mark* rate of their currency. When not abstaining from intervention, the *Bundesbank* conducts a policy of 'leaning against the wind' to counter disorderly exchange market conditions.[15] The *Banque de France* and the Bank of England follow the same policy of 'leaning against the wind' and try to avoid marginal interventions – at the limits of the EMS band – to maintain a two-sided risk.

In the mid-seventies the *Bundesbank* put more emphasis on its money market policy to control the growth of ZBG and, from 1988 of M3, through the interbank money market rate. A rise in the interbank rate both slows down the granting of credit by the banks to the private sector and also stimulates the demand by the public for assets outside ZBG and M3. The central bank indirectly controls the money growth by its money market policy, which means that the policy lag will be longer than in the case of direct credit controls.

In February 1985 the *Bundesbank* decided to fine-tune the money market by its repurchase agreements (*Wertpapierpensiongeschäfte*). The reason for this change was the large signalling effect of adjustments to both official rates by which the money market policy had lost its flexibility.

The result was that the interbank money market rate – *in casu* the call money rate – has depended less since then on the discount and Lombard rate and more on the *Pensionsatz*. From then on, in normal circumstances, the *Bundesbank* kept the repurchase agreements tight, i.e. smaller than the money markets expected. Moreover, the money market participants were focusing more and more on small adjustments in the *Pensionsatz*. So the interbank rate became increasingly volatile in the (very) short run as a consequence of the greater flexibility of the money market policy. Despite its volatility, the *Bundesbank* tries to keep the interbank rate between the Treasury bill rate and the Lombard rate, and thus within a band of 1 to 1½ points. While the *Pensionsatz* is very effective with regard to the interbank rate in the (very) short term, it has no effect on the debit and credit rates which the banks charge. On the other hand, by its discount and Lombard rate, the *Bundesbank* influences the interbank rate in the medium term and, thereby, also the debit and credit rates of the German banks.

In December 1986, the *Banque de France* decided to switch to completely market-oriented instruments to stabilize the French franc/*Deutsche mark* exchange rate, and at the same time has tried to control its monetary aggregates ever since. Once the decision was taken, the money market policy was developed very quickly and smoothly by the central bank. The official rates are determined solely by the Governor, after consultation with the Minister of Finance, and form the band within which the interbank money market rate fluctuates. In addition to this medium-term policy, the Governor fixes the amount and maturity of the calls for tender (*appels d'offres*) in the very short term. If there is a turbulent money market – e.g. the end of a cash reserve period – the *Banque de France* may decide to turn to direct interventions in the interbank market *(pensions à moins de 5 jours)* and eventually to open-market operations *(concours/reprises de liquidité)*. These money market operations are used for fine-tuning the interbank rate from day to day. In recent years, the *Banque de France* has kept itself increasingly aloof from influencing the interbank rate within the band of both official rates because of the unpredictable development of autonomous factors *(facteurs autonomes)* on the money market, such as the circulation of banknotes, the international reserves and the Treasury balance. According to the central bank, the money market should regulate itself between the official rates as limits for the interbank rate. As a consequence of the objective of exchange rate stability between the French franc and *Deutsche mark*, the *Banque de France* official rates are linked to those of the *Bundesbank*. Therefore, the *Banque de France* needs an additional and (partly) independent monetary instrument for controlling money growth in France. The cash reserve requirements are supposed to function as a partly independent and 'active' instrument beside the official rates. Hence, the *Banque de France* experimented twice – in June/July 1987 and May/June 1988 – with a contrary policy mix of both the official rates and the cash reserve ratios. However, these experiments proved that there was no independence at all between these monetary instruments.[16]

From August 1981 the Bank of England abandoned its Minimum Lending Rate as an official rate for the medium and long term. However, it reserves the right to announce this official rate on special occasions, e.g. on 8 October 1990, when the pound entered the EMS Exchange Rate Mechanism. The central bank usually applies its money market policy – i.e. dealing rates and money market operations – in order to stabilize the British pound/*Deutsche mark* exchange rate and to control money growth (M0). The Bank of England makes its interest rate views and intentions known by setting the level of short-term interest rates. It confines official influence to the shortest possible maturity range – recently to only one month – allowing market forces to have decisive influence beyond that maturity.[17] The transmission mechanism of short-term interest rates is supposed to run, apart from their impact on the exchange rate, through two direct channels. Firstly, higher interest rates raise the cost of current borrowing, making saving relatively more attractive and thus reducing current expenditure and money growth. Secondly, higher interest rates also reduce the disposable income of those who have already borrowed heavily and, thereby, expenditure and money growth. As a consequence of financial innovation, liberalization and debt accumulation, households and firms have become more sensitive to interest rate changes. In the United Kingdom the relevant indicator of monetary policy is not the interbank money market rate, as in Germany and France, but the base rate of clearing banks, comparable with the prime rate in the United States. That is the rate at which clearing banks will lend in the short term to high quality borrowers, e.g. large companies. By its dealing rates the Bank of England affects the base rates and thus the retail lending rates of the banks. Moreover, the central bank may influence, indirectly, the money market rates through arbitrage between the base and money markets and thereby the exchange rate. Clearly, the United Kingdom is out of line with the other EMS countries.

Convergence in Performance

After discussing convergence in the implementation of monetary policy during the eighties, we will now analyze convergence in monetary policy performance between Germany, France and the United Kingdom. This performance can be measured by the development of four key variables in both countries during the eighties: inflation rates, real exchange rates, real short-term interest rates (money market rates) and real long-term interest rates (capital market rates).

Table 4:
Inflation Rates in Germany, France and the United Kingdom*

Year	Inflation Germany	Inflation France	Inflation United Kingdom
1982	5.3	12.0	5.4
1983	3.3	9.8	5.3
1984	2.4	7.7	4.6
1985	2.2	5.8	6.1
1986	-0.2	2.5	3.4
1987	0.2	3.3	4.1
1988	1.3	2.7	4.9
1989	2.8	3.5	7.8
1990	2.7	3.4	9.5
1991	3.5	3.1	5.9

*   Annual rates of growth of Consumer Price Index (CPI) in Germany and France and Retail Price Index (RPI) in the United Kingdom

Sources: *Deutsche Bundesbank, Banque de France* and Bank of England.

The convergence of the German, French and British inflation rates (Consumer Price Index and Retail Price Index) has been quite remarkable in the period 1980-91. The inflation differential, i.e. the inflation rate in France and the United Kingdom minus that in Germany on an annual base, has declined to minus 0.4 and plus 2.4% points in 1991 (see Table 4). This has been the result of the stable development of the nominal exchange rate of the French franc *vis-à-vis* the *Deutsche mark* since 1986 and that of the British pound *vis-à-vis* the *Deutsche mark* since the end of 1990. Moreover, this stable development has resulted in converging targets and growth rates of the monetary aggregates in Germany, France and the United Kingdom since the mid-eighties (see Table 2).

As a consequence of the nominal exchange rate stability and the declining inflation differential, there was also a stable development in the real exchange rate between the French franc and the *Deutsche mark*, i.e. the nominal exchange rate corrected for the inflation differential, as of 1986 (see Figure 1).[18] This reflects that the terms of trade between Germany and France have not changed much since then. Very recently, until the currency crisis of September 1992, the same held for the real exchange rate of the British pound *vis-à-vis* the *Deutsche mark*. However, the performance of monetary policy in both pairs of countries cannot be judged by the development of the inflation differential and the real exchange rate alone because these variables refer only to the past and the present. To incorporate the inflationary expectations of the financial markets, we will turn to the development of the real interest rates in the short and long run. In case of nominal interest parity and the absence of exchange rate risk, differences in real interest rates between two countries reflect differences in inflationary expectations in both countries.

After a temporary divergence in 1987 and the first half of 1988, there is again some gradual convergence of the German and French real short-term interest rates, i.e. the nominal short-term interest rates corrected for the inflation rates (see Figure 2). The difference in the money market rates in Germany and France reflects the exchange rate expectations of the financial markets in the short run. These expectations are fed by the inflationary expectations in both countries in the short term. The markets still expect some depreciation of the franc against the *Deutsche mark* in the short run for which they ask a risk premium on the French money market. Obviously, it takes a long period of stability-oriented monetary policy for the *Banque de France* to earn a reputation in the financial markets.

The entrance of the British pound to the broad EMS band reversed the growing divergence of the German and British real short-term interest rates in October 1990. From then on the gradual convergence of both real money market rates has reflected that financial markets expect a depreciation of the pound against the *Deutsche mark* in the short run and, consequently, ask a risk premium on the British money market. The currency crisis of September 1992 proved

Figure 1:
The real exchange rate of the French franc and the British
pound vis-à-vis the Deutsche mark
(D = 100)

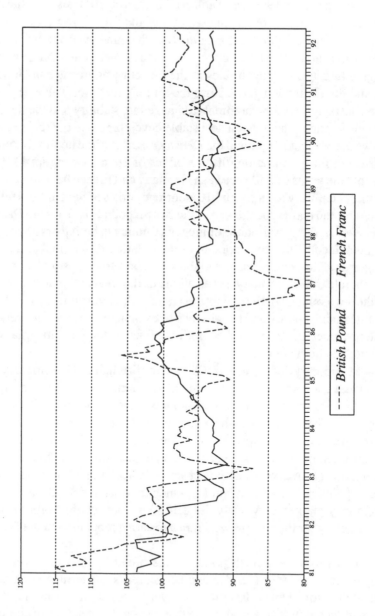

Source: *De Nederlandsche Bank*, Department of International Affairs.

them to be right.

Nevertheless, from the second half of 1988 until mid-1991 there was a strong convergence of the German and French real long-term interest rates, i.e. the nominal long-term interest rates corrected for the inflation rates (see Figure 3). The difference in the capital market rates in Germany and France reflects the exchange rate expectations in the long run and, thereby, the inflationary expectations in both countries in the long term. Apparently, the markets did not expect any depreciation of the franc against the *Deutsche mark* in the long run. Therefore, a prolonged monetary policy by the *Banque de France* directed at domestic price stability seemed to pay off. However, the monetary policy horizon has proved to be rather long and recently financial markets have again been demanding a risk premium on the French capital market.

Since the second half of 1988 the British real long-term interest has decreased considerably as a consequence of the accelerating inflation rate in the United Kingdom during the twilight of the Thatcher government. By entering the EMS Exchange Rate Mechanism and thus limiting inflationary expectations and the pound's exchange rate risk *vis-à-vis* the *Deutsche mark*, this trend was immediately reversed. From that moment on the British real capital market rate has increased substantially, even beyond the German real capital market rate. At the beginning of 1992, the financial markets were expecting some depreciation of the pound against the *Deutsche mark* in the long run, for which they asked a risk premium on the British capital market.

The declining inflation differential and – since 1986 – the stable real exchange rate indicate that the performance of monetary policy in Germany and France has already converged to a large extent. On the other hand, the present difference between the real short-term and long-term interest rates suggests that the *Banque de France* still has to gain more reputation in the financial markets, but will eventually succeed. The reverse side of the credibility medal is the loss of the *Banque de France*'s monetary policy sovereignty with respect to the *Deutsche Bundesbank*. This explains why France, more than Germany, wants to accelerate the evolution towards EMU. The United Kingdom, however, is just at the beginning of this road towards an Economic and Monetary Union. The floating of the pound since September 1992 and the loss of credibility of the British monetary authorities during the currency crisis makes it very unlikely that the United Kingdom will be in the core group should there be a two-speed EMU.[19]

Conclusion

Regarding the implementation of monetary policy, the convergence between Germany and France has accelerated since 1986 and has now reached a high

Figure 2:
The real short-term interest rates in France, Germany and
the United Kingdom (corrected for CPI)
Real yield on short-term capital
3-months moving averages

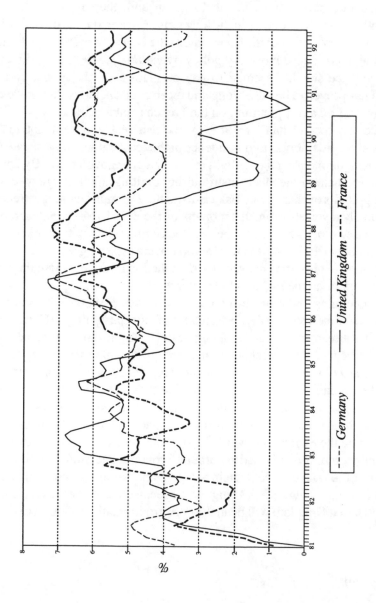

Source: *De Nederlandsche Bank*, Department of International Affairs.

Figure 3:
The real long-term interest rates in France, Germany and the
United Kingdom (corrected for CPI)
Real yield on long-term capital
3-months moving averages

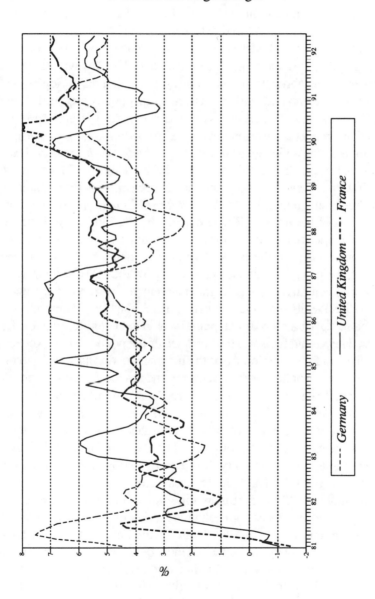

Source: *De Nederlandsche Bank*, Department of International Affairs.

level. This process was triggered by the large devaluation of the French franc against the *Deutsche mark* in March 1983. After that realignment, the French monetary authorities decided to turn to a restrictive fiscal and monetary policy to restore domestic price and exchange rate stability. Moreover, from 1985 the authorities have deregulated and liberalized the French financial markets in order to intensify competition between the financial institutions and to eventually bring down interest rates. With the decision of the Major government to bring the pound into the broad EMS band, the convergence between Germany and the United Kingdom has taken off since October 1990. However, this process of convergence was abrupted by the floating of the pound in September 1992. Furthermore, the implementation of UK monetary policy is quite different from that in Germany and France, both as regards its monetary target – M0 versus M3 (R), and its monetary instruments – i.e. no official rates or cash reserve requirements. The policy goals of the *Bundesbank*, the *Banque de France* and the Bank of England are actually the same, i.e. the stability of the domestic price level. However, it should be noticed that the objective of price stability is still not explicitly embedded in *Les Statuts de la Banque de France* nor in the Banking Act of the Bank of England. Legally, the Minister of Finance could force the *Banque de France* to stimulate economic activity, as he did in 1981; and the same holds for the Bank of England. Therefore, the test case for the French and British governments in the move towards EMU is their willingness to make their central banks legally independent of government instructions and to entrust them with the primary objective of price stability. Thereby, the French franc and in particular the British pound would gain credibility in the financial markets. This would facilitate the entrance of the pound to the Exchange Rate Mechanism and the functioning of the mechanism during stage two of EMU.

Money market policy, both in Germany and France, focuses on the interbank money market rate – i.e. the call money rate – as a monetary indicator. For that purpose the *Bundesbank*, as well as the *Banque de France*, try to keep the interbank rate within the band of their official rates and to fine-tune the interbank rate by their money market operations. The Bank of England, however, only provides its intentions for the very short term by setting the dealing rates. Interest rate policy in the United Kingdom focuses on the base rate of clearing banks as monetary indicator. There is still an important discrepancy with respect to the frequency and effectiveness of exchange market intervention in Germany, on the one hand, and France and the United Kingdom, on the other hand. This results from the diverging independence between these central banks in exchange market policy. Also, another test case for the French and British governments will be their readiness to give full responsibility for intervention to the *Banque de France* and the Bank of England.

Finally, in both Germany and France, monetary instruments are converging to a large extent as a consequence of the process of financial liberalization and integration in the Community. Nevertheless, the monetary instruments in the United Kingdom are very much out of line with those used in the other EMS countries because of the British preference to promote free competition between banks as much as possible. In Germany and France there is an obvious tendency to fully market-oriented, indirect instruments, such as:

– official credit facilities (quantities and rates) as an 'active' instrument in the medium term;

– money market operations (interbank and open market) as an 'active' instrument in the short term; and

– cash reserve requirements (ratios) as a 'passive' instrument in the long term, i.e. an 'automatic break' on monetary expansion.

Of course, these three instruments overlap as a consequence of their influence on the money market rate. Therefore, the monetary instruments of the central banks, including the *Bundesbank* and the *Banque de France*, tend to become more limited and less effective.

During stage two of EMU, from 1 January 1994, one of the main tasks for the European Community's central banks will be the (preparation of the) harmonization of their monetary instruments and targets. With respect to the targets there is a general tendency within the Community to control broad monetary aggregates and for the Committee of Central Bank Governors to strengthen *ex ante* coordination of monetary policy. Therefore, it is very well conceivable that the Bank of England will focus in future on the aggregate M4 instead of the wide monetary base. Regarding the instruments, we are just at the beginning of the convergence process. It can be expected that the Bank of England will again post a kind of Minimum Lending Rate, signalling its interest rate intentions for the medium term. Moreover, one could imagine an effective scheme of cash reserve requirements to be implemented in the United Kingdom as an 'automatic break' on monetary expansion. This would stabilize the income velocity of broad money and thus improve the precision of monetary control by the Bank of England. Also, the cash reserve ratios in Germany and France should be harmonized to create a level playing field for European banks and to further integrate the national money markets in the Community.

Finally, a convergence of policy horizon between the national central banks is needed with regard to the use of their instruments. The realization of price stability as policy goal demands a (very) long policy horizon covering not one, but many political cycles. A *conditio sine qua non* for such a long policy horizon will be the establishment of an independent *Banque de France* and Bank of England.

NOTES

1. Committee for the Study of Economic and Monetary Union (1989: 12).
2. 'Pöhl raises possibility of 2-speed monetary union', *Financial Times*, 12 June 1990.
3. Deutsche Bundesbank (1985: 103-128).
4. Banque de France (1986: 149-157) and W. Eizenga (1990: 1-6).
5. A. Cairncross (1988: 68); see also W. Eizenga (1991: 3-5).
6. The central bank money stock consists of the sum of currency and banknotes 'C', the cash reserve requirements for the banks against demand deposits 'D', time deposits 'T' and savings deposits 'S':
   ZBG = C + 0,166D +0,124T + 0,081S.
   H. Schlesinger (1983: 6-17).
7. The monetary aggregates in France are defined as follows:
   M1   = currency + banknotes + checkable demand deposits;
   M2   = M1 + non-checkable demand deposits + savings deposits;
   M3   = M2 + foreign currency deposits + time deposits + money market securities by banks (incl. CDs);
   M3R = M3 + *Organismes de Placement Collectif en Valeurs Mobilières* (OPCVMs)
   L   = M3 + contractual savings + Treasury bills + money market securities by non-banks (incl. CPs).
8. J.-P. Patat (1987: 299-308).
9. For the income velocities of M1, M2, M3 and M3R see Conseil National du Crédit (1991: 82).
10. The monetary aggregates in the United Kingdom are defined as follows:
    M0   =   notes and coins in circulation + banks' till money
    (wide monetary base) + bankers' balances with the Bank of England;
    M1   =   notes and coins in circulation + private sector non-interest bearing and interest bearing sterling sight deposits;
    £M3 =   M1 + private sector sterling sight and time bank
    (from May 1987:M3) deposits + private sector holdings of sterling CDs + public sector sterling sight and time bank deposits;
    M4   =   £M3 (or M3) + private sector holdings of building society shares and deposits and sterling CDs – building societies' holdings of bank deposits, bank CDs and notes and coins.
    Bank of England (1990). In this paper some consultative proposals are given by the Monetary Aggregates Group of the Bank of England for controlling money growth in the United Kingdom.
11. H.J. Dudler (1983: 19-20, 25).
12. Until 1986 the *Banque de France* used the *encadrement du crédit*, a system of quantitative controls on credit to the private sector. It was abolished because of its increasing complexity and distortion of competition and its declining effectiveness on money growth.

Y. Barroux and N. Dagognet (1990: 117-129).

13. R. Leigh-Pemberton (1987: 365-370); and Bank of England (1988). The monetary instruments were changed in August 1981 in order to strengthen their market-conformity and thereby their flexibility.

14. S.C.W. Eijffinger and A.P.D. Gruijters (1992); and G.J. Almekinders and S.C.W. Eijffinger (1991: 662-673).

15. S.C.W. Eijffinger and A.P.D. Gruijters (1991).

16. In June 1987 the official rates were reduced by a 1/4 point and in the following month the ratio for time deposits was raised by one point. Both official rates were also reduced by 1/4 point in May 1988, and the next month the ratios for savings and time deposits were raised by 1.5 and 0.5 points respectively.

17. For an excellent survey see J.C. Townend (1990). In contrast to the 'over-funding' of public sector debt in the first half of the eighties, the monetary authorities now use the 'full fund' rule which has a broadly neutral effect on liquidity.

18. In 1986 foreign exchange controls in France were considerably eased by instigating some not so onerous measures and also quantitative controls on credit were removed. See A. Icard (1990). For an empirical analysis of money market and capital market integration in the European Community, see J.J.G. Lemmen and S.C.W. Eijffinger (1992).

19. For an evaluation of the degree of convergence in the economic performances of Member States of the European Community see Bank of England (1991).

REFERENCES

Almekinders, G.J.; Eijffinger, S.C.W., 'Empirical Evidence on Foreign Exchange Market Intervention: Where Do We Stand?', *Weltwirtschaftliches Archiv*, vol. 127, 1991, pp. 645-677.

Bank of England, *Bank of England Operations in the Sterling Money Market* (London: October 1988).

Bank of England, 'Monetary Aggregates in a Changing Environment: A Statistical Discussion Paper', *Discussion Papers*, no. 47 (London: March 1990).

Bank of England, 'Convergence in the European Community', *Bank of England Quarterly Bulletin* (London: August 1991).

Banque de France, *La Banque de France et la Monnaie* (Paris: 1986).

Banque de France, *Compte Rendu 1989* (Paris: 1990).

Barroux, Y.; Dagognet, N., 'Analysis of the Relationship between Money Stock and Monetary Base: The French Experience during the Period of Quantitative Controls on Credit (1973-1985)', in Artus P. and Barroux Y. (eds), *Monetary Policy – A Theoretical and Econometric Approach* (Dordrecht: Kluwer, 1990), pp. 117-129.

Cairncross, A., 'The Bank of England: Relationships with the Government, the Civil Service, and Parliament', in Toniolo G. (ed.), *Central banks' Independence in Historical Perspective* (Berlin/New York: de Gruyter, 1988), pp. 39-72.

Committee for the Study of Economic and Monetary Union (chairman: Jacques Delors), *Report on Economic and Monetary Union in the European Community* (Luxembourg: April 1989).

Conseil National du Crédit, *Rapport Annuel 1990* (Paris, 1991).

Deutsche Bundesbank, 'Die Deutsche Bundesbank – Geldpolitische Aufgaben und Instrumente', *Reihe der Sonderdrucke No. 7* (Frankfurt am Main: April 1985).

Deutsche Bundesbank, *Geschäftsbericht 1989* (Frankfurt-am-Main: 1990).

Dudler, H.J., 'The Implementation of Monetary Objectives in Germany – Open Market Operations and Credit Facilities', in Meek P. (ed.), *Central Bank Views on Monetary Targeting* (New York: 1983), pp. 18-30.

Eizenga, W., 'The Banque de France and Monetary Policy', *SUERF Papers on Monetary Policy and Financial Systems*, no. 8 (Tilburg: 1990).

Eizenga, W., 'The Bank of England and Monetary Policy', *SUERF Papers on Monetary Policy and Financial Systems*, no. 10 (Tilburg: 1991).

Eijffinger, S.C.W, 'Over de beheersbaarheid van de geldhoeveelheid (On the controllability of the money stock)' (Amsterdam: Free University Press, 1986).

Eijffinger, S.C.W.; Gruijters, A.P.D., 'On the Effectiveness of Daily

Interventions by the Deutsche Bundesbank and the Federal Reserve System in the US Dollar-Deutsche Mark Exchange Market', in Baltensperger E. and Sinn H.W. (eds), *Exchange Rate Regimes and Currency Union* (London: MacMillan, 1992), pp. 131-158.

Eijffinger, S.C.W.; Gruijters, A.P.D., 'On the Short Term Objectives of Daily Interventions by the Deutsche Bundesbank and the Federal Reserve System in the US Dollar-Deutsche Mark Exchange Market', *Kredit und Kapital*, vol. 24, Spring 1991, pp. 50-72.

Eijffinger, S.C.W.; Schaling, E., *Central Bank Independence: Searching for the Philosophers' Stone*, Paper for the seventeenth SUERF Colloquium held in Berlin, Germany, on 8-10 October, 1992.

Icard, A., *Exchange Rates and Interest Rates inside the EMS – The French Experience*, Presentation to the IMF Visitors Center in Washington on 18 April 1990.

Leigh-Pemberton, R., 'The Instruments of Monetary Policy', *Bank of England Quarterly Bulletin*, August 1987.

Lemmen, J.J.G.; Eijffinger, S.C.W., 'The Degree of Financial Integration in the European Community', *Research Memorandum FEW 540*, Department of Economics (Tilburg: Tilburg University, 1992).

Patat, J.-P., *Monnaie, institutions financières et politique monétaire* (Paris: Economica, 1987).

Schlesinger, H., 'The Setting of Monetary Objectives in Germany', in P. Meek (ed.), *Central Bank Views on Monetary Targeting* (New York: 1983)

Townend, J.C., *The Orientation of Monetary Policy and the Monetary Policy Decision-Making Process in the United Kingdom*, Paper prepared for the Central Bank Economists Meeting held in Basle in November 1990.

ECONOMIC AND MONETARY UNION: A GERMAN CENTRAL BANKER'S PERSPECTIVE

Reimut Jochimsen

Introduction

In Maastricht, the European Council of Heads of State and Government marked out the trail towards a fully developed currency union in Europe, by completing the drafting for the European System of Central Banks (ESCB) in the final stage of the Economic and Monetary Union (EMU). This in turn is to be a part of the Treaty on European Union.[1] In the fields of democratic institution-building and Political Union in general, progress is only meagre and leaves much to be desired.[2] Of course, we have already progressed quite a considerable way along the path to EMU. On 1 July 1990, on the same day as the then GDR was included in the *Deutsche mark* currency area, the member countries of the EC launched the first of three stages in their further economic integration and ultimate monetary unification process. The second stage is scheduled to begin in one year's time, on 1 January 1994, and the third, in 1997, provided that the appropriate preconditions for convergence in the economic and financial worlds can be fulfilled by a majority of Member States, or at latest in 1999, by those which fulfil these preconditions, no matter how many actually reach that target.

The EC Heads of State and Government deserve recognition for having succeeded in reaching agreement at the Maastricht European Council meeting on the conditions to be fulfilled in order for Member States to be permitted to proceed to the third stage of EMU. Although this concerns necessary conditions only – albeit not sufficient ones! – this marks great progress in institutional and technical terms of an integrated economic, financial and monetary policy. It contains in particular the general objective of price level stability which is to be a central element of all the policies of the European Union. This progress holds true irrespective of the deficit in the political structure of the EC. This will continue to haunt us since the European Council meeting ended with respect to union as a whole with a lopsided limping result.[3] The European Council – with the exception of the UK and Denmark – has subscribed to the thesis that the irreversibility of the path towards

K. Gretschmann (ed.), Economic and Monetary Union: Implications for National Policy-Makers, 195–213.
© 1993 *European Institute of Public Administration. Printed in the Netherlands.*

Economic and Monetary Union could bring about new pressure to intensify political integration.

EMU: Economics, Politics or Polemics

STAGE THREE OF EMU: NEW APPROACH TO EUROPEAN INTEGRATION?

The definite time table for stage three for EMU came however as a complete surprise from the European Council. With this decision, the German Chancellor dropped the mandatory linkage of EMU to the parallel progress of political union, a precondition, a *conditio sine qua non* he had himself introduced in 1990. And with that he pushed aside the widespread consensus held in Germany that a common currency cannot function in isolation as the precursor for European integration, i.e. as a front-runner, a pioneer, without simultaneously creating the decisive elements of a political union. These elements would provide the necessary framework for consensus-building democratic decisions and the joint sharing of overall political responsibility for the union.[4] In history, there is not one positive example of a currency union which successfully preceded the political unification of the currency area.[5]

Additionally, in this context the still unresolved fundamental dimensions of the whole project emerge. What about the political viability of an Economic and Monetary Union with divergent membership and its repercussions on the cohesion of the institutional set-up? (Would this split prevent progress in political integration?) What about the nature of the market order of the European economic space in terms of industrial policy? Competition policy? Social charter? ('Fortress Europe' or liberal, world-open partner in trade?) What about admitting new members from EFTA and Central and Eastern Europe that want to join the Community or should be bound as strictly and as soon as possible to the Community? (The issue of 'widening' versus 'deepening' has not been solved, nor silenced by the Maastricht results – the perspective is simply still missing.)

The exact setting of the final date 1999 – enhanced by the notion of strict 'irreversibility' – marks a surprising departure from the decisions of the preceding European Council meetings (as well as from the finance ministers' meetings before Maastricht). Some argue that this signals courageous, pace-setting progress towards a European Union; others are bitter about a possible sacrifice of the criteria of convergency for calendric dates. This decision, in effect, represents a breach of the broad agreement that emerged after long discussions in 1990 and 1991.[6] Consequently, German public opinion was shocked by this new automatism of the 1999 deadline for the definite introduction of the common single currency and the simultaneous abolition of the *Deutsche mark*. The consensus prior to Maastricht on the participation of Member States in the final stage of EMU can be summed up in the following three principles to which the Twelve − including the United Kingdom − agreed:

(1) no Member State will be allowed to join EMU unless it has clearly fulfilled the entrance requirements to be stipulated in the Treaty;

(2) no Member State will be allowed to veto or block the EMU process altogether;

(3) no Member State will be obliged to join EMU's final stage, in 1996 or 1998 or later, just because it fulfils the preconditions.

It is the intention of the Heads of State and Government that the very decision, originally to be taken in 1996 or 1998, shall be advanced to the date of the ratification of the Treaty which was intended to be 1992. The future political circumstances and consequences of that calendric automatism cannot be anticipated in 1992 and, consequently, cannot be remedied in 1999 either. It seems to the observer that no one, neither government nor parliament, can undertake to make a juridical statement of irreversibility with such sweeping consequences, in such eventful times, seven years ahead of the intended event. The number of countries qualifying, the format of the further integration process with a possible split between the 'ins' and the 'outs', may even blow up the European Union. Even worse, this time-table automatism threatens to weaken the very cause of prior convergency and the hard adjustments needed in most Member States. The weaker ones among them might even calculate that, for political reasons, it will ultimately prove to be impossible for stage three to start without them. This, in turn, tends to place the burden on the Community and its stronger economies, namely, by not relying on the individual Member State's own capacity for restructuring, but rather, for fear of disparities at the start of the final phase, the stronger economies will soon be forced to start active crash programmes by organizing schemes of financial transfers before the transition to stage three, rather than being forced to do so anyway afterwards, and then possibly on an even larger scale. Thus, it seems certain that the envisaged 'cohesion fund'[7] to be set up in 1992 will just be the entrance door for more sweeping claims to resource transfers.

STAGE TWO OF EMU: THE NEED FOR CONVERGENCE

Built-in contradictions and the potential danger of conflicts of interest are also to be found with respect to the regulations for stage two. Because the progress towards convergence, which had originally been hoped for before stage two began,[8] has not been achieved, or was deemed unnecessary to be achieved by 1994, the substance of that stage will differ little from that of the one we are currently in. All the burden of adjustment and restructuring will thus be concentrated on the transition to stage three. Until the final stage is embarked upon, monetary policy will remain the sole and full responsibility of Member States. It is only right that this should be so. For one thing, the appropriate conditions for a common, unified monetary policy throughout the EC – as indicated – have not been fulfilled by far, and there can be no question of transferring responsibilities such as these on a step-by-step basis. Monetary policy is not amenable to any intermixing of areas of responsibility: it must be a unified policy from one single mould, albeit at national or at European level.[9] Germany's position on this is clear, namely that a stable currency takes precedence over a common one (though the objective naturally remains to achieve both simultaneously).

In the context of the European Monetary Institute (EMI) which is to be established by 1994 (its seat is still undecided) – the participating central banks will endeavour to intensify the information about and the coordination of their strategies and measures to a greater extent than has already been the case via the Committee of Governors under the current Rome Treaty (meeting ten times per year). On a parallel basis, the preliminary work required in advance of the fully-fledged currency union will be carried out under the auspices of the EMI.[10] (Here conflicting definitions as to its tasks obscure this preparatory role, e.g. by allowing exchange reserves management which nevertheless excludes any interference with the efficiency of any Member State's monetary policy). By the end of 1996, a report is to be compiled setting out the regulatory, organizational and logistical framework for the final stage to be decided upon and enacted by the European Central Bank at the time of its inception.

The criteria of convergence which have been established are not merely of a qualitative nature, and there are enough quantitative goals stipulated which have to be reached, though the overall picture is rather confused by a number of general clauses or terms which appear to be drafted in such a way as to sweep aside the hard edges of the criteria at the time of entering the final stage.

The countries' individual requirements are as follows:[11]

– A high degree of price stability. Before it may enter the third stage of Economic and Monetary Union, any Member State's inflation rate may not be more than 1½ percentage points in excess of that of the three best performing EC countries in terms of price level stability.

– Secondly, the government's financial position must be sustainable over a longer term. This is assumed to be the case if net government borrowing per year is not in excess of 3% of gross domestic product at market prices, and if accumulated government debt does not exceed 60% of GDP. A very broad definition of 'government' is used for these purposes, local municipalities and social insurance schemes.

– The third convergence criterion is the requirement that a potential participating country in EMU must have kept its currency within the normal fluctuation margins (i.e. the band of ± 2¼%) in the European Monetary System's (EMS) Exchange Rate Mechanism for at least two years, without strong tension arising or any devaluation being asked for.

– Finally, the fourth requirement is that the durability of the degree of convergence a Member State has achieved should be reflected in the judgement of the capital markets. The measure of such market confidence is taken to be the yield on long-term government bonds in the country concerned, which may not be more than two percentage points higher than that of the best performing three Member States.

One had wished for rather more in certain places. That applies, for example, to the area of government finances, where unfortunately a rule that there should be an upper limit on borrowing equal to the level of net fixed government capital formation (the so-called 'golden rule') could not be agreed upon.[12] Even worse, adherence to these ratios is not a matter which seems to be taken particularly seriously. The ratios are intended only as guidelines for arriving at what will ultimately be an 'overall assessment' of whether a country's government finances would qualify it for participation in the final stage. One can only hope that the discretionary leeway thus granted will not be used wrongly. The most crucial omission, however, concerns any reference to an absolute low inflation rate or target of effective price level stability; all references in this sense are to 'best performers'. Every member country ought to be clearly aware that it must not be allowed to participate in a common currency unless it fulfils the convergence requirements. These have indeed been set at an exacting level and necessitate, for realization, sweeping programmes for restructuring budgets and deflating the demands on the economy, otherwise the Union, right at the outset, will be burdened with countries which are unfit and this, in turn, will lead them to press for objectively needed assistance, corresponding to the degree of discrepancy right from the beginning.

A sufficient amount of convergence in fundamental economic parameters is an absolutely essential prerequisite if the completely developed currency union is to function without frictional losses or even not to be blown apart by growing disparities.[13] We know very well from recent experience in Germany what consequences can result from a poorly prepared common currency area. Of course, it will not be necessary for any EC member countries to cope simultaneously with the results of a complete change of economic and political system and the sudden and hasty opening up of borders which had previously been hermetically sealed, as has been the case with the new *Länder* of the Federal Republic of Germany. Nevertheless, there exists quite substantial differences in productivity levels within Western Europe. These do not *per se* necessarily lead to disruptions or discrepancies. However, it is a matter of quite different political visions, perspectives and programmes which represent undecided dilemmas and built-in contradictions in the conception of the European Union Treaty and its realization.[14] This is clearly recognized and, indeed, forms the backdrop to the demands being made, especially by the southern Member States, for major increases in the transfer payments they receive via the EC. And this is a matter for political judgement: what kind of a common market do we want? A system of rational factor allocation by efficient markets or a political entity with dominant equalization mechanisms, common welfare aspirations and political solidarity suspending undesired market results? Do Member States joining at the third stage have to comply in advance with the convergence criteria – or does the EC first have to help them to reach these by transfers which then are also likely to continue throughout future periods?

The Proposed Anchor for Stability: The European System of Central Banks

THE ESCB AND THE GERMAN POSITION

When the final stage of currency union starts, for which the go-ahead ultimately needs to be given according to a complex procedure some time from 1996 onwards, the new European System of Central Banks (ESCB) will be formed, encompassing the national central banks of the participating countries, together with the European Central Bank (ECB), which has then also to be established. When that step is taken, the nation states entering the Monetary Union will lose their sovereignty over monetary policy altogether which, in the case of Germany, calls for changes in the Constitution. From that point on, the course of monetary policy will be set on a uniform basis, a single monetary policy for all participant countries of the ESCB.

The Germans have been following this project very attentively, and also with some concern. The question which arises for Germany is whether the ESCB can be expected to be just as resolute on the fundamental issues of safeguarding the value of a currency as Germany's monetary policy has been in the past (even if everything is not quite as one would wish right at the moment). The Vice-President of The Netherlands' Central Bank, Professor Szasz, portrayed our situation quite succinctly during a hearing on EMU held by a committee of the German *Bundestag*: he explained that it would be the Germans above all who, having held the currency anchor role in the EMS up to the present time, would be called upon to renounce their formative influence over monetary policy. This has made it all the more important from

Germany's point of view that, at least as far as the institutional framework is concerned, it should do everything within its power to ensure that the possibility is open for a future European central bank to maintain at least as good an orientation to stability as that which has been characteristic of the German and Dutch central banks.[15]

According to the agreements now reached, the ESCB will essentially have the same objectives and tasks assigned to it as those of the *Deutsche Bundesbank* today. Yet, although the outcome in this respect does meet Germany's wishes to a large extent and although it also marks a substantial improvement in the 1989 Delors Report[16] and in the Draft Statute drawn up by the central bank governors themselves in 1990, it does not mean to say that all worries have been eliminated even within the narrower context of Monetary Union (I have referred briefly to the other worries before).

The individual tasks of the ESCB will be the following:[17]

– to define and implement the monetary policy of the Community;

– to conduct foreign exchange operations in accordance with the relevant terms of the Treaty;

– to hold and manage the official convertible currency reserves of the Member States; and

– to promote the smooth operation of payment systems.

The paramount objective of the future European System of Central Banks is to ensure stability in the value of money. The ESCB is also intended to act in support of the overall economic policy in the Community, only to the extent that scope remains after this prime obligation.

STRIVING FOR PRICE STABILITY: BETWEEN SCYLLA AND CHARYBDIS

The priority given to ensuring stability is a natural consequence of the fact that the instruments available make monetary policy the area best suited to taking care of this objective. It does not, of course, follow that too generous a money supply will by logical necessity lead to an inflationary process. Yet any relatively long phase of general price increases is barely conceivable unless the funds are made available to feed it. Fundamentally though, control of the rate of growth in the money supply can do no more than lay down an operating framework. Whether that framework is then used in the form of higher growth or of higher inflation is ultimately determined by other economic participants such as the State by means of its fiscal policy, mainly by taxation, expenditure, methods of financing, etc., the social partners in their collective bargaining on wages, the investors and consumers as well as savers. The extent to which these groups will bear their share of responsibility for a policy of stability depends on the modes of behaviour which are often heavily dependent on values and patterns and, thus, also manifest themselves in a country's monetary culture and tradition of stability-mindedness. Even if for no other reason than differences in historical and more recent experiences, leaving aside for a moment differences in political priorities, that culture is undoubtedly not uniform across Europe. That in turn makes it all the more important that the central bank is able to ensure on its own independent authority that solid defences are built up against any inflationary floods.

That having been said, it is not merely a matter of the social nature of monetary policy determining that the stability objective ought to be entrusted to one particular body. In our view, stability is of such extraordinary significance that it needs to be looked after separately. Stability of money may not be everything but, without stability, anything amounts to nothing. Stable money is not only indispensable for social reasons – I am sure there is no need for me to elaborate any further on how inflation makes itself felt as a tax on savings and financial assets and thus in the distribution of income and wealth – but stable money is also an essential precondition for the capacity of the price system to fulfil its allocative, steering function to the optimum and to create an investment climate for growth and employment.

Happily, it is no longer very common for policy-makers – at least in Europe nowadays – to assume that a ready supply of easy money will act as a remedy for weak economic growth and employment problems. The idea has long ago proved to be illusory that a trade-off is possible between the level of employment and the rate of price inflation. Expensive experiments in monetary policy have soon tended to go awry, and have usually resulted in both higher unemployment *and* higher inflation at the same time. At the world economic summit meeting in London in 1977, the participating Heads of State and Government rightly asserted that 'inflation is not a cure for unemployment but one of its causes'.[18] When price signals are falsely interpreted because they have been distorted by the falling real value of money, misallocation of resources occurs accompanied by structural upheavals and losses in growth and employment (accompanied by a flight out of monetary – nominal – assets into real values of property, land, buildings, etc., starting vicious upward price spirals.)

Even though these are known dangers, tensions still repeatedly arise between economic and financial policies oriented towards growth and employment goals on the one hand and monetary policy oriented towards price-level stability on the other. Although these have seldom been severe, there have also been conflicts between the German Government and the *Bundesbank* in the past. One can assume that the course of the country's economic history would have been different if the *Bundesbank* had had to submit to the Government's will when it came to the crunch.

We know from our own experience that there can only be any real sense in giving priority to the obligation to maintain stability if the central bank is autonomous on matters of monetary policy *vis-à-vis* the government of the day. A number of academic studies have confirmed that there is a positive correlation between the degree of independence available to the central bank and its success in maintaining stability. There are, of course, exceptions but, on closer inspection, they do not necessarily run counter to that correlation.[19] Rather, they are more likely to reflect the fact that some central banks, though *de jure* they may be required to carry out the directions of their government, in reality have a great deal of autonomy. A good example of this situation is to be found in The Netherlands. Conversely, one cannot rule out the possibility that a substantially autonomous central bank, for whatever reasons, might be wary of coming into conflict with its government and economic groups and may in effect behave as if it were subservient to it or them. Informal connections play a part in this, which are very difficult to detect in an academic analysis. Thus, it may very well turn out that the ESCB, for all its institutional independence, etc., could still follow quite a different course from that of the *Bundesbank* in the past and present.

There is ultimately another very straightforward consideration which would indicate the urgent need for the priority obligation for stability to be backed up by an autonomous role for the monetary authorities. That is simply that governments inevitably need to devote themselves to several different economic objectives at once. If, for example, something happens to the severe detriment of the objective of maintaining a high employment level, a government which depends on the need to be re-elected will do what it can to put that situation right, even if it impairs the fulfilment of other objectives to which it may have been much closer. Hence the stability of the value of money is accorded less importance by governments 'targeting systems', for they see it as one among a number of objectives and often it appears to them to be amenable to compromise, particularly since the consequences of 'sin' only show up in full later. An independent central bank has no need to make any such compromises and, indeed, it must not make them for the sake of its first priority of maintaining stability and defending its medium and long-term record of credibility.

However, still more is needed in order to perform the stability tasks required of a central bank. For one thing, the provision of loans to government bodies must be rigorously constrained or excluded altogether. There are more than enough examples in German history of what can happen when it is possible for the central bank to be misused by an irresponsible government which decides to 'help itself'. The wording of the Maastricht Treaty is still firmer in fending off any such temptations than Germany's *Bundesbankgesetz*. Albeit on a strictly limited basis, the latter does at least allow short-term advances to be made to the Federation or to the *Länder*, whereas the ESCB will be prohibited from granting loans of whatever nature to any government bodies.

On the other hand, there is as yet no clear-cut practical definition at hand of the task of promoting the smooth operation of the payments system: to be 'lender of last resort' in Germany under all circumstances allows only for lending against collateral, while the Anglo-Saxon and Scandinavian traditions include functions of a 'lender of last resort' even without collateral, in cases where this proves unavoidable. It is obvious that such a difference in approach is reflected in normal bank operations as well as supervision and the central banks' role in this. (For instance, the Bank of England is also the supervisory body for the credit institutions while this task in Germany is executed by a separate federal office.)

FOREIGN EXCHANGE FLANK: WHO'S IN CHARGE?

Unfortunately, however, the foreign exchange flank has not been so well covered. This, without doubt, is a weak point in the European Central Bank constitution as drawn up in Maastricht. The exchange rate regime (fixed or floating) and any official central rates against third countries' currencies will ultimately be decided by the Council of Economic and Finance Ministers (ECOFIN).[20] If there is no system of fixed exchange rates and no formal agreements have been concluded with third countries, the Council is entitled to lay down general orientations on exchange rate policy. Certainly, it is true, that the Council can only lay down policies in this way after first completing complex consultation procedures. In particular, the Council is obliged to solicit the views of the ECB in an endeavour to establish a compromise which will be reconcilable with the stability objective. Furthermore, the general orientations on currency policy are not permitted to impair the ESCB's priority aim of stability. Nonetheless, the upshot is that the future European Central Bank's ability to operate foreign exchange policy will be crucially and continuously dependent on obtaining the agreement of politicians.

The *Bundesbank* has had its own painful experience of how monetary policy can be impeded by such shared decision-making competence. At the end of the 1960s, towards the end of the Bretton Woods system of fixed exchange rates, the federal government of the day refused for months to implement a revaluation of the *Deutsche mark* for which the *Bundesbank* was urgently calling. It was not until the federal election was over, in September 1969, that the government finally yielded to the urging from Frankfurt. Under Bretton Woods rules the *Bundesbank* had to purchase all the US dollars offered at the fixed rates (though in effect they were depreciated by the inflationary effects of the financing of the Vietnam War) and thus to swell the *Deutsche mark* circulation while the goods purchased by price bidding were shipped abroad – a classical case of imported inflation. In the interim period, the Federal Republic was swamped several times over by huge waves of speculation. On a number of occasions, in November 1968, in September 1969, and again in 1972 and 1973, dealings on the foreign exchanges were suspended for a short cooling-off period.[21] Until the Bretton Woods system eventually came to an end, the hands of the German monetary authorities were tied. During that period, which was characterized by recurrent international currency crises, monetary policy-makers frequently felt they were at the mercy of the ups-and-downs on the world's financial markets. It was not until the *Deutsche mark*'s exchange rate against the dollar was finally floated in 1973 that the *Bundesbank* regained the scope it needed to do its job, namely to exercise control over the money stock, and was able to begin the cleaning-up operation.

These experiences made a deep impression on our thinking towards exchange rate agreements. Other Member States, and indeed also the European Commission, quite often tend to see things rather differently. Faced with the very volatile conditions which often move exchange rates between particular currencies quite some distance away from where one would expect to find them on the basis of so-called fundamental factors, e.g. purchasing power parities, they occasionally show a much greater preference for political management of the foreign exchange markets. The Plaza Agreement (1985),[22] the Louvre Agreement (1987)[23] and the discussion of what have been termed 'target zones' have all been staging posts in the debates surrounding this topic.

Of course, it would be helpful if exchange rates were to follow rather more gentle paths. Yet that is not something which can be forced on the markets simply by setting maximum fluctuation margins and having the central banks defend them. To achieve the desired greater balance, it is necessary to dig deeper. The foreign exchange markets will not be rid of crucial disruptive factors until all major industrial countries are – among other things – steering the same course with the same importance attached to achieving or maintaining price stability, and giving price stability precedence, in case a choice is needed, over exchange rate stability.

Our experience has been a similar one with the regional or continental system of fixed exchange rates – the 'grid' – which the European Monetary System represents. After frequent realignments in the early years, the system has now been operating for quite some time, namely since January 1987, virtually without disruption. The main reason for this is that – in the EMS's core countries at least – the objectives and of course the results of different national economic policies, as expressed in inflation and interest rates, are much closer together now than they were in the early years because it has been understood that frequent depreciations may be self-defeating operations. These functional relationships ought not to be lost sight of whenever a future Europe with its Economic and Monetary Union thinks it necessary to enter into negotiations with the USA or Japan about target zones or even stricter relationships.

Quite apart from perceived differences in economic policy, on a world scale there are also other factors which have an important influence on exchange rates and which are not so prominent in the regional arena. Time and again, political instabilities or economic crises and military conflicts tend to generate a major restructuring of investment portfolios. We know from the period of the Bretton Woods system and also from the early years of the EMS that any attempts to arrest the accompanying exchange rate fluctuations by means of market intervention have very often done no more than actually reinforce the speculative tendencies already existing.

Against the background of experiences such as these, a reserve banker inevitably has a feeling of some unease when faced with the prospect of political bodies deciding in rather cumbersome procedures how much scope a central bank should be permitted in the pursuit of its foreign exchange policy. Of course, it is possible that a division of responsibilities along such lines could function well. On the whole, that has been the case in Federal Germany. However, it took a long time to reach that situation and – as I have briefly outlined – a lot of painful experience was needed before we attained the current degree of cooperation. It would be fatal to have to go through the same learning process all over again on the European level; this could very well endanger the primary objective of price stability in the crucial years ahead. I very much hope that the political sphere and the central bank will rapidly develop a constructive relationship in Europe which is appropriate to their common objective, rather than obstructing one another in jealous disputes over decision-making authority.

Concluding Remarks: National Central Banks, the ESCB: What We Can Learn from German Experience

Just as economic and monetary policy in general will have to reorganize their relations both on the European level and in most member countries, so too the reserve banks in Europe will find themselves operating in a new environment. Like the European Central Bank itself, they will become integral parts of the European System of Central Banks. Once the third stage begins, there will be just one uniform monetary policy for all participating countries, as determined by the Governing Council of the ECB. That will leave no more room for any nations or indeed regions to go their own ways.

Germany's reserve bank has been made acutely aware of this by past experience. At the end of 1950, in the early days of the Federal Republic, the Berlin Central Bank decided for its own regional policy reasons and the insular location of West Berlin in the midst of the GDR, not to go along with an increase in the discount rate decided upon by the Central Bank Council. This it could do under the system then existing in the Federal Republic. The idea was to give a further boost to the reconstruction of Berlin by keeping interest rates low. However, even at that early stage in the development of the post-war German financial system, this interest rate differential of 0.25% was a short-lived affair. The spread in rates encouraged savers to deposit their money in West Germany proper, where it would obtain a better yield, while would-be borrowers began to come increasingly to Berlin. The Berlin Central Bank soon had to put a stop to its deviation from the common front established by all the others. In the United States too, presumably for similar reasons, although the regional reserve banks were entitled (till the 1930s) to apply for their own discount rates, a deviating rate has not been set since the 1920s. It is accepted today that the individual Federal Reserve Banks do not have room for such separate initiatives and the Board of Governors, which is required to confirm the interest rates applied in the regions, has always insisted on uniform rates throughout this vast continent.

Any distinct regional monetary policy could only possibly be enforced with the aid of a comprehensive system of quantitative controls. Yet intervention of that nature could hardly be reconciled with the overall regulative model of an open market economy with free competition which was again underlined in the Treaty of Maastricht.

However, even though monetary policy can only be pursued on a uniform, undivided basis, and even though there must not be any 'grey areas' of responsibility for such policy, there nevertheless remains some degree of scope for both federative elements, i.e. for the application of the principle of subsidiarity. Individual Member States have some influence over the common monetary policy established in as far as each of their central bank governors has a seat on the Governing Council of the ECB. Even if those national central bank governors are not permitted to act as mere representatives of their own countries' interests and must orient their actions to the aims and objectives of the ECB, remaining independent of any directives from government bodies, they will, by their cooperation in the Governing Council, ensure that the ECB's decisions are based on a broad process of discussion intended to establish consensus. That, in turn, will secure greater acceptance for those decisions, which will be a particularly crucial matter in a Europe with a single monetary and currency policy. In view of the productivity differentials which still persist, the necessarily uniform monetary policy will make its effects felt very differently from one region to another.[24]

Of course, it is true that national central banks will lose their most important functions in the final stage and, the greater their independence has been in the past, the greater their loss of functions will be. Yet they will still have some substantial jobs to do. The form of cooperation and division of tasks which we practice within the *Bundesbank* system, between the *Landeszentralbanken* and the Directorate in Frankfurt, is quite similar to what one could imagine in the ESCB, and also to what has so far been hinted at in the draft Statute.

The preserves of the Directorate are the functions of acting as fiscal agent for the federation, managing special assets of the federal government and dealing with financial institutions which perform central tasks for the country as a whole. To these tasks can be added foreign exchange dealings and open market operations.[25] However, in the latter case, the *Landeszentralbanken* already provide important and extensive assistance. All technical processing work relating to repurchase agreements in securities trading, which is the predominant open market activity in Federal Germany in terms of volume, is carried out by the *Landeszentralbanken*. Central bank funds, with an average monthly volume of approximately DEM 130 billion, are currently made available to financial institutions via four-week or eight-week tenders. The *Landeszentralbanken* receive offers from the participating banks in their own areas, examine and keep records of the drawers, and manage the accounts of financial institutions as well as the securities used as collateral. All that is done at the central level is to decide whether such transactions should be conducted, what volume and what rates will be appropriate, for which the Central Bank Council (in which the presidents of the *Landeszentralbanken* sit with full voting power alongside the members of the Directorate) has to empower the Centre.

The *Landeszentralbanken* are still more closely interlinked with the financial institutions in their respective areas by means of all the other dealings they have with them. This applies especially to their management of the bill discounting business which is accorded high priority in Federal Germany and to the implementation of minimum-reserve-asset policy. In the latter case, the *Landeszentralbanken* not only administer compulsory deposits but also monitor reported reserves. Indeed, from time to time, staff go to the banks themselves to check that the appropriate regulations are really being properly adhered to. In the same manner, the so-called 'Lombard' credits are extended, i.e. unlimited short-term overdraft against collateral which the *Landeszentralbanken* administer for their client banks.

Apart from doing the bulk of the work in implementing monetary policy, the *Landeszentralbanken* or their subsidiary departments are also largely responsible for managing the flow of payments, and for supplying notes and coin. For example, at its headquarters in Düsseldorf, the *Landeszentralbank* in *Nordrhein-Westfalen* maintains the largest computer centre for clearing payments on the Continent.[26] In EMU there will be no need any more for the national central headquarters to function as the eye of a needle for payments from one country to another, but there is scope for broad cooperation, e.g. between *Nordrhein-Westfalen* and The Netherlands, without recourse to a centralized European pool.

The *Landeszentralbanken* also provide important auxiliary and consultancy services to the banking supervisory authority. The Federal Banking Supervisory Office (*Bundesaufsichtsamt für das Kreditwesen*), which is responsible for this task, is in fact only a relatively small organization, without any subsidiary branches. Thus the 'long arm of the law' is extended on its behalf around the country by the *Landeszentralbanken*. They collect and collate the necessary reports from the financial institutions, examine accounts and then pass everything on, adding comments and recommendations as needed, to the supervisory office in Berlin. Based on these findings, the latter takes whatever measures may be deemed necessary, in the execution of which the services of the *Landeszentralbanken* are used where expedient.

Finally, the *Landeszentralbanken* also carry out the fiscal-agent function for their own *Land* governments and their administrative departments, also assisting the Directorate in stock exchange or money market dealings which form part of its fiscal-agent function at the federal level to facilitate the emission of federal financial bills and securities.

All these activities provide the *Landeszentralbanken* with deep insight into the business dealings of financial institutions and the overall economic processes occurring in the country. An essential part is played in that by their involvement in the bill discounting business. Because we develop a good idea of the credit standing of the joint parties to bills of exchange, we also come into close contact with a wide variety of companies, get to know their balance sheets and, hence, gain a good impression of the overall financial and economic condition of the corporate sector. The experience and information they are thus able to collate make the *Landeszentralbanken* important providers of information in the overall process of establishing the policy line in the monetary and currency spheres. From my own perspective, this is an indispensable element in ensuring the direct practical relevance of our work in the *Bundesbank*'s Central Bank Council. This helps to alleviate the dangers of losing touch with reality when sitting 'at the high table'.

This, or something along these lines, could also act as the model for the division of tasks in the future European System of Central Banks. So far, little discussion has taken place regarding these concrete matters, with the exception of the secretariat at Basle of the Committee of EC Governors, which has started on money concepts. In that respect, we have a lot of work ahead of us and the time available in which to carry it through is tight indeed. As in other areas, the work which now needs to be done should also conform to the maxim that centralization should be kept to the absolute minimum necessary.

There can be no doubt that the decision-making competence on monetary policy must be concentrated in one single body. However, when it comes to the technical implementation of that policy, recourse should most definitely be made to the existing infrastructure of national and regional central banks. Given that the regional differences around Europe are undisputedly much greater than those within the Federal Republic of Germany, it will be more important than ever to make good use of the insights and experience thus obtained. A structure of subsidiarity in Europe's central bank system would not only be the proper kind of structure, but would also be extremely helpful in achieving the system's purposes.

NOTES

1. See Commission of the European Communities (1992).
2. See Jochimsen (1992), pp. 319-342.
3. See Jochimsen (1991a).
4. Idem., op. cit.
5. See *Deutsche Bundesbank* (1990).
6. See Committee for the Study of Economic and Monetary Union (1990); Centre for Economic Policy Research and 'Paolo Baffi' Centre for Monetary and Financial Economics (1991).
7. Art. 130d of the Draft Treaty on the Foundation of the European Community (abbreviated as EC Draft); Protocol on the economic and social cohesion.
8. See European Council (1990).
9. See Jochimsen (1991b), pp. 73-81.
10. See Art. 109 F EC-Draft; Protocol on the Statutes of the European Monetary Institute.
11. Cf. EC Draft, Protocol on the criteria of convergence in Art. 109 j.
12. Art. 104 C merely stipulates that this 'should be taken into account' among other factors when 'considering' that an 'excessive deficit' exists.
13. Committee for the Study of Economic and Monetary Union (1990) op. cit.
14. Jochimsen, (1991a) op. cit.
15. See Szasz (1991).
16. Committee for the Study of Economic and Monetary Union (1990), op. cit.
17. See Art. 105 EC Draft.
18. Statement of the Heads of State and Government meeting, London (1977).
19. Alesina (1989: pp. 55-98).
20. Cf. Art. 109 EC Draft.
21. Emminger (1976).
22. Ministers of Finance and Central Bank Governors of France, Germany, Japan, the United Kingdom and the United States (1985).
23. Ministers of Finance and Central Bank Governors of Canada, France, Germany, Japan, the United Kingdom and the United States (1987).
24. Jochimsen (1991a) op. cit.
25. *Deutsche Bundesbank* (1989).
26. *Landeszentralbank* in *Nordrhein-Westfalen* (1992).

REFERENCES

Alesina, Alberto, 'Politics and Business Cycles in Industrial Democracies', *Economic Policy*, no. 8 (1989), pp. 55-98.

Centre for Economic Policy Research and 'Paolo Baffi' Centre for Monetary and Financial Economics, Bocconi University, *The Road to EMU – Managing the Transition to a Single European Currency* (Milan: 1991).

Commission of the European Communities, 'Treaty on European Union', *Official Journal*, no. C 191, 1992.

Committee for the Study of Economic and Monetary Union (Delors Committee), 'Report on Economic and Monetary Union in the European Community', (in German), in Bofinger, Peter (ed.), *Der Weg zur Wirtschafts- und Währungsunion in Europa* (Wiesbaden: 1990).

Deutsche Bundesbank, 'The Deutsche Bundesbank. Its Monetary Policy Instruments and Functions', *Special Series*, no. 7, 3rd edition (Frankfurt a.M.: July 1989).

Deutsche Bundesbank, 'Statement by the Deutsche Bundesbank on the Establishment of an Economic and Monetary Union in Europe', *Monthly Report of the Deutsch Bundesbank*, vol. 42, no. 10, October 1990.

Emminger, Otmar, 'Deutsche Geld- und Währungspolitik im Spannungsfeld zwischen innerem und äußerem Gleichgewicht (1948-1975)', in Deutsche Bundesbank (ed.), *Währung und Wirtschaft in Deutschland 1876-1975* (Frankfurt a.M.: Knapp, 1976), pp. 485-554.

European Council, Conclusions (in German) of the Presidency of the Summit of 27 and 28 October 1990 in Rome (special meeting), *Bulletin des Presse- und Informationsamt der Bundesregierung*, no. 128, 6 November 1990.

Group of Seven, Statement of 23 December 1987, *Auszüge aus Presseartikeln*, no. 93, 28 December 1987.

Heads of State and Government, Statement made at the meeting at Downing Street, London, *Bulletin des Presse- und Informationsamtes der Bundesregierung*, Bonn, 11 May 1977, and *Auszüge aus Presseartikeln*, no. 29, 13 May 1977.

Jochimsen, Reimut, 'The Key Elements of Financial and Economic Policy in the Context of European Integration and a Consideration of its Regional Aspect' (in German), Aachen Paper, October 1991, *Auszüge aus Presseartikeln*, no. 86, 14 November 1991a.

Jochimsen, Reimut, 'Subsidiarity in the Area of Economic and Monetary Union', in *Subsidiarity: The Challenge of Change*, Proceedings of the Jacques Delors Colloquium 1991 of the European Institute of Public Administration (Maastricht: 1991b), pp. 73-81.

Jochimsen, Reimut, 'Die Europäische Wirtschafts- und Währungsunion. Sachstand und Perspektiven', in Görgens, E. and Tuchfeldt E. (eds), *Die Zukunft der wirtschaftlichen Entwicklung – Perspektiven und Probleme, Festschrift für Ernst Dürr* (Freiburg i. Br.: 1992), pp. 319-342, reprinted in *Auszüge aus Presseartikeln*, no. 16, 17 February 1992 (Deutsche Bundesbank).

Landeszentralbank in Nordrhein-Westfalen, *Bericht über das Jahr 1991* (Düsseldorf: 1992).

Larosière de, Jacques, 'Die Europäische Wirtschafts- und Währungsunion, ein wesentlicher Beitrag zur internationalen Inflationsbekämpfung', in Presse- und Informationsabteilung der Französischen Botschaft in Bonn, *Frankreich Infor*, 91-33, 8 October 1991.

Ministers of Finance and Central Bank Governors of France, Germany, Japan, the United Kingdom, and the United States, Statement made in New York on 22 September 1985, *Auszüge aus Presseartikeln*, no. 62, 23 September 1985.

Ministers of Finance and Central Bank of Governors of Canada, France, Germany, Japan, the United Kingdom, and the United States, Statement made in Paris on 22 February 1987, *Auszüge aus Presseartikeln*, no. 15, 23 February 1987.

Szasz, A., Member of the Board of Directors of the Nederlandsche Bank, Statement made before the Finanzausschuß of the German Bundestag in Bonn on 18 September 1991, *Auszüge aus Presseartikeln*, no. 69, 19 September 1991.

SECTION 3:

SPILL-OVERS RESULTING FROM EMU

THE IMPACT OF AN ECONOMIC AND MONETARY UNION ON SOCIAL AND ECONOMIC COHESION: ANALYSIS AND ENSUING POLICY IMPLICATIONS

Willem Molle, Olaf Sleijpen, Marc Vanheukelen*

Introduction

The question has often been raised in economic literature as to whether increased economic integration in Europe would promote regional development in the less prosperous countries of the EC and thus decrease disparities among the Member States, or whether it would have the opposite effect.[1] This last possibility in particular has focused attention on the importance of a European regional policy to avoid or overcome national and regional disparities.

Two major events in the history of the EC have contributed to the formulation, setting-up and strengthening of a Community regional policy. First, the enlargement of the Community to include Denmark, United Kingdom and Ireland in 1973, which led to the creation of a European Fund for Regional Development in 1975 (EFRD); second, the completion of the internal market, better known as the '1992 project', together with the enlargement of the Community to include Spain and Portugal in 1986, which led to a doubling of the structural funds in the period 1989-1992. In both cases, the fear that the widening and/or deepening of the European integration process would undermine cohesion in the Community brought forward a more active policy aimed at bridging the gaps in prosperity between the rich and poor regions in the EC (Padoa-Schioppa, 1987).

The creation of an EMU, together with greater emphasis on the need for solidarity between Member States[2] has once again focused the attention of politicians and economists on the threat of increased disparity between Member States which could be entailed when this stage of integration is put into practice. Fears are being voiced that such an increase in disparity would jeopardize economic cohesion in the European Community and, once again, the question of the need for an increased policy effort to decrease disparity in income levels in the Community arises.

In this chapter we contribute to this debate by trying to answer two questions:

---

* The views expressed in this chapter are those of the authors. The article was completed in autumn 1992.

K. Gretschmann (ed.), Economic and Monetary Union: Implications for National Policy-Makers, 217–243.

(1) What are the consequences of an Economic and Monetary Union on cohesion in the Community, and

(2) Given these consequences, does an Economic and Monetary Union impose new needs and constraints on EC cohesion policy?

This chapter is structured as follows: the section on 'Foundations' provides a definition of cohesion, indicates a way to measure it and shows how it has evolved over the past decades. The following sections deal with the economic effects of EMU on regional disparities. EMU implies a number of changes with respect to the present situation. Of these we have picked three for further analysis. First, we deal with the effects of the increased allocative efficiency that is caused by the introduction of a single currency. Next, we analyze the implications of the loss of the exchange rate as a policy instrument. After that we consider the impact of European constraints on national fiscal policy and, finally, we discuss the effects of convergence of monetary policies. This analysis shows that, although risks and opportunities are present, major changes in the EC regional balance are not likely. On the basis of that conclusion we attempt to answer the question of whether EMU calls for new EC initiatives with an appreciable budgetary incidence.

The starting point of this chapter is the current pallet of EC policy instruments available. It should be noted that this chapter does not cover, or only tangentially, the long-term convergence/divergence tendencies in the EC, and then only those tendencies that are wholly or largely related to EMU: the substance of this chapter is on the nexus between EMU and cohesion.

Foundations

DEFINITION

With the adoption of the Single European Act in 1987, economic and social cohesion has become a clear treaty obligation of the EC. The Maastricht Treaty on European Union has confirmed this objective and has slightly revised its wording. The new Article 130a reads:

> In order to promote its overall harmonious development, the Community shall develop and pursue its actions leading to the strengthening of its economic and social cohesion. In particular the Community shall aim at reducing disparities between the various regions and the backwardness of the least-favoured regions, including rural areas.[3]

Social and economic cohesion is an ill defined concept. It is probably best described as the degree to which imbalances in economic welfare between countries or regions in the EC are socially and politically tolerable. In other words, disparities may not lead to actions by national governments that could endanger the good functioning of the EC. At the same time however, the objective goes beyond a pure equity concept. It aims to reduce the gap in real income per capita, not by mere inter-regional transfers, but by fulfilling some structural conditions for poorer regions to surpass the growth rate of the Community as a whole.

This definition is not very operational. Therefore, for practical purposes, social and economic cohesion is measured by indicators such as the regional differences in the level of income per capita, (un)employment, the productivity per head of the working population, and the availability and accessibility of environmental goods, cultural infrastructure, leisure activities, etc.[4] Cohesion is thought to improve, if differences in regional disparities decrease. To bring that about, the lagging regions need to catch up, that is to say they need, with respect to these indicators, to outperform the prosperous ones in growth terms.

This catching-up can be stimulated, on the one hand, by policies aiming at a more efficient use of resources in the production of goods and services in all European regions (i.e. by a regional policy that aims at shifting the European economy in the direction of the production-possibility frontier). On the other hand, it can be encouraged by equity-based policies that stress the role of a 'fair' income distribution and other social matters, (i.e. by a regional policy focused upon shifting the aggregate European economy along the production-possibility frontier).

In practice the EC has never made a clear distinction between efficiency (allocation) and equity (redistribution) considerations in its regional policy. Indeed, the Regional Fund, like the other Structural Funds (the Community's prime cohesion instruments), combines allocative and distributive functions. However, the allocative function is of prime importance as the Funds mostly use specific grants for developing elements of the regional (infra)structure with a view to matching the quality of the business environment in the prosperous regions.

PAST RECORD

In the past the EC has gone through different stages of integration. We will review how real income disparity has developed in the EC throughout these different phases of economic integration. EMU is a logical step in the process of economic integration (Molle, 1990a), and tracing back the history of the Community with respect to cohesion serves as a proper point of departure for our analysis.

The disparity between EC countries is the indicator that is of utmost importance for cohesion.[5] Figure 1 below gives the development of GDP per capita between the Member States in a long-term (1960-1992) perspective (weighted variation coefficient of GDP per capita); Figure 2 gives the evolution of disparity in GDP per capita (in ECU/PPS)[6] between regions within the Member States of the EC.

Figure 1:
Weighted Variation Coefficient of GDP per Capita for the EC (1960-1992)
(in PPS)

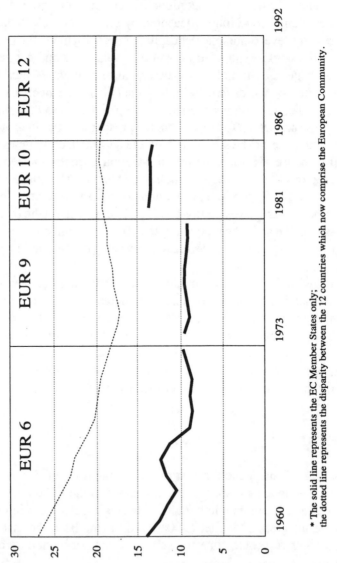

Source: Vanheukelen, 1992.

Figure 2:
Evolution of Income Disparities in Member States (1960-1988)
(in ECU/PPS)

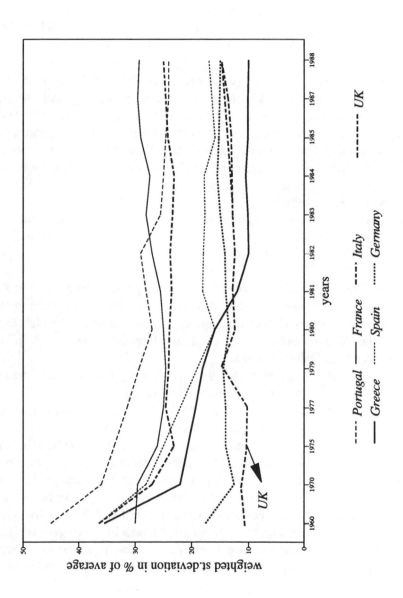

Source; Boeckhout et al., 1991.

From these figures and from other studies that have analyzed this development over a longer period (e.g. Molle, 1990b, Boeckhout et al. 1991, Vanheukelen 1992), we see different developments in different periods. *Disparities among Member States* narrowed in the period 1950-1973, as regards both the original Member States and those that were to join later. The oil crisis altered this trend, but much less so far for the then nine EC Member States; the relative economic fate of Spain, Portugal and Greece worsened significantly from 1975 to 1985. However, since 1986, a smooth but clear pattern of overall convergence has been again observable.

Disparities among regions is the next indicator that is relevant in the discussion on cohesion. Boeckhout et al. (1991) conclude that regional disparities are correlated with disparities among countries (during the period 1950-1989). However, instead of stabilizing, they slightly decreased in the eighties. The diverging trend that can be observed is a result of a deterioration in the position of regions in the weaker countries of the Community, on the one hand, and a relative increase in the position of regions in the European heartland. Recently, this tendency has levelled off.

Income per capita not only varies at international level, but also within countries, as Figure 2 reveals (small countries like Belgium, The Netherlands, Denmark, Ireland and Luxembourg have been omitted). From this it appears that:

    – in France (after an initial decrease) and, to a lesser degree also in West Germany and the United Kingdom, disparities have gone up slightly; in other Member States income disparities decreased and stabilized in the eighties;

    – from 1960 onwards, income disparities have been fairly small in West Germany and the United Kingdom;

    – in Italy, Portugal and especially France, income disparities have been considerably higher than in the countries mentioned before.

This decrease in disparity levels in the EC in the period 1960-1973 seems to be related to market integration, mostly to the liberalization of trade and capital flows (Molle, 1990b), and less to increased labour mobility (Molle and Van Mourik, 1987, 1989, Van Mourik, 1988). These results are especially interesting for an EMU with predicted large capital flows and no exchange variability (Morsink and Molle, 1991). It can also be shown that the degree of convergence is correlated to aggregate economic growth (Molle, 1990b): a hypothesis supported by the data above, as temporary downturns in convergence coincide with periods of decreased economic activity. Hence, in so far as aggregate economic growth benefits from EMU, there is the likelihood of increased cohesion.[7]

Allocative Efficiency

MECHANISMS UNDERLYING THE EFFECTS OF EMU ON ALLOCATIVE
EFFICIENCY

The creation of EMU implies the adoption of a single currency by 1997 or,
ultimately, by 1999. This is beneficial for allocative efficiency. The Commission
report on the benefits and costs of EMU[8] spells out the main advantages
associated with a single currency. EMU decreases exchange rate uncertainty and
transactions costs. Although exchange rate variability in the EC is already very
low, thanks to the Exchange Rate Mechanism, there still are exchange risks to
be faced by traders as well as by investors. There is of course the possibility of
hedging this risk, but this involves significant costs, especially for the greater
number of European firms, namely the small and medium enterprises. Besides,
for private households, who traditionally pay the highest price when converting
cash from one currency to another,[9] it is hardly practical to hedge exchange risks.

These static allocative efficiency gains of a single currency rate are rather
obvious, but more interesting are the expected dynamic gains. The latter have
been the object of an interesting debate, centring chiefly around the following
three issues.

– As far as the impact of *fixed exchange rates* on trade is concerned, the
empirical evidence is not conclusive. On the one hand, one can refer to the more
global studies that have been undertaken, namely by the IMF (1984) or Perée
and Steinherr (1989). Whereas the former study finds no convincing negative
effect of exchange rate variability on trade, the latter does. On the other hand,
in a more European context, Bini-Smaghi (1987) and Sapir and Sekkat (1989)
found a significant negative effect on trade flows, but in both cases very small.
Interesting, however, is a recent study by Huijser and Stokman (1992), which
took a more sophisticated approach in evaluating the impact of exchange rates
on trade flows for The Netherlands, arguing along the lines set out by Bini-
Smaghi (1990), namely that the problem in measuring the influence on trade lies
in the high degree of aggregation. Their study is based upon a sectoral
desegregation of trade flows (volumes) and their respective relationship with
several variables, including exchange rate variability (expressed as weighted
standard deviations of three-monthly changes in nominal terms). Their conclusion
is that the effect of exchange rate variability on trade is significant and negative
for four out of the five sectors in their research.

– With respect to the influence on capital movements, *foreign direct
investments* are of particular interest. Morsink and Molle (1991) have found that
the variability in the average monthly real bilateral exchange rate[10] is a
significant factor in explaining direct investment flows in the Community, i.e.
an increase in variability leads to lower investment flows, while a decrease in

variability favours direct investments.

– Finally, the disappearance of exchange rate uncertainty has an influence on growth. In EMU, the interest rates could fall throughout the Community (decrease in risk premium for exchange risk), thus stimulating the demand for capital, investment and also overall economic growth (CEC, 1990). But one should be very careful in making a final assessment of these long-term growth prospects. It is true that lower interest rates, via a decrease in risk premiums, influence investments, but strategic business expectations are probably more important (CEC, 1990).[11]

The subsequent question to be addressed is how these predicted effects of EMU, i.e. increased trade, direct investments and overall economic growth, will affect regional income disparities.

TRADE

It can be argued that EMU will have a similar effect as the '1992 project': both undertakings encourage trade by abolishing trade barriers in Europe, i.e. physical, technical and fiscal barriers in the single market programme, and monetary barriers (different currencies) in EMU. Studies on the impact of '1992' reveal an increase in welfare for the Community as a whole. For instance, Smith and Venables (1988) assess the welfare gains of the '1992 project' in an industry case study, taking into account imperfect competition and economies of scale. Their results indicate considerable welfare gains. Due to the fact that EMU, through its dynamic effects discussed above, could have a similar effect on trade as the abolition of trade barriers, welfare should increase throughout the Community.

With respect to the regional effects of trade, we might consider exchange rate variability as an impediment to trade, just like tariffs or other trade barriers. Existing empirical research on the trade integration effects on regions could then also have validity in assessing the impact of exchange rate variability on regional trade. The results of these studies are not conclusive: they do not support the hypothesis that progressive integration would lead to an increase in the level of disparities, but neither do they show that trade integration will lead to a decrease in cohesion.

For example, in their study on changes in regional accessibility[12] due to integration, Keeble, Owens and Thompson (KOT study, 1981,1982) show that after the enlargement of the EC in 1973 the peripheral regions of the original Six benefited more, in relative terms, than the central regions. Total employment grew most in the peripheral regions and least in the central ones, while unemployment increased more in the central regions and least in the peripheral ones.

Integration through international trade in industrial products between EC and EFTA has had a different effect on each of the 58 German regions (Peschel, Haass, Schnöring, 1979, and Peschel, 1978, 1982). Integration has slightly favoured the more densely settled regions in Germany and has, in fact, favoured those regions that are closest to the geographic centre of the EC. A very comprehensive study by Peschel (1988), the only study known based on an explicit (partial equilibrium) model of inter-regional trade, in order to quantify static integration effects relating to the foundation of EFTA and EC for 73 regions in Scandinavia and Germany, indicates among other things that (1) the variance of integration effects among the regions of each individual country is low and (2) that no centre-periphery pattern can be observed with respect to price or quantity effects of integration.

We may suppose that the increased trade brought about by EMU will have similar effects as the trade created by earlier stages of integration. From past experience we may conclude that it is likely to have beneficial effects on Community economic growth and probably on social and economic cohesion and, at the same time, that empirical research does not support the old conjecture that increased integration via increased trade will favour central regions more than peripheral ones. However, with respect to regional effects of trade, it is very difficult to predict precisely which regions will gain from EMU, and which ones may lose.

DIRECT INVESTMENTS

A second factor that can promote economic development is an increase in direct investment flows from the richer to the poorer Member States (Petrochillos, 1989). EMU, by eliminating exchange rate uncertainty, will eliminate one risk factor and hence may stimulate direct investment flows.[13] In order to assess the regional impact of increased direct investment on disparity levels, we should examine whether a link exists between the growth of lagging regions and direct investments.

Table 1 below shows the inflow of direct investments in the lagging Member States, as well as the degree of convergence, expressed in relative GDP per capita.

The data for the period examined suggest that only Spain and Portugal gained considerably in terms of direct investments[14] (to a lesser degree Greece) and, in terms of convergence, Ireland, Spain and Portugal. From this data, it is possible to conclude that an increase in direct investments could lead to convergence.

Table 1:
Direct Investment (DI) and Cohesion (relative GDP per capita 1985-1990)
Direct investments in millions of US dollars
GDP/capita (PPS) (EC 12 = 100)

Member State	1985	1986	1987	1988	1989	1990
Greece						
DI	447	471	683	907	752	1005
GDP	50.7	50.1	48.4	48.6	48.7	47.1
Ireland						
DI	164	-43	89	92	85	99
GDP	62.5	60.7	61.8	62.4	64.9	68.3
Spain						
DI	1968	3451	4571	7021	8428	13841
GDP	70.4	70.6	72.5	73.4	74.6	75.5
Portugal						
DI	255	239	466	922	1737	2123
GDP	50.7	51.8	51.8	52.7	53.8	56.0

Source: IMF (1990), CEC (1991).

The trends depicted above do not match the divergence school's argument saying that, due to agglomeration economies, economic integration does not lead to an increase in direct investments in peripheral regions.[15] In the case of Portugal and Spain, there is simultaneous convergence and growth of direct investments in the examined period. Direct investment has considerably increased in Spain and Portugal, probably caused by the accession of both countries to the EC and the forthcoming integration effects. As far as Greece is concerned, there is no visible link between direct investments and convergence (the relationship even seems to be negative!), while Ireland's catching-up can be explained by endogenous economic performance, though Ireland received a considerable amount of direct investments before 1985 and there could be a time lag in the effects on convergence.

As noted before, EMU in general will promote investment throughout the Community, which could be beneficial in terms of convergence especially for lagging regions with a high borrowing capacity. However, the structural endowments of the regions will finally determine which regions will gain more than others.[16] The lagging regions, which are relatively more attractive to investors, can perhaps attract more direct investment than some more prosperous regions, which could lead to convergence of real income. But, also after the establishment of EMU, there will still be regions suffering from large structural deficiencies and lack of investments. EMU is only likely to change this to a limited extent and it is especially in those regions that the Community structural funds can play a supportive role.

MUTUAL REINFORCEMENT BETWEEN TRADE AND INVESTMENTS

The third argument is constructed on the two previous lines of thinking, namely that the increases in both trade and direct investments are closely related and reinforce the (regional) growth process. In the traditional neo-classical theory, trade and capital flows are considered to be substitutes.[17] However, new trade theory, taking into account the role of multinational enterprises, imperfect competition and economies of scale, argues that the emergence of intra- and inter-industry trade sets in motion a process of simultaneous increase in trade and direct investments. The findings of Morsink and Molle (1991) indeed reveal a complementary relationship between trade and direct investments. As the increase in trade in the Community is mainly the result of intra-industry trade (Molle 1990a), it can be expected that the reinforcing process between trade and direct investments, caused by fixed exchange rates, will foster economic development. Again, the effect of this on regional growth differentials, and hence on cohesion, is unclear.

CONCLUSIONS

In general, EMU is expected to increase trade and investment flows in the Community as a whole. But, on the basis of results of current empirical economic research, the repercussions of these effects on regions are inconclusive. Much of the impact at regional level depends on other meso- and micro-level regional variables.

It may well be that EMU will contribute to closing the gap in incomes between countries, but the question remains: what will happen to differences in incomes between regions within Member States. In the light of subsidiarity, this problem is of course of lesser concern to the EC. The role of EMU in this perspective will probably be so small that we will not go into this matter. It should however be noted that regional disparities within EC Member States have recently gone up again (not only in Italy, the best example of the 'North-South' problem, but also in France, the United Kingdom and Belgium). These examples of regional disparities within already existing currency areas indicate that EMU is no guarantee for cohesion.

The Loss of the Exchange Rate as Policy Instrument

Abandoning the exchange rate can also have implications for economic policy-making, as the exchange rate may be used to adjust for problems of internal and external balance due to demand and/or supply shocks. As the economies of 'cohesion countries' have not reached a durable equilibrium, fixing exchange rates could thus threaten the convergence process.

The traditional optimal currency area (OCA) theory stipulates that a group of countries or regions not representing an OCA[18] should not fix exchange rates because the occurrence of asymmetric shocks necessitates individual adjustments via the exchange rates (Mundell, 1961). Eichengreen (1990), for example, argues that Europe is indeed not an OCA and hence should design a mechanism that can replace the exchange rate as policy instrument. Low factor mobility especially could impose difficulties whenever it is no longer possible to adjust via the exchange rate.[19] However, it has never been the objective of the Community to have massive flows of workers from one country to another. Indeed, political preferences in Europe are clearly towards bringing jobs to people, rather than the reverse.

FEASIBLE OR NOT?

We should, however, first assess whether the exchange rate instrument really is a feasible policy instrument, i.e. whether there is a long-term relationship between nominal and real exchange rates. If this is not the case, the arguments above hinge upon incorrect assumptions and the hypothesis that fixing exchange rates will endanger cohesion does not hold.

As to this issue, it should be noted that a country needs a change in real exchange rate in order to alleviate the impact of durable economic shocks while, at the same time, it is only the nominal exchange rate that can be changed directly. A nominal devaluation will initially lead to better terms of trade and an improvement in the trade balance.[20] However, increased import prices, due to the devaluation, will have their impact on the domestic price level, leading to an adjustment of nominal wages, domestic prices and a reversal of the initial real depreciation. If wage indexation is rather low, the catch-up process will be set in motion more slowly.[21] Empirical evidence shows that there is a degree of correlation between nominal and real exchange rates (CEC, 1990), however the impact of nominal exchange rates on real exchange rates does not persist in the long run. The main advantage of the nominal devaluation is that it can 'front-load' a real exchange rate depreciation, but ultimately a change in real factor prices is necessary for a long-run change in terms of trade. Hence, nations cannot rely exclusively on the nominal exchange rate to improve competitiveness, but have to implement more structural measures. Thus, by fixing the exchange rates, social and economic cohesion is not threatened, at least not in the long run.

Besides, recent EMS experience has shown that it is possible to have a system of almost fixed exchange rates without a large system of income transfers to cushion shocks. The fact that the economies of the EC are becoming more alike decreases the chances of large asymmetric shocks or, in the case of an external shock such as a new oil crisis, makes it possible to act in a more coordinated manner. It should be noted, however, that this is only true of the core Member States of the EMS, because the southern 'cohesion countries' joined the EMS but recently (Spain and Portugal) or are still outside the Exchange Rate Mechanism (Greece). This observation underlines the fact that for countries that are going through an accelerated phase of modernization, exchange rate fixing is a serious policy constraint.

EMPIRICAL RESULTS

The recent German monetary unification gives us a good example of what can happen when two countries, which are not an OCA, form a monetary union. The wages in the peripheral regions (the former GDR) with low productivity increased to the level of the high productivity regions, causing a massive emigration towards the more prosperous regions in the union. Although such a development seems unlikely in a Economic and Monetary Union because of large and persistent cultural differences (both countries in our example had the same cultural backgrounds or at least the same language), this worrisome prospect could be used to argue that Europe needs a system of regional transfers in order either to alleviate massive potential migration or to absorb possible asymmetric shocks that might occur.

Many authors have expressed their concern with respect to the impact of fixed exchange rates and a common currency on regions. E.V. Morgan (1973), for example, stresses the existence of strong rigidities that exist between regions that impede the normal adjustment process via supply and demand. Morgan takes the example of South Wales confronted with a fall in coal sales. A fall in the price of coal is unlikely due to the rigidity of costs, especially the rigidity of wages. So unemployment will ensue, spending power will be reduced, and South Wales will be faced with a decrease in consumption of domestic goods. The existence of rigidities in factor markets, notably wages, will not lead to adjustments via factor flows between regions and hence – according to Morgan – a devaluation might reduce many of the frictions that impede price changes.

The fact that monetary integration between countries or regions with pronounced differences in development could have exactly the reverse effect of monetary integration between countries or regions with a similar development has also been argued by Stahl (1975) by comparing two cases of regional development, West Germany and Italy, in the period 1961-1969. The former stands for a monetary union between homogeneous regions and the latter represents a monetary union with very high levels of disparity. The idea developed by Stahl and Giersch (1965) is that a monetary union will lead to harmonization of wages, through collective bargaining or *de facto*, while regional productivity levels may develop differently. In the case of two relative homogeneous regions, the approximation of wages will not be pronounced or permanent and the positive effects of increased integration (see subsection on allocative efficiency) might increase productivity and compensate for the increase in nominal wages. However, monetary integration between unequal partners should be avoided as the productivity gap cannot be bridged through the positive effects of monetary integration, creating a consistent disparity between regions. Stahl's research has indeed supported this theory as his results show that regional approximation of wages in Italy overcompensated for the regional convergence of productivity; whereas in Germany, unit labour costs hardly increased in the poorer regions. Hence, a system of transfers would be necessary in the Italian case to alleviate the negative consequences of monetary integration. However, this line of thinking hinges upon the important assumption that wages will automatically adjust to the highest level in a monetary union due to the downward rigidities of wages, the power of collective bargaining and the level of social protection. Hence this issue is probably more important in the light of Social Union in Europe and not so much a topic for EMU. If workers in one country know that excessive wage claims will not be bailed out by other countries, the 'wage demonstration' effect is unlikely to take on major proportions.

CONCLUSION

Summarizing the results of this section leads us to conclude that EMU might impose difficulties on the 'cohesion countries'. Although there is no long-term relationship between nominal and real exchange rates, the lagging countries can still use changes in the nominal exchange rates to trigger temporary adjustments. For the core members of the EMS, EMU will impose no problems with respect to the loss of the exchange rate. However, for the recent EMS members, we should not completely rule out the exchange rate as policy instrument because their exchange rates are still in an adjustment phase.

Loss of Fiscal Autonomy

The envisaged EMU Community entails more than just the irrevocable fixing of exchange rates, it also calls for other constraints on national economic policy. Part of these new 'rules of the game' are closely related to pursuing the main objective of the future European Central Bank, i.e. the maintenance of stable prices in the Community. The broad constraints on national (fiscal) economic policy arising from the Maastricht Treaty are basically fourfold:

(1) The formulation of broad guidelines for Community economic policy, as well as the monitoring of national economic performances with a view to achieving closer policy coordination;[22]

(2) The prohibition of access to central bank credit facilities for all public authorities; however, the purchase by the ESCB on its own volition of debt instruments issued by public authorities is allowed;[23]

(3) The avoidance of excessive government deficits, as reflected in the ratio of government deficit to GDP and the ratio of government debt to GDP, possibly leading to sanctions against Member States failing to respect recommendations to this effect;[24]

(4) As for the accession to the third stage of EMU, Member States have to fulfil five criteria two of which are related to the budget.[25] These criteria should, however, not be seen as absolute figures, but should be regarded upon as indicators for making a long-term perspective assessment of the budgetary position of EC Member States. The deficit must in principle not be higher than 3% of GDP, whereas the debt must not exceed 60% of GDP or, if it does, then it must be declining at a 'satisfactory pace'.

It is possible to distinguish a broad range of direct and indirect effects of the loss of macroeconomic flexibility, which are all related to the nominal convergence process that is necessary to fulfil the EMU criteria. In order to structure the analysis, the discussion will be organized around four topics:

– the role of increased policy coordination and cohesion;

– the deflationary bias of the convergence process;

– the necessary restructuring of the national budgets and the impact on national regional policies;

– the loss of inflation tax as a source of revenue for poorer Member States.

THE ROLE OF INCREASED POLICY COORDINATION AND COHESION

In the context of the traditional Mundell-Fleming model of stabilization in an open economy with fixed exchange rates (domestic monetary policies are targeted towards stabilization of the exchange rate and not for domestic stabilization purposes), the effectiveness of fiscal policy increases. In accordance with this theory, one can argue that EMU should always be accompanied by a system providing for EC-wide fiscal policy coordination as an instrument to stabilize income. First of all, symmetric shocks hitting EMU as a whole should be cushioned by the joint efforts of all the States involved and, secondly, as argued by Meade (1990), a unified monetary policy with decentral fiscal policies could be inconsistent. Besides, as mentioned before in this chapter, stable and sustainable growth in the Community, brought about by increased policy coordination, could be beneficial for cohesion.

Hence, although increased policy coordination means a loss of fiscal autonomy, with perhaps political costs for Member States, the effect on cohesion can only be assessed to be positive, to the extent that policy coordination leads to sustainable growth in EMU, promoting cohesion.[26]

THE DEFLATIONARY BIAS OF THE CONVERGENCE PROCESS

As can be inferred from the Maastricht provisions regarding the process towards stage three of EMU, nominal convergence in terms of price inflation has been imposed as a precondition. The experience of the EMS has shown that countries with high inflation rates and loose fiscal policies face considerable costs in the stabilization process of their currencies, as fixed exchange rates could only be sustained by tending to the low (German) inflation rates. Table 2 shows that four of the five 'cohesion countries' (Greece, Portugal, Italy and Spain) are faced with the need to lower their inflation rates and hence to adapt to a rather tight fiscal and monetary policy. In so far as tight macroeconomic policies can influence the growth perspectives of regions, the establishment of EMU and the accompanying process of nominal convergence put these poorer Member States of the Community in a more disadvantageous position. Hence, the deflationary bias of the nominal convergence process would, *ceteris paribus*, temporarily threaten the convergence process. However, this would partially be an unfair judgement of EMU, since the EMS framework will force Spain, Portugal and Greece to lower their inflation rates anyway. Indeed, EMU offers the opportunity to lower the inevitable costs of disinflation.[27]

THE NECESSARY RESTRUCTURING OF THE NATIONAL BUDGETS AND THE IMPACT ON NATIONAL REGIONAL POLICIES

The necessary reduction in public spending and debt in order to stabilize prices and to allow a sound fiscal policy to be maintained has not only well-known macroeconomic implications, but also directly alters the composition of the budget of the Member States. Cutting the deficit implies cutting expenditures or levying taxes. The transition towards EMU has been seized on by many governments as a political argument for large cuts in the public budget. In the

Table 2:
Budget Deficit, Public Debt and Inflation Rates in the EC

Member State	Budget Deficit (% GDP), 1992 est.	Public Debt (% GDP, 1991)	Inflation latest rates (91) in %
B	-6.0	129	2.8
DK	-2.1	67	2.3
D	-3.4	46	4.2
E	-3.9	46	5.6
FR	-2.0	47	3.1
GR	-13.3	96	17.8
IRL	-2.5	103	3.5
I	-9.9	101	6.1
L	+2.6	7	2.6
NL	-4.0	78	4.9
P	-5.4	65	9.6
UK	-5.0	44	4.5

Source: CEC (1991, 1992).

long run, restructuring of national public finance will probably improve the macroeconomic stability of the Member States and hence their growth capabilities but, in the short run, transitory problems are likely. Particularly important in the context of this chapter is the possible influence the restructuring of the budget could have on national regional policies (in terms of budget expenditures). Table 3 shows average expenditure per capita for the period 1975-1983 for some EC Member States.

Table 3:
National Regional Policies: Public Spending per Capita (1987)
In Pounds Sterling/Purchasing Power Parity

Member State	Total Expenditure (million)	Spending/Cap.	
		per capita of the whole population	per capita of the population of the recipient regions
B	71	7	22
DK	7	1	6
D	350	6	20
FR	55	1	3
IRL	124	35	35
I	2404	42	117
NL	50	3	14
UK	602	11	27 [1]

[1] 27 for Great Britain and 56 for Northern Ireland

Source: Yuill, D. et al. 1990.

Ireland and Italy, two of the five 'cohesion countries', have relatively large expenditure on regional policies. We must however note that regional policies consist of more than just subsidies provided by public authorities, and that the indicated data only give a partial view of national regional policy-making. In some countries, regional policies consist largely of subsidies; in other countries, regional policies are more structural supply-side policies consisting of, for example, more tax benefits. Besides, many other policies have regional elements, for instance, technology policy or industrial policy in a broad sense. Perhaps most important of all is the impact of the social security systems and direct taxation, both of which have a clear regional dimension. Not only are regional policies affected, but also other expenditures, such as investments in infrastructure (telecommunication, transport), could be endangered in the 'cohesion countries'.[28] Hence, the transition process of budgetary convergence in particular could threaten, at least in the short run, cohesion among EC regions. The EC structural funds could perhaps provide some opportunities to alleviate these negative consequences on the level of income convergence.

THE LOSS OF INFLATION TAX AS SOURCE OF REVENUE FOR POORER MEMBER STATES

The *One Market, One Money* report identifies the loss of seigniorage as one of the cost elements of the establishment of an Economic and Monetary Union, ranging from 0.21 % of GDP for Italy to 1.13 % of GDP for Greece (as far as the peripheral Member States are concerned).[29] Seigniorage is money creation that can serve as a source of revenue for the government because central bank liabilities are largely non-interest bearing.

In EMU, countries cannot set their inflation rates independently in order to raise revenue by inflation tax. This is not only true of EMU, but also of the EMS. Hence, if a country sets an inflation rate which is incompatible with stable (or fixed) exchange rates, it will be penalized (Grilli, 1991).[30] In EMU these costs will be even higher than in the EMS. However, Grilli (1991) also argues that the existence of unsustainable deficits makes it necessary to find new means of revenue as tax increases become more difficult: 'many economists believe that several of the countries...are not following fiscal policies which are sustainable in the long run. Sooner or later these countries will have to undertake budget adjustments which may well involve resorting to seigniorage revenues.' (Grilli, 1991). Grilli suggests that incompatibility would exist between budget restructuring and the decrease in seigniorage revenues in EMU. It is true that EMU will impose some budgetary constraints on countries with high debt, however it is not likely to lead governments to increase seigniorage revenues. The high-inflation countries in particular (notably the poorer Member States) cannot afford to raise inflation any higher, as this will not only have severe consequences for the EMS but would also affect growth levels (CEC, 1990), which could lead to an increase in disparity levels instead of convergence. Furthermore, the scope for raising seigniorage has already been strongly restricted by the 1992 programme which rules out capital controls.

To conclude, seigniorage is still an important source of revenue for 'cohesion countries' and EMU will cut this means of income. This could lead to some short-run transitional problems, but negative effects on cohesion will probably be moderate and temporary. In the long-run, however, the costs of seigniorage would probably cause an increase in the level of income disparity. Furthermore, revenue from seigniorage can always be replaced by revenue from an explicit tax which is often more efficient and definitely more equitable.

CONCLUSIONS

The four issues taken up in the previous considerations make it possible to extract a conclusion with respect to cohesion and the loss of fiscal flexibility in EMU. The arguments presented try to answer the question: to what extent does the loss of fiscal autonomy constitute a threat to the level of convergence? It is true that the adaptation process which the poorer Member States need to go through imposes a transitory burden on their economies: the necessary nominal convergence and accompanying loss of fiscal policy flexibility, due to the conditions spelled out in the Maastricht Treaty, make it necessary to adjust public finance and thus partly undermine the potential of fiscal policies as a stabilization instrument. As this convergence process is harsher for the 'cohesion countries' (see Table 2), they are probably in a more disadvantageous position. But, in the long run, cohesion probably depends much more on structural adjustments (supply-side) than fiscal policies (demand-side). Curtailing the deficit will probably improve the poorer Member States' macroeconomic stability, fostering growth capacities and hence prospects for increased cohesion in the EC.

Cohesion and Convergence of Monetary Policies

In this light, the issue of the extent to which unification of monetary policies endangers regional development and cohesion has to be addressed: if there is a case for a considerable degree of decentralization of monetary policies in the light of social and economic cohesion, then EMU could have a negative impact on disparity levels.

According to Fleming and Cordon (1971/1972), one monetary policy with one inflation rate will increase unemployment more in the poorer regions. The argument is that each region has its own Phillips curve and exchange rate flexibility (thus different monetary policies) which permit each region or country to select its preferred position on their Phillips curve. In a monetary union, there will only be one inflation rate: the regions suffering from the stronger inflationary pressures (in the EC the 'cohesion countries') will have to pay more in terms increased unemployment, hence monetary union would endanger cohesion.

Two critical remarks should be made with respect to this theory. Firstly, the theory of the Phillips curve is highly disputed: there might be a relationship between unemployment and inflation rates in the short run, but there is no evidence whatsoever that this relationship persists in the long run, to the contrary. Secondly, Williamson (1975) argues that this theory provides no reason for expecting that the peripheral regions will be the ones with the highest unemployment, since the theory does not provide a rationale for assuming that the peripheral regions will be prone to suffer more serious wage pressures than the others.

It has been shown that a positive relationship exists between economic growth and price stability (CEC, 1990). A unified monetary policy through an independent central bank (aiming at price stability) will benefit overall economic growth in the Community. As mentioned before, a positive impact on growth for the EC as a whole is likely to lead to a decrease in regional disparity levels.

This 'triangle' between central bank independence, price stability and economic growth is not only valid for stage three of EMU but also for the transitional period, as the Treaty explicitly asks Member States to adopt legislation leading to increased central bank independence.[31] Especially the 'cohesion countries' score very low on central bank independence. Hence, the 'cohesion countries' in particular will gain relatively more from greater monetary policy credibility associated with central bank independence.

General Conclusion: Implications for EC Cohesion Policy

The second question raised in the introduction to this chapter related to the changes in policy which the Community has to make in order to cope with the impact of EMU on cohesion. Table 4 below summarizes the main conclusions of our analysis of this question.

The overall picture that emerges from the analysis is that whereas the 'cohesion countries' have more 'homework' to do in the transitional period of EMU, they stand to gain relatively the most from this further deepening of the economic integration process. Future Community policies in favour of the 'cohesion countries' should therefore be formulated with these findings in mind.

Table 4:
EMU and Cohesion: The Main Conclusions

	MICRO	MACRO		
	ALLOCATION	LOSS EXCHANGE RATE	LOSS FISCAL POLICY	LOSS MONETARY POLICY
IMPACT ON COHESION	positive if overall growth will decrease disparity levels; regional impact of trade and investments effects of EMU not clear-cut	negative, as 'cohesion countries' do not (yet) witness their equilibrium exchange rate	short-term: negative for some 'cohesion countries', long-term: positive, as sound public finances will probably foster growth	positive, thanks to central bank independence, price stability and growth (for the EC as a whole and for the 'cohesion countries' individually)

NOTES

1. For an extended overview of the literature on the regional impact of the integration process, see for example Norbert Vanhove and Leo H. Klaassen (1987: 230-262).
2. Protocol on economic and social cohesion, Treaty on European Union, *Official Journal* 1992, C 191/93.
3. Art. 130a, Treaty on European Union, *Official Journal* 1992, C 191/26-27.
4. Op. cit. p. 418, Molle (1990a).
5. Also widely used are measures on (un)employment rates.
6. Purchasing Power Standard (PPS), equivalent to Purchasing Power Parity (PPP).
7. One should not confuse correlation with causality: the forces that bring about this correlation remain largely unexplained.
8. CEC, *One Market, One Money*, 1990.
9. Static bank note transaction costs were estimated to lie between 13 and 20 billion ECU (1990 prices), *One Market, One Money*, 1990, p. 65.
10. Nominal exchange rates corrected for inflation differentials.
11. One should note that the neo-classical model of growth, which underlies this reasoning, is based upon the assumption of firms producing one (possibly composite) product with capital and labour under constant returns to scale and perfect competition.
12. Accessibility should be defined as the economic potential of a region. However, the question remains whether accessibility can be used to measure the impact of trade on regions. This is only true if regional development depends on regional accessibility (Bröcker and Peschel, 1988).
13. Also promoting direct investment flows are the provisions on capital liberalization, see new Articles 73b to 73g, Treaty on European Union, *Official Journal* 1992, C 191/8-9.
14. This can probably be attributed to the large borrowing capacity of both economies (Molle and Morsink, 1991).
15. Direct investments tend to flow to those regions with the largest stock of economic capacities. As these are the richer regions, the increase in direct investments to those regions will lead to larger disparities in income (so-called 'backwash effects').
16. For an overview of factors determining investment decisions of firms, see *One Market, One Money*, 1990, chapter 9, pp. 218-219.
17. Heckscher-Olin theorem.
18. An optimum currency area is characterized by (1) similarity in economic shocks hitting the countries or regions and (2) large mobility of labour among the countries or regions.
19. Changes in relative prices between countries or regions can be brought about either through factor movements or through changing the (real) exchange rate.
20. Given that the Marshall-Lerner condition will hold true.
21. The formal expression underlying this line of reasoning: $P=wP + aP^*$, where P, represents the domestic price level and P^* the foreign price level, w the degree

of wage indexation, and a measures the importance of imports for the domestic economy.

22. Art. 103, Treaty on European Union, *Official Journal 1992*, C 191/11-12.
23. Art. 104 and 104a, Treaty on European Union, *Official Journal 1992*, C 191/12.
24. Art. 104c, Treaty on European Union, *Official Journal 1992*, C 191/13.
25. Art. 109j, Treaty on European Union, *Official Journal 1992*, C 191/20.
26. We should note, however, that the whole argument hinges upon the traditional Mundell-Fleming world, which is a stylized model. Other authors have doubts about the positive effects of fiscal policy coordination (Frankel and Rockett, 1988).
27. As a follow-up to the Maastricht Treaty, bond yields of the Southern EC Member States decreased considerably and converged to the German rates. Markets seemed to have discounted the positive impact of EMU on these Member States. However, the troubles about the ratification of the Treaty in Denmark led to exactly the opposite effect, i.e. an increase in divergence between bond yields.
28. Even in the absence of specific regional policies, budget contraction will normally harm poorer regions relatively more.
29. *One Market, One Money* (1990: 120-123).
30. It should be noted that in many EC countries it is not the government but the central bank which has the prime responsibility for price stability. In those countries where the central bank controls inflation (and has as prime objective the stabilization of prices), inflation tax is partly made ineffective as a source of revenue. As this is the case in most core Member States and the poorer Member States have less tradition in central bank independence, EMU will lead anyway lower seigniorage as central banks have to become independent in the process towards stage three of EMU (see also the section on cohesion and convergence of monetary policies).
31. Art. 107 and 108, Treaty on European Union, *Official Journal 1992*, C 191/15.

REFERENCES

'All Saints Manifesto for European Monetary Union', (unsigned), *The Economist*, 1-7 November, 1975.

Bini-Smaghi, L., 'Exchange Rate Variability and Trade Flows', *mimeo*, University of Chicago and Banca d'Italia, 1987.

Boeckhout, I.J. et al., *Developing Prospects of Lagging Regions and Socio-Economic Consequences of the Completion of the Internal Market in the EC* (Rotterdam: NEI 1991).

Borts, G.H.; Stein, J.L., *Economic Growth in a Free Market* (New York: Columbia University Press, 1984).

Bröckler, J.; Peschel, K., 'Trade', in Molle, W., and Cappellin, R., (eds), *Regional Impact of Community Policies* (Aldershot: Avebury, 1988), pp. 127-151.

Cappellin, R.; Molle, W., 'The Co-ordination Problem in Theory and Policy', in Molle, W., and Cappellin, R., (eds), *Regional Impact of Community Policies in Europe* (Aldershot: Avebury, 1988), pp. 1-22.

Commission of the European Communities, 'One Market, One Money, An Evaluation of the Potential Benefits and Costs of an Economic and Monetary Union', *European Economy*, no. 44, 1990.

Commission of the European Communities, *The Regions in the 1990s; Fourth Periodic Report on the Social and Economic Situation and Development of the Regions of the Community* (Luxembourg: 1991).

Commission of the European Communities, Treaty on European Union, *Official Journal* 1992, C 191.

Cordon, W.M., 'Monetary Integration', *Essays in International Finance*, no. 93, Princeton, April 1972.

Eichengreen, B., 'Is Europe an Optimum Currency Area ?', *CEPR Discussion Paper*, no. 478, London, 1990.

European Parliament, 'A New Strategy for Social and Economic Cohesion After 1992', *Regional Policy and Transport Series*, no. 19 (Luxembourg: 1991).

Fleming, J.M., 'On Exchange Rate Unification', *Economic Journal*, September 1971, pp. 467-488.

Frankel, J.A.; Rockett, K.E., 'International Macroeconomic Policy Coordination When Policy-Makers Do Not Agree on the True Model', *The American Economic Review*, vol. 78 (3), pp. 318-339, 1988.

Giersch, H., 'Marktintegration, Wechselkurs und Standortstruktur, fundamentale Fragen künftiger Währungspolitik', *Frankfurter Gespräche der List Gesellschaft*, 1965.

Grilli, V., 'Seigniorage in Europe', in De Cecco, M., and Giovannini, A., (eds), *A European Central Bank? Perspectives on Monetary Unification Ten*

Years After the EMS (Cambridge: Cambridge University Press, 1989), pp. 53-79.

Huijser, A.P.; Stokman, A.C.J., 'Export en Wisselkoersonzekerheid' *Economisch Statistische Berichten*, pp. 1176-1179, 1991.

International Monetary Fund, 'Exchange Rate Variability and World Trade', *Occasional Paper*, no. 28 (Washington DC: IMF, 1984).

International Monetary Fund, *Balance of Payments Statistics*, vol. 41, Yearbook (Washington DC: IMF, 1990).

Keeble, D.; Owens, P.L.; Thompson, C., (KOT), The Influence of Peripheral and Central Locations on the Relative Development of Regions, Final Report, Cambridge, 1981.

Keeble, D.; Owens, P.L.; Thompson, C., (KOT), 'Regional Accessibility and Economic Potential in the European Community', *Regional Studies*, vol. 16, 1982, pp. 419-432.

Meade, J.E., 'The EMU and the Control of Inflation', *Oxford Review of Economic Policy*, vol. 6 (4), pp. 100-107, 1990.

Molle, W.; van Mourik, A., 'International Movements of Labour under Conditions of Economic Integration, The Case of Western Europe', *Journal of Common Market Studies*, vol. 26, pp. 317-342, 1988.

Molle, W., *The Economics of European Integration (Theory, Practice, Policy)* (Aldershot: Dartmouth, 1990a).

Molle, W., 'Will the Completion of the Internal Market Lead to Regional Divergence?', in Siebert, H. (ed.), *The Completion of the Internal Market* (Mohr: Tübingen, 1990b), pp. 174-196.

Morgan, E.V., 'Regional Problems and Common Currencies', *Lloyds Bank Review*, October 1973.

Morsink, R.; Molle, W., 'Direct Investments and Monetary Integration', in Commission of the European Communities, 'The Economics of EMU: Background Studies for European Economy, no. 44, 'One Market, One Money'', *European Economy*, special edition no. 1, 1991.

Mourik, van A., 'Testing Factor Price Equalisation in the EC: An Alternative Approach; a Comment', *Journal of Common Market Studies*, vol. 26, pp. 79-86, 1987.

Mourik, van A., 'Countries; a Neo-Classical Model of International Wage Differentials', in Molle, W., and Mourik, van A., (eds), *Wage Differentials in the European Community; Convergence or Divergence* (Aldershot: 1989), pp. 83-103.

Mundell, R., 'A Theory of Optimum Currency Areas', *American Economic Review*, September 1961, pp. 657-665.

NIESR, *A New Strategy for Social and Economic Cohesion After 1992* (London: 1992).

Padoa-Schioppa, T., *Efficiency, Stability and Equity, a Strategy for the*

Evolution of the Economic System of the European Community, Internal Document (Brussels, 1987).

Perroux, F., 'Note sur la notion de pôle de croissance', *Economie Appliquée*, no. 7, 1955.

Perée, E.; Steinherr, A., 'Exchange Rate Variability and Foreign Trade', *European Economic Review*, no. 33, pp. 1241-1246, 1989.

Peschel, K., 'Auswirkungen der europäischen Integration auf die grossräumige Entwicklung in der Bundesrepublik Deutschland', *Informationen zur Raumentwicklung*, Heft 11/12, 1978, pp. 963-976

Peschel, K.; Haass, J.M.; Schnöring, Th., 'Auswirkungen der europäischen Integration auf die grossräumige Entwicklung in der Bundesrepublik Deutschland', *Schriftenreihe 'Raumordnung' des Bundesministers für Raumordnung, Bauwesen und Städtebau*, Bad Godesberg, 1979.

Peschel K., 'International Trade, Integration and Industrial Location', *Regional Science and Urban Economics*, vol. 12, 1982, pp. 247-269.

Petrochillos, G.A., *Foreign Direct Investment and the Development Process* (Aldershot: Avebury, 1989).

Richardson, H.W., *Regional and Urban Economics* (Harmondsworth: Penguin Books, 1978).

Sapir, A.; Sekkat, K., 'Exchange Rate Variability and International Trade, The Effects of the European Monetary System', *mimeo*, Université Libre de Bruxelles, 1989.

Siebert, H., *Regional Growth Theory: Theory and Policy* (Scranton: International Textbook Company, 1969).

Smith, A.; Venables, A.J., 'Completing the Internal Market in the EC, Some Industry Simulations', *European Economic Review*, vol. 32, pp. 1501-1525, 1988.

Vanheukelen. M., *Cohesion, Convergence and Conditionality: EC Redistributive Policy in the Perspective of EMU*, (Brussels: mimeo), June 1992.

Williamson, J., 'The Implications of European Monetary Integration for the Peripheral Areas', in Vaizey, J. (ed.), *Economic Policy and Regional Policy* (Dublin: Gill and MacMillan, 1975), 1975, pp. 105-121.

Yuill, D. et al., *European Regional Incentives*, 10th edition (London: Bowker Sauer, 1990).

THE IMPACT OF ECONOMIC AND MONETARY UNION ON MEMBER STATES' FISCAL POLICIES

Paul van den Bempt

Introduction

The aim of this chapter is to evaluate the implications of the Maastricht Treaty on the fiscal policies of the EC Member States.

In the first section, an examination will be made of the functions fiscal policy can perform in the chosen institutional arrangement (i.e. EMU), characterized by a fixed exchange rate regime with a common monetary policy conducted by the European System of Central Banks (ESCB) and a fiscal policy essentially left in the hands of the Member States. In the following section, we will analyze the main provisions concerning macroeconomic and budgetary policies as they are laid down in the Maastricht Treaty. In this respect, it should be noted that a distinction has to be made between the role of fiscal policy during the transitional stage two of EMU and the significance of fiscal policy in the final stage three. In the third section, an assessment will be made of the extent to which present national positions in macroeconomic and budgetary policies will have to be altered in order to comply with the criteria conditional for transition to the final stage of EMU. It is clear, in this respect, that compared with the present *status quo* some Member States may face serious problems.

In the light of the Maastricht Treaty, it could be argued that the role of the Community budget ought to be reconsidered because up till now the Community budget, mostly in conjunction with the national budgets, only has a redistributive or allocating function. However, the Community budget as such will, at least in the near future, not be used for stabilization purposes. Whether EMU does represent a case for redefining the function of the EC budget for objectives concerning macroeconomic stabilization, will be the issue in the last section of this chapter.

In all items to be addressed, it seems that the heart of the matter lies in the division of competences and the degree of national autonomy in the area of fiscal policy between the Community and the Member States.

K. Gretschmann (ed.), Economic and Monetary Union: Implications for National Policy-Makers, 245–261.

Constraints on and Leeway for Fiscal Policies in a System of Fixed Exchange Rates

EMU in its provisional shape lays down the following framework in which fiscal policies have to be embedded:

– A regime of fixed exchange rates between the EC Member States (but not *vis-à-vis* third countries) scheduled for stage three. Up to this point, realignments, although political undesirable, are still basically possible.

– A set of macroeconomic and budgetary criteria laid down in the Maastricht Treaty, bearing a major impact on both monetary and fiscal policies in the Member States during the different stages of EMU:

1) in stages one and two, monetary policy will not be centralized, although closer coordination is to be achieved, while national fiscal policies will be subject to some constraints;

2) the aim of monetary and fiscal policies in the transitional period will be to foster and achieve satisfactory economic convergence; the latter will be the prerequisite for a fully fledged EMU;

3) the use of the exchange rate as an instrument of adjustment will become increasingly restricted and will finally disappear, increasing the burden of adjustments on national fiscal policies.

ON THE WAY TO EMU: BETWEEN SHOCK ABSORPTION AND FISCAL CONVERGENCE

It is clear that the role of fiscal policy will become essentially different while proceeding towards the final stage of EMU. Economic theory has taught that if monetary policy cannot be used efficiently as a tool for economic stabilization and adjustment because it is exclusively centred on bringing down inflation to the lowest level possible in the Community, fiscal policy has to take over and thus becomes more important. However, it is subject to some serious limitations.

Firstly, it is evident that the fiscal policy stance of the major Community Member States can have quite substantial external effects on the other members. Hence, the degree of coordination between the actions of these countries has to be advanced as far as possible if divergent developments (e.g. 'beggar-thy-neighbour' policies) are to be avoided in the Community. This is probably not a foregone conclusion as is shown by the consequences of the large increase in the German budgetary deficit in the wake of unification. Since the spill-overs from their fiscal policy measures are less significant, smaller Member States may probably retain more freedom in the use of their fiscal policy, provided they do not jeopardize their chances of achieving convergence. Due to the fact that in the transition period monetary policy will not yet be centralized, we can assume that the asymmetry of the EMS will continue until the beginning of the final stage, with the *Deutsche mark* playing the anchor role. This fact, combined with the need to avoid macroeconomic shock waves being transmitted in the Community, puts severe constraints on the manoeuvrability of the national fiscal policies of the major Community countries.

Secondly, external shocks coming from outside the Community could give rise to different reactions from the individual Member States. If these shocks are symmetric, they will not be detrimental to the convergence achieved by the Member States and mark a clear case for increased fiscal policy coordination. However, if these shocks are asymmetric, Member States will need some freedom to react on an individual basis. The leeway for individual policy-making is restricted by the need for convergence as laid down in the Maastricht Treaty. In order to avoid a situation of conflicting objectives and forthcoming pressures at national as well as at Community level, it is necessary to create a framework incorporating both the possibility of increased coordination of fiscal but also monetary policies between Member States *vis-à-vis* third countries, as well as the possibility of being able to react to specific national disturbances, provided that fiscal policy can serve as first-best solution to these problems. Such a scheme would be better than the present situation in the EMS where the strong position of the *Deutsche mark* and the related influence of the *Deutsche Bundesbank* on other Member States' monetary policies can lead to suboptimal results for individual Member States. This applies not only to the external dimension, as the exchange rates of the European currencies *vis-à-vis* the US dollar and the Japanese Yen are influenced decisively by the *Bundesbank* but also, as already mentioned before, to the internal dimension because the individual national fiscal policies could jeopardize the position of the respective Member State in the EMS.

FISCAL POLICY IN THE FULLY FLEDGED EMU

EMU will not only entail fixing exchange rates but also the introduction of a single currency, probably the ECU. This will have, next to the full liberalization of capital flows in the Community, a strong integrating effect on the European capital markets which will provide the opportunity to fund national budget deficits in the same currency. This means, on the one hand, an increase in the stock of capital within reach for the governments (with perhaps related decrease in interest rates) and a greater transparency of the market for government bonds.

We can also assume that, before becoming members of EMU, countries will have created the necessary conditions to ensure sound public finances. In this respect, it should be noted that EMU does not allow for excessive deficits. Therefore, the Maastricht Treaty has laid down certain devices for preventing Member States from overborrowing. Opinions diverge on how this should be done. Some experts place their confidence in market forces, assuming that supposedly lax budgetary policies will be 'punished' by the financial markets via higher interest rates, reflecting increased risk premiums. Others are of the opinion that markets are not able to impose such restraints.

There can be no doubt, however, that significant deterioration in budgetary stance in individual Member States cannot be tolerated for longer periods, due to the risk of raising nominal and real interest rates throughout the Community, thereby crowding out investment and reducing economic growth. The budgetary position of a country is closely related to its fiscal policy and budget deficits could be considered as attempts to practice 'beggar-thy-neighbour' or 'free-rider' policies. However, one cannot, of course, completely rule out the necessity to alter the budget in the pursuit of a fiscal policy responding to shocks in the short term. Nonetheless, the imperative of coordinating these actions will be strong because of the degree of convergence required in the second stage and the third stage of EMU.

The Provisions of the Maastricht Treaty with Respect to Fiscal and Budgetary Policies

Given the requirements which EMU imposes on fiscal and budgetary policies, we will first review the provisions laid down in the Maastricht Treaty regulating fiscal and budgetary policy, in order to be able to make a final assessment of the provisions of the Maastricht Treaty with respect to position of the Community and the Member States. These provisions have been tailored in accordance with the imperatives upon budgetary and fiscal policy in each stage of EMU and a short comment on the substance of the stages and the criteria used to trigger the transition from the one stage to the next should be helpful to obtain a correct understanding of the intentions implicit in the Treaty.

THE TRANSITION TO EMU

EMU has been devised as a three-tiered undertaking. Stage one started already on 1 July 1990. Its primary objectives have been to consolidate progress already made within the EMS with regard to economic convergence and exchange rate stability, to secure the implementation of a genuine internal market and effective freedom of movement of factors of production, as well as to organize an intergovernmental conference in 1991 preparing EMU. In order to support these objectives, some new Community legislation on the coordination of economic policies entered into force in parallel.

The transition to stage two is to start on 1 January 1994. It will be automatic, although the Council will make an assessment; firstly, of the progress made in economic convergence, notably with regard to price stability and public finance and, secondly, of the implementation of the directives concerning the single European market. Stage two will be a crucial one, since it should promote satisfactory convergence of the national economies of the Member States which is necessary for promoting the passage to the next and final stage. From the institutional point of view, this stage introduces a series of institutional innovations, not only in the field of fiscal and budgetary policy, but also in the area of monetary policy as evidenced by the proposed setting up of a European Monetary Institute. The major tasks it has been assigned are to lay down the groundwork for establishing the ECB, promote the strengthening of the exchange rate mechanism of the EMS and the use of the ECU, and to monitor the changes in national central bank statutes in order to make all central banks independent.

Stage three is the final one, starting with the creation of the European System of Central Banks, the irreversible interlocking of intra-Community parities of the currencies of the Member States and, finally, the introduction of a single currency, probably the ECU. The procedure to be set in motion for the transition to the final stage is a complex one and the following explanation does not enter into its various aspects in detail. In the first place, the Treaty specifies that member countries can only participate in the final stage if they satisfy certain economic convergence criteria. The position of the Member States will be judged by the Commission authorities on the basis of four criteria:

– the absence of excessive deficit (the deficit must not exceed 3% of GDP and the debt-to-GDP ratio must not be higher than 60%);

– a sufficient degree of price stability, i.e. inflation rate in the country concerned should not be higher than 1.5 percentage points than the average of the three best performing countries in terms of price stability;

– nominal long-term interest rates should not be higher than 2 percentage points of the three best performing countries in terms of price stability;

– observance of exchange rate stability, that is the Member State's currency should be in the narrow band of the exchange rate mechanism of the EMS during the two years preceding the transition to the final stage.

On the basis of these criteria, the Community institutions will make an assessment of the economic performance of each Member State in order to determine whether there is an adequate majority of Member States (and which ones) ready for entering stage three on 1 January 1997 (at present that has to be seven Member States). Before the end of 1996, the Heads of State and Government will decide by qualified majority whether stage three is to start in 1997, following recommendations of ECOFIN, based on a report from the Commission and the European Monetary Institute on the conformity of Member States with the convergence criteria.

If no majority of Member States can enter EMU, the next attempt to start the final stage will be much easier. The Council must apply the procedure mentioned above every two years at least and, in any event, the last stage of EMU starts for those countries satisfying the convergence criteria at the latest on 1 January 1999, whether they are a majority or not. The Member States that do not satisfy the criteria will have a special status as 'Member State with a derogation', which leaves them out temporarily but also deprives them from participation in certain decisions (e.g. those to be taken by the ECB Governing Council). In this respect, the United Kingdom has a special status: it is not compelled to participate in the third stage even if it complies with the convergence criteria, but it can apply for membership at any time, subject to scrutiny by the competent Community bodies. These procedures apply three principles agreed during the negotiations: the obligation to participate (except for the UK), no right of veto against EMU, and no discrimination between Community countries. It should be noted that in all cases decisions related to EMU membership are taken according to the agreed Community procedures (qualified majority voting) and not through intergovernmental cooperation.

GENERAL PROVISIONS WITH RESPECT TO MACROECONOMIC POLICY

Macroeconomic policy-making should take place in an environment where monetary policy is centralized at Community level and Member States have the actual power to take decisions in the field of fiscal and budgetary policies, of course in conformity with predetermined Community rules or plans. These may involve common actions but at present they are principally aimed at achieving convergence of economic performance.

In the first stage, the coordination of economic policies has already been reinforced by the adoption of a procedure on broad guidelines containing confidential recommendations. Multilateral surveillance of national economic policies has been organized to check whether these policies are consistent with the recommendations and do not endanger the correct functioning of EMU. If Member States' policies do not allow the goals set by the Community to be achieved, special recommendations may be addressed to them. At present, the only sanction, in case of a dissenting Member State, would be the publication of these recommendations. Member States have also been invited to draw up so-called 'convergence programmes', which should outline how their economic policies are designed to meet the convergence criteria. The European Parliament is kept informed about economic policy in general and the results of multilateral surveillance and may question the President of the Council on these matters.

These procedures are also applied in stage two. It is evident that the scrutiny of national economic policies will become closer as the possible starting date of stage three approaches and the need the comply with the convergence criteria increases.

With respect to stage three, the same mechanisms continue to be applied.

However, the need to use them will probably decline as, on the one hand, the economic situation of each participating Member State is deemed to be satisfactory almost by definition by then and, on the other hand, no new (more compelling) provisions enter into force except with regard to budget discipline.

PROVISIONS ON FISCAL AND BUDGETARY POLICIES

Whereas prescriptions concerning macroeconomic policy are worded in very general terms and may even seem to be rather loose, the provisions on fiscal and budgetary policies are much more precise and even open up the possibility of severe sanctions, at least in the final stage. Three main provisions can be distinguished:

1. Constraints on Monetary Financing of National Budgets. In EMU the funding of national budgets should be organized in such a way that the inflationary impact is minimized and should not be at cross purposes with the policy of the European Central Bank which aims at price stability throughout the Community. As a consequence, Member States must:
– abolish any forms of monetary financing of public deficits, notably via credit facilities or direct purchase by the central banks of instruments of public debt being issued; this rule applies to national central banks as well as to the ECB;
– abolish privileged access by public authorities to financial instruments and markets;
– leave the responsibility for the public deficit up to the Member State, with no bailing-out obligations for others;
These prescriptions apply to the entire public sector and, at the latest, from the start of the second stage (1 January 1994).

2. Rules of Conduct for Budget Deficits. The Treaty imposes on Member States an overall rule of behaviour for budget discipline and avoidance of excessive deficits. Application of this rule is already recommended in the first stage of EMU, a logical precaution as, on transition to the second stage, Member States are expected to have orderly public finances even if this is not an obligatory condition.

3. Excessive Deficit Procedure. In order to avoid excessive deficit, the public finances of each country are constantly reviewed by the Commission and reference can be made to quantified criteria as described in the Protocol to the Treaty. A special procedure of mutual surveillance is applied which can lead, at least in the final stage, to the application of sanctions if the Member State does not comply with the recommendations addressed to it by the Council.

Excessive deficits are defined as a state of affairs that can be officially declared by the Council on the basis of a Commission report if and when a Member State does not comply with the following criteria:

– a ratio of actual government deficit to gross domestic product of 3 per cent;

– a ratio of government debt of 60 per cent to gross domestic product.

The Commission will have to interpret these figures taking into consideration the dynamics of these criteria, i.e. it will observe whether countries with higher figures make substantial progress in the direction of the values attached and it will of course recommend remedial action if the situation is deteriorating. The definition of government in this context is taken in the widest sense, i.e. it includes national, regional, local government and social security authorities. The criteria serve as a trigger mechanism which may prompt the Commission to hear the Monetary Committee. Having heard the opinion of the Monetary Committee, the Commission will decide independently whether it is necessary to submit to the Council an opinion stating that there is a risk of an excessive deficit in the country concerned.

As a follow-up, a complex procedure of multilateral surveillance could be started in which the Council, after an overall assessment that a particular Member State has an excessive deficit, may act by qualified majority. This procedure could eventually lead to a formal recommendation by the Council, to be made public if the Member State does not take any measures to curtail the deficit (which is in fact not different from the surveillance procedures in stage one and two described above). From the third stage onwards, positive sanctions may also be taken if the Member State does not comply. This mechanism will not be applied to those Member states which have a derogation or, for that matter, the UK. It can be applied to all the EMU members if they fail to put into practice the recommendations of the Council which will henceforth become a Council decision. Four types of sanctions can be taken:

– an obligation imposed on the Member state to publish additional information on the state of its finances when it wants access to the financial markets;

– a recommendation addressed to the European Investment Bank to revise its lending policy *vis-à-vis* this member country;

– the imposition of fines;

– constitution of non-interest bearing deposits.

The Provisions of the Maastricht Treaty and their Implications for National Budgetary and Fiscal Policies

The EMU Treaty definitely imposes a system of fixed internal exchange rates on the Community Member States. Following the rules established for the transition to the third stage, changes in parities would still be basically possible until at least the end of 1996. This possibility may however simply be a theoretical one (except perhaps for countries with derogation) as a devaluation would undermine the credibility of the country's monetary policy and could have long-lasting adverse consequences for it in terms of inflation, especially in a Community committed to price stability. This may explain (and possibly justify) the insistence in the Maastricht Treaty on budgetary discipline.

Several types of fiscal action are indeed inappropriate in the framework drawn up for EMU. For example, in the not too distant past, some countries tried to relieve their unemployment problems by making recourse to expansionary expenditure policies and doing so without consulting the partner countries. In France, in 1981-1982, such a policy immediately led to an upward jump in the budget deficit, a sizeable deterioration in the balance of payments, accelerated inflation, a large loss in reserves and, finally, to successive (small) devaluations of the French franc in May 1983. In the run-up to the third stage of EMU, before parities have been irreversibly fixed, a massive deterioration in the budget balance of a major Community country could create credibility problems and trigger speculation against that country's currency. Without monetary accommodation, a sizeable increase in the budget deficit would raise nominal interest rates attracting capital from abroad. This could be a compensatory factor and prevent a deterioration in the overall balance of payments, but this would only hold if confidence in the currency could be maintained.

A deterioration in the budget balance due to cyclical factors would not have such an effect since we may suppose that it would be correctly interpreted by the market and also because there is a strong possibility that a recession would affect the entire Community more or less simultaneously. Joint action against such a development, if undertaken, would prevent divergencies in the balance of payments of the various countries. In fact, the assessment of 'budget discipline' will have to be undertaken in a medium-term perspective and on the basis of budget balances corrected for cyclical factors (both the Commission and the OECD Secretariat have undertaken and published studies on methods to be used for this purpose).

The problem of excessive deficits seems even more tricky after the third stage has been entered. Given the liberalization of capital movements and the full integration of capital markets which will take place when a single currency is created, a heavy deficit in a major country is likely to raise nominal and eventually real interest rates in the entire Community, creating the danger of crowding out.

As already mentioned, opinions differ on the strategy to adopt in such a case: some think that the market will apply suitable sanctions (no funds will be lent or interest rates will become prohibitive, the example usually quoted being the failure of New York State); others believe that action by the Community is necessary. The Maastricht Treaty more or less tries to support both approaches. On the one hand, as already explained, monetary financing by central banks is forbidden, as is bailing out by one or more member countries (except in the context of a Community corrective action), and governments have no privileged access to financial markets. On the other hand, sanctions can be imposed (see above) if the country, having received a recommendation from the Council, fails to take the necessary steps.

It should be mentioned in passing that there is no guarantee in the Maastricht Treaty, except perhaps mutual surveillance correctly implemented, against 'too virtuous' fiscal policies being applied by a major country which would impart a deflationary bias to the Community economy. This fear was in certain minds over fiscal policy in Germany, but events have proved that a rather opposite course is being taken. Anyway, it has not been proved that budgetary restraint is by necessity deflationary: it may slow down economic growth in the short term, but ensure faster growth in the medium term if it contributes to the correction of imbalances.

BUDGETARY PROBLEMS IN SPECIFIC MEMBER STATES

This leads us to examine the cases of Italy, Belgium and Greece, where budget discipline is insufficient and the criteria mentioned in the relevant protocol may prove difficult to achieve by 1997, and the cases of The Netherlands and Ireland, which seem to have fewer problems in promoting convergence.

As evidenced by Table 1, five countries may be compelled to make constant efforts to meet the criteria relating to excessive deficits as their position in 1991 was well above the relevant figures (3% of GDP for the deficit and 60% of GDP for the gross public debt). The evolution during the last ten years shown by the Table gives us some insight into the causes for the present situation and some indications as to future developments and problems.

To sum up, Ireland and especially The Netherlands are mild cases to cure, Belgium and Italy serious cases and Greece very serious. The core explanation of this diagnosis rests not only on the level of public debt but also on the size of the related unavoidable interest payments and the so-called 'snowballing effect' which has already taken place and may be triggered off again at any time. According to a well-known arithmetic rule, if the effective average interest rate on the public debt is higher than the rate of increase of nominal GDP, the public debt will automatically increase due to interest payments (at a rate which is the

Table 1:
Borrowing Requirement, Public Debt and Other Budgetary Indicators
as a % of gross domestic product

	1981					
	B	**GR**	**IRL**	**I**	**NL**	**EC**
Net borrowing	12.8	11.0	13.4	11.4	5.5	5.3
Interest payments	8.0	3.2	7.4	6.2	4.4	3.7
Primary surplus	-4.8	-7.8	-6.0	-5.3	-1.0	-1.6
Public debt	89.7	34.2	79.8	59.9	50.3	45.5
Current revenue	44.7	28.8	38.4	34.3	54.0	41.8
Total expenditure	57.5	39.9	51.8	45.8	59.5	47.1
Effective interest rate on public debt	9.6	10.2	9.6	10.5	9.2	8.4
	1991					
Net borrowing	6.4	17.9	4.1	9.9	4.4	4.1
Interest payments	10.9	13.2	8.3	10.2	5.9	5.0
Primary surplus	4.5	-4.6	4.2	0.3	3.1	0.9
Public debt	129.4	96.4	102.8	101.2	78.4	60.3
Current revenue	44.5	35.1	40.4	42.6	51.8	43.3
Total expenditure	50.9	53.0	44.5	53.7	56.6	47.4
Effective interest rate on public debt	8.5	13.9	8.1	10.2	7.5	8.3

Source: CEC (1991).
Notes: EC = Community average : in the second box data refer to 1990; interest rate
         calculated by dividing interest payments by average gross public debt.

difference of the two rates divided by one plus the rate of increase of GDP and multiplied by the ratio of public debt to GDP). An increase in the public debt (always quoted as a percentage of GDP) will only be avoided if the primary budget balance (the deficit minus interest payments) is increased accordingly. In the more distant past (e.g. in the seventies) such problems were 'solved' via inflation, often leading to negative real interest rates. It is more than obvious that 'solutions' of this kind cannot be applied in the EMS and EMU or only maybe by countries that stay out for quite some time and provided that economic agents behave irrationally. The chances of a successful redress in this field therefore depend, among other things on a) the level of public debt, b) progress already made, c) the preparedness to reduce expenditure (or alteratively to raise taxes) and, d) future developments in interest rates, inflation and real growth.

In *Belgium*, very substantial progress was made between 1981 and 1988 in reducing the budget deficit (it was actually halved from 12.8% of GDP) while at the end of this period the ratio of public debt to GDP started to decline slowly. This progress was due to severe cuts in non-interest expenditure leading to a sizeable primary surplus. The deceleration of economic growth, with long term interest rates staying high despite the decline in inflation, led to a renewed (small) increase in the public debt. The government's target is to bring down the deficit from its present level (close to 6.5%) to the 3 per cent region in 1996. If nominal interest rates remain at their present level and since nominal growth exceeding 6 to 7 per cent seems unlikely, a primary surplus of some 4.5 per cent of GDP (the 1991 level) would only slightly overcompensate for the expansionary effect on public debt. If the government succeeds in reducing the overall deficit to 3 per cent of GDP in 1996-1998, which would raise the primary surplus, a more substantial decline in the debt rates could be expected. This task seems difficult to achieve and, even in this case, only one of the two criteria would be met.

The position of *Italy* looks worse. True, the level of public debt is lower than in Belgium, but the budget deficit is much higher and virtually made no improvement in the eighties; there is also no primary surplus. Interest rates are higher than in Belgium and inflation is even further above that of Belgium, which in a sense relieves the Italian budgetary position somewhat. Nevertheless, the expectation is that nominal growth will remain below the effective interest rate in the near future, so that the necessity of creating a very substantial primary surplus, already implied in the budgetary target for 1996 (1998) with a reduction of 6 percentage points is the more pressing. If inflation accelerated in Italy (an unlikely development in Belgium), the task would be easier, but would put the country in a different league from the point of view of the foreign exchanges.

The position of *Greece* does not need much comment: public expenditure literally exploded in the eighties (from 40% of GDP in 1981 to 55% in 1990 with a deficit rising to 20% of GDP!). Greece is presently benefiting from Community assistance, subject to severe economic conditions. Even if the positive results, which have begun to materialize, become more substantial, the high level of public debt (now near 100% of GDP) is a severe handicap. Continued strong inflation will probably alleviate the debt problem but, for several reasons, this excludes Greece for a considerable time span from the inner circle.

In *Ireland* the position looks somewhat troublesome but only from the point of view of the public debt. Thanks to severe curtailments in public expenditure and strong growth in 1987-1990, the debt level has already fallen from 122 per cent in 1987 to below 100 per cent. This reduction is expected to continue and, in view of this, it should not be too difficult for the Irish authorities, barring a prolonged recession, to reduce the budget deficit further between now and 1996.

The budgetary situation in *The Netherlands* appears to be manageable and it should be possible to attain the budget norm in 1996, considering the intentions of the Dutch authorities in this field. The debt ratio is lower than in the countries mentioned above (less than 80%), effective interest rates are also much lower, a primary surplus has appeared since 1988 and is rising slowly and total expenditure continues to decline as a percentage of GDP.

Other countries of the Community find themselves in a more comfortable position and should easily satisfy the criteria. One exception might be Germany, because of the heavy burden imposed by the transfers to the East German *Länder*. The deficit might be high in the next few years (4 to 5%), but it is to be expected that the German authorities will want to reduce it substantially before 1996.

National Budgets and the Community Budget

The constraints imposed on national fiscal policies by the Maastricht Treaty are, as can be inferred from the previous sections, rather global. They leave intact the choice of national parliaments and governments to determine the composition of public expenditure and revenue and its level, as long as the budget balance and its financing conform with the rules explained in the section on 'The Provisions of the Maastricht Treaty with Respect to Economic and Budgetary Policy'. However, current developments in the area of the Community budget and Community policies, partly as a consequence of the Maastricht Treaty, give rise to a few exceptions to this principle.

Firstly, the harmonization of indirect taxes introduces some rigidity in public revenue, to the extent that its rates have to be fixed within certain limits. After protracted negotiations, the Council decided in June and December 1991 to fix minimum standards for VAT and minimum rates for excise duties. The provisional regime still allows for some flexibility, but a definitive regime is expected to come into force in 1997.

Secondly, the Community imposes some constraints in the area of common policies. Some are wholly financed via the Community budget, such as the common agricultural policy or external policy, while other policies are co-financed by the Community and the Member States, e.g. structural policies and technology policy. The Maastricht Treaty introduces some new policies, notably the creation of a so-called 'Cohesion Fund'. This is to be financed by the Community budget for countries with a per capita GNP of less than 90 per cent of the Community average and is to be used for investment in environment and trans-European networks. In addition, it is expected that the application of the Treaty, in its foreign policy component and taking account of developments in Eastern Europe, will give rise to higher expenditure on foreign assistance.

In view of this, and due to the fact that new financial perspectives had to be established for 1993-1997, the Commission proposed a new budgetary framework known as 'Delors II', which has the following characteristics:

– the various expenditure categories are planned to develop according to Table 2 below; the relative share of the common agricultural policy is further reduced (specific limit, i.e. no increase higher than 74% of GNP growth is being maintained) whilst that of structural operations (structural funds and cohesion fund) increases and expenditure on R&D and external action also rises;

– in order to meet new demands, the Commission proposes to raise the total of the general budget to 1.37 per cent of GNP by 1997; the relevant VAT rate is to be reduced to 1 per cent, the VAT base would be capped at 50 per cent of GNP for all countries and the GNP-related contribution would continue to make up the difference.

The 'Delors II' package seeks to enhance the redistribution effect of the EC budget on the receipts as well as the expenditure side. It will strike the reader that this redistribution takes place at the state or regional level and not at the interpersonal level, as is the case in federal or unitary states.

The present and future situation of the Community budget in comparison with the public finances of the Member States gives rise to the following comments:

– the total volume of the Community budget will probably not exceed 1.4 per cent of Community GDP in the next few years, even if this does not live up to the Commission's expectations. This is to be assessed against budgets of 45 to 50 per cent of GDP for most Member States. It is obvious that the Community budget cannot substitute for Member States' own 'stabilization policies' except when it contributes directly and considerably to individual (smaller) Member countries. In this context, it is important to note that Ireland, Greece and Portugal are already benefitting from very substantial net transfers (up to 5% of their GDP) from the Community budget.

– due to the differentiating effect of the various expenditure and revenue mechanisms, the impact on the balance of payments (or public finances) of the individual Member States diverges markedly, which is of course a positive and, to some extent, a deliberate move when it is in favour of a less prosperous country and to the detriment of a more wealthy country, but this is not always the case. At present, Germany is by far the largest contributor, followed by France, the UK and, to a much smaller extent, Italy. Belgium is more or less in balance, but Denmark and The Netherlands are net receivers, the former to the tune of more than ECU 400 million. The new proposals of the Commission would raise Italy's net payments very substantially and also those of Denmark, Belgium and The Netherlands. This has become a source of dispute with most of these countries arguing that this development is contradictory to their obligation to reduce their deficit for the final stage of EMU.

   – as can be seen from Table 2 below, the Community budget covers a very narrow range of activities compared with national budgets, 80 per cent of total expenditure being devoted to agriculture and regional policy. An additional leverage effect is given by the loan activities of the European Investment Bank and various smaller funds administered by the Commission. Besides, the main function of the Community budget is still an allocative one, even in the framework of regional policy, where the principal aim is to improve the infrastructure and to stimulate investment.

Table 2:
Financial Perspectives: Commitment Appropriations (billions ECU 1992)

	1987	1992	1997
I Common agricultural policy	32.7	35.3	39.6
II Structural operations	9.1	18.6	29.3
III Internal policies	1.9	4	6.9
IV External action	1.4	3.6	6.3
V Administrative expenditure	5.9	4	4
VI Reserves	0	1	1.4
TOTAL	51	66.5	87.5

Source: CEC (1992).

One major issue is to determine whether action should be undertaken preferably at the Community level (trans-European infrastructure networks are a good example) and the extent to which it substitutes for expenditure on national level. In the final analysis, the answer to these questions will determine the volume of the Community budget and the degree to which it complements national budgets. Moreover, as long as the Community budget, due to its size, cannot fulfil the task of a macroeconomic stabilizer, national budgetary and fiscal policies still require considerable national leeway.

Concluding Remarks

Fiscal policy will no doubt have an important role to play in the construction of EMU, particularly in the transitional stages in order to promote convergence and to ensure the stability of the Union. Once the final phase is reached, member countries will have a greater degree of autonomy, provided sound public finances are maintained.

The framework established by the Maastricht Treaty is not flawless in this respect. One can regret, more and more so as the final stage becomes nearer, the opposition between a largely centralized monetary policy and the decentralized approach of economic and budgetary policy. The success of the transitional stages will largely depend on the strength with which the Council applies the criteria regarding budget discipline and on the willingness of the member countries to comply with this discipline. An improvement in the present German budgetary position will be crucial to provide a stabilizing force.

BIBLIOGRAPHY

Commission of the European Communities, 'Intergovernmental Conferences: Contributions by the Commission', *Bulletin of the European Communities*, Supplement 2/91 (Luxembourg: Office of Official Publications of the EC (OOPEC), 1991).

Commission of the European Communities, 'One Market, One Money', *European Economy*, no. 44 (Luxembourg: OOPEC, 1990).

Commission of the European Communities, 'Annual Economic Report 1991-1992', *European Economy* no. 50, December 1991.

Commission of the European Communities, 'The Economics of EMU', Special edition, no. 1, *European Economy* no. 44 (Luxembourg: OOPEC, 1991).

Commission of the European Communities, 'The Community's Finances between Now and 1997', *Communication from the Commission to the Council and Parliament*, (COM(92) 2001 final), Brussels, 10 March 1992.

Committee for the Study of Economic and Monetary Union, *Report on Economic and Monetary Union in the European Community* (Luxembourg: OOPEC, 1989).

Europe Documents, no. 1759/60, 'Text of the Treaty on European Union', *Agence Europe*, Brussels, February 1992.

Paul de Grauwe et al, *De Europese Monetaire Integratie: vier visies* (The Hague: Wetenschappelijke Raad voor Regeringsbeleid, 1989).

Elena Flores and Peter Zangl, 'La structure financière de la Communauté face aux défis présents et futurs', *EUI working paper*, EPU no. 91/9 (Florence: European University Institute, 1991).

Alexandre Lamfalussy, 'Macro-Economic Coordination of Fiscal Policies', in Committee for the Study of Economic and Monetary Union, *Report on Economic and Monetary Union in the European Community* (Luxembourg: OOPEC, 1989).

Tommaso Padoa-Schioppa et al, *Efficiency Stability and Equity* (Oxford: Oxford University Press, 1987).

Paul van den Bempt, 'Quelle politique budgétaire pour l'Europe?', *'de Pecunia'*, revue du CEPIME, vol. II, no. 2-3 1990.

Paul van den Bempt, 'National Fiscal Policies in an Economic and Monetary Union', *European Business Journal*, London, 1991.

CONCLUSION

BY WAY OF CONCLUSION:
WILL POLICY-MAKERS BE EMUSED?

Klaus Gretschmann

The leeway for *national* economic policy-making has narrowed down considerably over the past decade because market forces and capital mobility have made many policy measures largely inefficient. This holds true – with some modification – both for all EC Member States and for all kinds of sectorial policies, not least, however, for monetary policy in Europe. Concerning the latter, the *Bundesbank* sets the pace and course, and the monetary authorities of the other Member States have to follow suit, in order to avoid unpleasant economic consequences resulting from 'deviant' behaviour and the financial markets' reaction to such.

EMU will bring about a change in this *political* asymmetry and it will open up new options and extended leeway for a less Germanic and more European monetary policy. Whether Europe will benefit *economically* from such a regime switch, is very much contested. Some policy-makers in the monetary arena are afraid that such a European monetary policy will be – due to the soft-currency countries' political preferences – laxer and less stability-oriented than today's. Others are concerned that there might be too heavy a deflationary bias due to the convergence criteria which every country wanting to be eligible for EMU is required to fulfil. Some critics maintain that both tendencies might complement each other: during the transitional phase to EMU, deflation may reign in some (overindebted) countries, whereas in a fully-fledged EMU, inflationary tendencies may prevail. Be that as it may, in both cases, national economic policy-makers will be faced with the need to take action: they will either have to counter deflation by setting growth incentives, or neutralize the propellants of inflation by incomes policies and budget constraints.

Since, in an EMU, the exchange-rate instrument is no longer at the disposal of national economic agents, and monetary policy is centralized in a genuine supranational institution, the European Central Bank, there will be a strong need for increased flexibility and for a more significant role for national fiscal policies. However, even fiscal policy is in chains: firstly, EMU involves strict criteria on national debt and fiscal deficits which limit any enhanced role for

K. Gretschmann (ed.), Economic and Monetary Union: Implications for National Policy-Makers, 265–281.
© 1993 *European Institute of Public Administration. Printed in the Netherlands.*

budgetary action. Secondly, national tax policies are also restricted by EC tax harmonization and coordination for more allocative efficiency. Therefore, there will be high hurdles for national tax and budget authorities.

Difficulties may arise against this background in finding the right policy mix (monetary, fiscal, incomes policies) and in coordinating these policies for 12 national economies which differ greatly in size, structure, level of development and economic potential. Policy mix and policy coordination, however, will gain in significance if asymmetric macroeconomic shocks (hitting the Member States to a varying extent) cannot be excluded. Since monetary policy is centralized and fiscal policies restricted, the only national tools which remain are labour-market and incomes policies. The deployment of these is, however, extremely difficult and conflictive, and warrants the inclusion and consensus of all relevant national actors (unions, employers associations, regional authorities, etc.). Since labour-market and incomes policies cause considerable externalities in a single European market, the situation for national policy-makers, which have to take into account such spillovers, will become much more complex. At the same time, individual economic agents as well as weaker Member States will call for a European system of fiscal support, fiscal equalization and federal transfers in order to absorb macro-shocks. This may soon translate into demands for a fully-fledged system of fiscal federalism in the EC, which will make the setting-up of new institutions necessary. These institutions will represent new players in the arena of European economic policy-making and the increase in the number of those involved will make coordination more difficult. However, these new institutions may attach more weight to a centralized European fiscal policy as a counterpart to centralized monetary policy, with the consequence that a Fiscal Union may be the 'national' complement to an EMU.

In this *'Eigendynamik'* of integration, the EC policy-makers are faced with just two choices: either be merely the willingless objects of such structural developments, or actively give this process shape and form. In both cases, they will be confronted in the years to come with increased demands, less national leeway, more coordination and cooperation requirements, more complex tasks, new institutional structures, etc. Whether, in the face of all this, they will be EMUsed or EMUted, remains to be seen.

In what follows, we will analyze in some detail some of the elements of the scenario described above.

Riding High on Inflation ...

In spite of the fact, that many EC Member States have proven their general commitment to monetary stability in the framework of the European Monetary System (EMS), a standard argument against EMU and in favour of more national monetary sovereignty claims that once EMU is in place, on-average anti-inflation performance in the EC will be considerably lower than it is under present EMS rules. Since, in EMS, the *Bundesbank* sets the admitted rate of inflation, and since the ERM translates these into Member States' monetary policies, the *Bundesbank*'s strict anti-inflationary stance guarantees a high rate of stability also in the other countries which are less averse to inflation.

The willingness and motivation to 'join the club' and give up national sovereignty in monetary affairs can be ascribed partly to a cooperative spirit within the Community. Standard economic theory suggests that independent monetary policy leads to suboptimal outcomes due to externalities from individual one-sided action. Coordination, so the argument goes, can achieve much better results. *Bundesbank*-'enforced' cooperation is considered to be conducive primarily to price stability but in the long run also to growth and employment in Europe. Another proposition suggests that willingness to accept losses in national sovereignty results from potential political benefits of self-binding elements in the EMS. National monetary authorities swap portions of their autonomy for import of stability by shadowing *Bundesbank* policies. Such behaviour helps national policy-makers fend off interest-group claims for more relaxed monetary and economic policies. They can and indeed do point to the fact that despite their (alleged) willingness to correspond to such suggestions, 'unfortunately' they are unable to do so because of international ties and their embeddedness in EC monetary arrangements. Therefore they maintain not to have a choice.

Yet, admittedly, national monetary policy-makers do not always represent anti-inflation protagonists which can use EC-imposed discipline to better implement their stability policies. For many countries and in quite a few cases, there are also incentives for accepting higher rates of inflation than the *Bundesbank*-dominated EMS admits.

Incentives for inflation in national economies come from various sources, the most important of which are (1) political pressure for accommodating expansive fiscal policies during recessions, for structural adjustment or for coping with demographic shifts (Gretschmann, 1991) and (2) the opportunity to generate government revenue by attenuating the real value of government debt and deficits. As the literature on inflation tax (Mankiw, 1987) has taught us conclusively, inflation can be used as part of a nation's tax system. Although it may not be considered an optimal instrument, in a world of second best, it may have some appeal (Fratianni, v. Hagen, 1992, pp. 165): the larger the costs of 'normal' tax collection, the stronger the tax resistance and evasion, the lower the money velocity and the higher a country's debt/GDP ratio, the more tempting it is for a country to have a high inflation tax and reap seigniorage revenues.

In an EMU, only one inflation rate for the whole Union can be fixed; variability across national inflation tax rates is no longer possible. At the same time delegates of each Member State on the ECB Board represent different combinations of the abovementioned factors, and, hence, they have different preferences about how much inflation should be admitted. Since the future ECB, according to the statutes laid down in the Protocol to the Maastricht Treaty, is basically designed as a 'one man one vote' institution (Article 10.2 of the Protocol on ECB), every Member State has one vote and this does not take into consideration a country's economic strength or monetary significance. Under a simple majority rule, watered-down compromises will be the probable outcome of decisions on the adequate Community inflation rate.

Moreover, another mechanism – currency competition – which prevails in a system of several national currencies and which entails an automatic tendency to curb inflation, will get lost in an EMU. Under currency competition, a high inflation rate in a country may be detrimental because this will prompt private agents to restructure their portfolios and increase the share of assets they will wish to hold, denominated in low inflation currencies. The resulting shifts in the demand for different currencies diminish the inflation-prone Central Bank's ability to reap seigniorage revenues. Equilibrium is reached when the loss through currency competition outweighs the gains from inflation tax. This equilibrium no longer holds in a monetary union with just one currency, a system in which by definition currency competition is abolished and consequently the potential costs of inflation, in terms of intra-Community portfolio shifts, are lower. National policy-makers will thus be faced with a new constellation both in terms of revenue-oriented and tax-oriented (anti)-inflation policy.

For the union as a whole, the system change may lead to a higher on-average inflation rate. On-average may, however, mean that some countries may have a lower rate than before, whereas others will fare worse than before. Probably countries like Germany and France with a fine anti-inflation record, will lose little seigniorage but may be pushed to accept higher inflation and their stability policies will lose credibility also on the fiscal side. On the other hand, soft-currency countries may lose substantial seigniorage (due to higher inflation) but will better perform in credibility because the ECB may on average exert a stricter monetary control than the former national Central Banks of those countries did. Therefore, regardless of whether or not the welfare effects of a monetary union will be positive or negative over the union as a whole, there will be redistributive effects among the national economies involved, i.e. there will be winners and losers. National economic policy-makers will have to analyze thoroughly which side they will be on.

... or Deflationary Bias on the Way to EMU

Most of the analyses of EMU up till now reflect the fear of *higher* inflation in a monetary union. Nonetheless, there are also voices spelling out worries of too much deflation and too much austerity embodied in the design of transition towards EMU.

Some political economists assume that EMU will be an elitist club of 'autonomous' national Central Bankers sitting on the management board of the ECB-to-be and representing there primarily the interests of capital owners in Europe. With the exception of the *Bundesbank* and the *Nederlandsche Bank*, which have been independent of political instructions (see Table 1) in EMU Central Bankers will shake off political control and, hence, may be less interested in employment issues or in supporting the general economic policies of the (still existing) national Member States (Katseli, 1987). Whereas those critics, who believe that EMU is an 'exercise in more inflation', view EMU as inherently vulnerable to political influence and national interests, others are afraid that EMU – under the control of the ECB, the 'apolitical' guardian of price stability – could render economic policies, especially budgetary policies in some countries so rigid that growth and employment might suffer. In particular, there are serious worries that the *convergence criteria*, which the Maastricht Treaty has established for countries to become eligible for EMU, may have a deflationary bias for those who have to strive hard to fulfil the criteria.

As is well known, the Maastricht Treaty provisions foresee that in order to be eligible for EMU, every Member State has to fulfil the following conditions: a country's inflation rate must not be higher than 1.5% above the average of the best three performing countries; its debt to GDP ratio must not exceed 60%; its deficit is not to be more than 3% of GDP; the long-term interest rate must not be higher than 2% above the average of the 3 best performing countries in terms of price stability and the country must be participating in the ERM (under normal conditions) for the two years preceding EMU. A closer look at Table 2 reveals that for a number of countries, quite some effort and painful adjustment will be necessary to make them 'convergent enough' for EMU. Problems will emerge for Italy, Belgium and Ireland in particular in getting their debt/GDP ratio drastically down from more than a 100% of GDP. According to the 1992 data, only two EC Member States would be ready for EMU right now, and they are France and Luxembourg. Denmark has a good chance of getting its debt below 60% and could soon join the distinguished club. Ireland and Belgium seem to have insurmountable problems on the debt side, whereas The Netherlands might have a chance of getting their house in order. Whilst Britain has a good record in all the criteria but has an option to opt out of EMU, the Mediterranean countries are in economic trouble and have little chance of fulfilling the criteria.

Table 1:
Central Bank Independence in EC Member States

Central Bank	Independent from instructions	Monetary stability as legal objective	Terms of office of the direction	Loans to government
Deutsche Bundesbank	yes	yes	8 years, no recall	only to a very limited extent
Bank of England	no	no	4 to 5 years, no recall	no legal restriction
Banque de France	no	no	indefinite, can be recalled at any time	upper limit
Banca d'Italia	no	no	indefinite, can be recalled at any time	no restriction in case of legal authorization
De Neder-landsche Bank	*de facto*	yes	7 years, recall is more difficult	only to a very limited extent
Banque Nationale de Belgique	close cooperation required	no	3 to 6 years, recall is more difficult	unlimited
Central Bank of Ireland	far-reaching	yes	5 to 7 years, no recall	left to the discretion of the bank
Danmarks Nationalbank	far-reaching	no	indefinite, recall is more difficult	formal agreement on restriction
Banco de España*	no	no	3 to 4 years, can be recalled at any time	unlimited
Banco de Portugal**	partly	no	5 years, recall is possible	only to a very limited extent
Bank of Greece	no	no	3 to 4 years, can be recalled at any time	far-reaching possibilities

*   Change in the central bank law has been announced towards more independence.
** The 1991 central bank law has been changed fundamentally.

Table 2: Convergence Criteria: The Entrance Ticket to EMU

Member State	Inflation 1992 (GDP deflator) in %	Gross Public Debt 1992 (% of GDP)	Deficit (gen. govt. net borrowing requirement) % of GDP 1992	Long-Term Interest Rate 1992 (Yield on govt. securities) in %	Two Years Member of ERM/ No Devaluations	Number of Criteria Fulfilled
Belgium	2.5	132.2	- 6.7	8.8	yes	3
Denmark	2.2	62.7	- 2.6	8.9	yes	4
Germany	4.8	44.0	- 3.2	8.0	yes	3
Greece	15.9	106.7	-13.2	20.8	no*	0
Spain	6.1	48.4	- 4.7	12.2	no*	1
France	2.8	50.1	- 2.8	9.1	yes	5
Ireland	3.0	98.7	- 2.5	9.2	no*	3
Italy	5.2	107.2	-10.7	12.4	no*	0
Luxembourg	3.5	6.8	- 0.4	7.9	yes	5
Netherlands	3.1	79.8	- 3.8	8.2	yes	3
Portugal	9.5	66.2	- 5.4	11.8	no*	0
UK	5.2	45.9	- 6.6	9.1	no*	2
Target for EMU	4.0	60	3	10.0	yes	5

Source: OECD; Eurostat; Annual Economic Report 1993 by the EC Commission; own calculations.
* Ireland devalued in early 1993; UK and Italy left ERM during EMS crisis in Sept. 1992; Spain and Portugal had to devalue during the same crisis; Greece has not been a member of the ERM.

The loose canon on deck is Germany, since, despite *Bundesbank* efforts, the fundamentals in Germany indicate a move away from the targets (inflation and interest rates, deficits, etc.) due to the long-term burden from unification. But without the Germans, a monetary union is a *Fata Morgana*, because how could a European currency and a European Central Bank compete with the *Deutsche mark* and the *Bundesbank*? Neither the idea of a monetary union without Germany, the economic giant of the EC, nor the assumption that Germany may be forced into EMU against its will through a Treaty automatism (by 1999 at the latest), are remotely realistic.

Against the background of the data presented above, it is clear that most of the EC Member States will have to embark on a difficult journey, if they want to joint the EMU club: painful adjustment and stabilization programmes will have to be implemented. Calculations show that, for instance in the case of Italy, an annual budget surplus of over 1% of GDP would be required for the next 6 years to bring their debt down to reasonable size. Such switches in the national economic systems may be a healthy cure in economic terms, but it may cause social unrest and political trouble. Government expenditure would have to be cut down drastically with serious implications for its beneficiaries and with the consequence of a negative multiplier effect. Wages will have to be kept low with the consequence of the unions withdrawing support and even the cutting-down of the deficit may bring along some corresponding temporary disequilibrium bearing upon capital markets (Böttger et al, 1981).

In order to avoid demanding too great a stabilization effort from candidate countries and in order not to instill too much austerity and deflation into some of the national economies, the fiscal convergence criteria are set out in the Maastricht Treaty as recommendations or guidelines rather than as hard-numerical rules (Article 104b): both figures in excess of 3% deficit and of 60% debt could be tolerated, the Treaty says, if they can be considered as temporary or exceptional, or if they show a declining trend. It goes without saying that the *Bundesbank* is not too enthusiastic to see this kind of writing on the wall.

This softer interpretation may give national economic policy-makers more leeway on the way to EMU but it also carries some uncertainty. On the one hand, they have to find out how much austerity their constituencies are willing to accept and, on the other hand, they have to form expectations about how far off the mark they may be in being accepted as an EMU member. As we know from fiscal psychology, citizen-taxpayers are normally inclined to make sacrifices in good times, i.e. in booming economies, whereas in times of recession, the safeguarding of achievements prevails. Moreover, from an economic point of view, it is much more difficult to get debt and deficit down during recessions and in economic slumps, whereas inflation and interest rates have a self-lowering tendency at these times. In a boom, the reverse holds true. Therefore, a crucial element for success or failure is the future economic development in the EC Member States.

Exchange Rates and Macro-Shocks: Foregone Necessity or Superfluous Tool?

In a fully-fledged EMU, exchange rates will be eliminated since there will be only one single currency being legal tender in the whole Union. This implies that diverging trends in competitiveness in individual countries can no longer be accommodated by realignments; also, macroeconomic shocks can no longer be absorbed by exchange-rate adjustment.

Admittedly, exchange-rate flexibility is not a magic potion, making painless adjustment possible or permanently offsetting the effects of idiosyncratic real shocks. Depreciation itself can boost domestic inflation (via import prices), and the awareness that currency can be allowed to slide may encourage firms to concede higher wage increases than otherwise. Nonetheless, depreciation can be a useful tool when other policies fail, or meet strong political resistance. Most importantly, however, exchange-rate operations may help policy-makers buy time. Temporary income losses can be bridged and bolstered.

With the exchange rate renounced as a shock-absorber and with monetary policy centralized and determined at supranational level, national economic policy-makers are faced with a limited choice of action when national economies are threatened or even hit by asymmetric macroeconomic shocks. The toolbox at their disposal will be thinned out in EMU.

Some economists argue that this will not be a major problem, since the probability of such shocks is rapidly declining in the EC (Commission of the EC, 1991). If shocks are industry-specific rather than country-specific and if the EC Member States have a sufficiently diversified industrial structure and enough intra-industry trade, than shocks will work symmetrically and can be dealt with in a coordinated manner or at European level. In this case, intra EC exchange rates would not play a great role in any case. Moreover, if the 1992 project will contribute to making wages and prices in EC Member States more flexible, wage and price movements may well replace exchange-rate adjustment (Frenkel, Goldstein, 1992). Eventually, if monetary union is flanked by a system of fiscal equalization or embedded in fiscal federalism, country-specific shocks can to a large extent be cancelled out by countervailing tax and transfer reaction (Eichengreen, 1990).

Yet, there is very little empirical evidence that the probability of country-specific shocks is particularly low in the EC (Bayoumi, Eichengreen, 1992). Neither is there convincing argument that price and wage flexibility has been increased. It is also abundantly clear, that the EC lacks a system of fiscal equalization (Vanheukelen et al, 1992). Therefore, the opposite proposition seems to hold true, viz. that the probability of asymmetric shocks has recently grown, for the following reasons:

- Reform processes in Central and Eastern Europe bear very different consequences for individual EC Member States in terms of migration, commodity trade and capital movements.

– German unification has represented a serious asymmetric shock for its EC partners with both direct effects (import demand and growth impulses for individual Member States) and indirect consequences (interest-rate policy of the *Bundesbank*) (BIS, 1992: 133; Ranki, 1992).

– Different industry clusters and industrial cores in the different Member States have evoked different national industrial policies (Nicolaides, 1992) with different degrees of protectionism involved, which entail asymmetric effects in a common market.

Idiosyncratic shocks indeed strengthen the case for national-policy autonomy and suggest that significant costs are associated with its sacrifice. Consequently, national policy-makers have to look twice before they leap, and they have to be particularly careful to see what policy instruments will last with them for coping with such shocks.

If adjustable exchange rates are renounced, the need for adjustments will bear down fully upon relative wages, since interest rates will – in EMU – be largely harmonized through ECB action. To avoid unemployment in structurally weaker countries or in shock-affected economies, either members of the national workforce will have to migrate to the more prosperous regions of the Union, or they will have to accept wage levels (made very transparent and comparable by the single currency) well below Community average. The proponents of rapid monetary union tend to assume quite blandly that the two sides of industry are aware of this additional responsibility that they face, and that they will respect this in the interest of the economy as a whole. In reality, though, it is rather doubtful whether this mechanism would bite effectively and equally in every EC Member State.

Taking into account that labour-market flexibility and mobility in Europe is low (mobility rate of below 1% of EC workforce) and considering that it is questionable whether Europeans will be willing to accept the wage-side consequences from higher intra-EC labour mobility, and since monetary policy will no longer fall under national responsibility, more national flexibility and more diversity in fiscal policy-making will be called for (Healy, Levine, 1992).

National Fiscal Policy in Chains ...

If the President of the German *Bundesbank* is right, then, in the future, national fiscal policy will be strictly delineated in its responsibilities and will be given very little leeway for independent action.

In a system where national monetary competences are lost and where access to seigniorage as well as to tax revenues is reduced, national debt finance is bound to fill the gap. This is not without problems, since, in an EMU, the Community as a whole will be affected by national spillovers (van der Ploeg, 1990). Macroeconomic consequences from national action involve external exchange-rate effects, union interest rates, and Community balance of payments. Therefore, in the Maastricht Treaty, it has been acknowledged that a monetary union is basically an irrevocable community of mutual solidarity which needs to avoid free-rider attitudes. Two restrictions have been incorporated: first, that the European Central Bank should not finance budget deficits by monetary expansion; and second, that binding fiscal rules would be required to limit the freedom of national governments in budgetary policy.

The main reason for these rules is that some analysts fear that, in an EMU, national policy-makers might be tempted to shift incidence of taxes from their constituencies to citizens of other countries through overborrowing. In this case, the interest-rate increases, i.e. the burden will be distributed over the Community in its entirety, whilst the benefits (from higher expenditure) can be contained nationally. Others, however, argue that the financial markets will automatically discipline national governments' desire for a 'free-ride' by means of price and quantity constraints on credits reflecting the respective 'country risks'. In case of a no-bail-out rule, such that no country can count on support from the EC, markets would attach tags of different risks to the national borrowers and the interest rates would spread correspondingly. In this case, neither binding rules nor multilateral surveillance would be necessary.

Without deciding at this point on whether constitutional rules or market forces are better apt to cope with 'moral hazard' in EMU, one thing seems to be uncontested, and that is the vulnerability of a monetary union through non-cooperative behaviour. No matter how, the exploitation of a common-pool situation by individual participating Member States has to be avoided.

A related issue is how to best cope with national – non-conjunctural – financial needs. In this field, the role of tax policy has long been veiled by the emphasis on debt-financing. As long as the EC is not a federal entity but rather an intergovernmental body, national preferences of citizen-taxpayers will definitely vary with respect to level and composition of government expenditures. With limitations imposed on debt-financing, the state share in GDP is a function of the tax load that taxpayers are willing to shoulder. In other words, differences in expenditure preference will be reflected in differences in national tax rates. As European labour mobility is low (due to cultural and linguistic diversity), and since capital mobility is high, national policy-makers will have to go for the immobile tax base, i.e. personal income taxes. However, national tax policies are a poor substitute for budgetary policies, because taxation of income is detrimental to capital formation and savings (allocative effect), is difficult to implement (tax evasion), has undesirable distributive effects (capital owners v.

workers) and does not lend itself – without major revenue loss – to fighting recessions (insufficient impulses for growth and employment). If income taxation were eventually harmonized at EC level, national leeway would narrow down drastically.

Similarly, difficulties may emerge from the restricted ability of national governments to conduct counter-cyclical macroeconomic policies, since, in an EMU and under deficit rules, there may be little leeway for pump-priming through deficit-spending. Therefore, either a centralized mechanism to coordinate national fiscal policies or the resort to Community stabilization funds will be necessary to even out cyclical fluctuations. Previous experiences of international coordination have not shown any promising results. Rather, the time lags associated with fiscal-policy operations are getting longer, when agreement has to be reached at a supranational or intergovernmental level. The undesired result may be a pro-cyclical effect of fiscal-policy measures. In other words, for the sake of national stabilization policies, Member States should have highly flexible budgetary instruments at their disposal. It may appear to be paradox that – in order to avoid undue appropriation of Community savings – national deficit capacities will be limited, which in a different context – anti-cyclical policy – are strictly necessary.

Also, at the interface of fiscal and incomes policies, problems will arise. To propose a blueprint for a suitable policy mix in EMU is not difficult in theory: centralized monetary policy is supposed to be combined with a decentralized tax policy and a restrained national budgetary policy and both have to be complemented by a regionally differentiated (marginal productivity) wage and incomes policy. However, in practice, it is hardly possible to enforce differentiated wages in a union. As the example of German unification demonstrates, divergent levels of material well-being will not be accepted over a longer span of time. If monetary union (with one currency making wage positions comparable and differences visible) is accompanied by wage claims and increases geared to the real income of the more prosperous and more productive countries, it would tend to divide rather than unite Europe.

... Or the Missing Chain of Policy Coordination

Eventually, in a system where monetary policy is allocated to a supranational agency, whereas other economic policies still fall within the responsibility of numerous national economic agents and institutions, coordination is required at all levels. Price stability is not simply and exclusively the result of monetary policy; if fiscal and incomes policies do not cooperate, the result will be disappointing. The same holds true the other way round: growth cannot be achieved through fiscal action and incomes policies alone, the flanking support of monetary policy is required.

Moreover, coordination is also needed from a microeconomic point of view. A single monetary policy, which is combined with several decentralized national fiscal policies and various regional wage and incomes policies, inevitably makes it extremely difficult, if not impossible, for the economic agents to form rational and reliable expectations. A single indivisible monetary policy can hardly be made consistent with as many fiscal and incomes policies as there are Member States. A consistent result is even less probable, since an established mechanism for adjustment of different policies at national level is missing in EMU. At national level there is intensive dialogue and exchanging of views between the policy-makers responsible for fiscal policies and those responsible for monetary and other policies. This dialogue takes place largely in the framework of informal discussions and personal contacts. With fiscal policies being decentralized and fragmented nationally, the European Central Bank, as the monetary authority in EMU, lacks a necessary European counterpart, so that effective informal agreement can barely be achieved.

But what body, if any, on the fiscal, or more generally, on the economic side could balance the ECB's strong control over monetary affairs? As long as there is no counterpart, disequilibrium prevails, making not only coordination more difficult and more costly, but also making conflicts between monetary and fiscal policy-makers possible, plausible and probable. Much depends on whether the Community will soon take on an enhanced role in economic – and maybe social – policy-making. Such a development will not be to everyone's taste. Those with major reservations against the model of a federal Europe will hesitate and rather accept a lopsided structure with preponderance, that is with more coherent institutions and a consistent policy, on the monetary side. Along such lines, Fratianni and von Hagen (1992: 166) have pointed out that the examples of Germany and Switzerland seem to suggest that a particularly fine record in price stability can be achieved whenever there is *no* strong central government as countervailing power to monetary authority but rather fiscal decentralization and policy fragmentation. However, this argument does not carry much conviction since despite fiscal federalist structures (German *Länder* and Swiss Cantons), the *federal* budget alone is of a significant size in both countries (ca. 17% of GDP). The centrally-managed Community budget, in turn, is a very small fraction of Community GDP (1.15%) and is likely to remain a very small part of total public sector spending in the Community.

On the Way to Fiscal Union?

If, in an EMU, state tasks – whether in the field of allocation or stabilization policies – can only be carried out to a limited extent at national level, as they can only receive restricted national financing, the pressure increases at supranational level (i.e. on Brussels) to take on these tasks to a larger extent. However, this would mean that the EC budget, which has so far hardly been suitable either as a provider or as a stabilizer due to its low fiscal volume, will have to be drastically increased. MacDougall (1992) has recently recommended an EC budget of at least 5% of Community GDP as being necessary for EMU. This would be an increase of more than 300% compared to the status quo. However, if there is not much room to manoeuvre in tax policy, no responsiveness in wages policy and no flexibility in labour-market policy, if the monetary policies (through EMU) and fiscal policies (through binding budget regulations) are in chains, and if the exchange-rate mechanism (through the elimination of national currencies) is abolished, then the only way for a regionally and nationally differentiated economic policy is to effect financial transfers between the Member States in the sense of an EC fiscal equalization scheme.

It may be a truism that interregional transfers are a necessary element in every unequally developed community or union in which policy-makers strive for an equalization of living conditions and material well-being. In general, the findings of the famous MacDougall report (1977) demonstrate that in mature federations and in Unitary States, fiscal equalization schemes reduce regional income inequalities by up to between 35% and 45%. The necessary budgetary means to achieve this aim (net transfers) amount to about 4% of GDP. The EC, for its part, spends about 0.3% of Community GDP on Structural Funds which fulfil a similar function of regional equalization. This is clearly too little if regional disparities are to be evened out.

Moreover, in federations, cyclical fluctuations or macroeconomic shocks are automatically and efficiently offset through lower payment of taxes and/or social insurance contributions from the federal budget as well as through receipts of unemployment benefits. For example, in the United States, a state in recession contributes less to the federal budget as its tax revenues drop, while at the same time, federal aid to this state automatically increases. Accordingly, a mechanism of automatic stabilizers stimulates activity in states where the economy is in a slump and slows it down in the ones where it is booming. However, the federal budget must be of a sufficient size. The Community budget in its present size and composition will not lend itself to such a function.

Nonetheless, a monetary union, if it is to work reasonably well, will have to involve elements and entail mechanisms which work in such a direction: to syphon off income from high-income regions with overemployment and to redirect it to low-income regions with unemployment. Also, financial means will have to be activated to cushion income and demand against macro-economic shocks (Vanheukelen et al, 1992). In particular, if societies do not want to accept the pressure for more labour mobility and migration resulting from uneven economic development and unbalanced growth in the face of the absence of the exchange rate mechanism, demands for more convergence, more equalization and more cohesion, involving significant increases in the EC budget, will emerge. Moreover, if a monetary union, with one single '*numéraire*', makes disparities more visible and obvious, the push towards more political measures for fiscal equalization will be reinforced. As a consequence, this may sooner or later trigger a move to integrate the national budgets, the national social security systems and the national system of fiscal federalism into one system of Euro-Fiscal, Social and Regional Policy, the 'European Fiscal Union'.

The crucial issues for such a tendency to surface are the following:

– Is there political will among the Community net payers (Germany, France, UK and in the future possibly Austria and Sweden) to increase their financial contribution?

– Are these countries economically and politically able to contribute more funds and give away national financial sovereignty?

– Can the potential beneficiaries from more transfers and from a larger EC budget actively influence this tendency?

– What is the probability of asymmetric shocks and what are the positive spillovers from anticyclical policies for the EC as a whole?

As regards questions one and two, doubts may be justified both with respect to the degree of financial solidarity on the part of the 'donors', which, as the Edinburgh summit and the refusal of Delors' five-year budget plan (financial preview) have demonstrated, may have reached their limits. Question three may be answered with a cautious 'yes', in particular since the net payers often need the support of the net receivers for political issues in order to go ahead with integration. As regards question four, we have already explained above why the probability of asymmetric shocks, and hence potential positive effects from Community action, may increase rather than decrease.

If these findings are correct, the trend towards Fiscal Union is ambivalent: even though monetary union is *de facto* just a halfway house '*en route*' to a fully-fledged European Economic and Fiscal Union – which supposedly is on the hidden agenda of EC policy-makers – there are still many impediments and obstacles in the way. This makes it extremely difficult for national policy-makers to form firm expectations about the future course of events. Whereas there is considerable uncertainty attached both to any scenario on EMU and to the possible consequences and effects for national policy-making, the following is for certain: the consequences, ramification and effects of EMU, whether it succeeds or fails, are likely to differ enormously across the EC Member States.

The reason is that the economic fundamentals, as well as the policy-making approaches, still differ widely. But is it not exactly this political, economic, administrative and cultural variety, which constitutes Europe's unique attractiveness? In this vested tradition, national policy-makers will probably not

take on EMU as a supranational challenge, but as a national affair – EMUsed
or not!

REFERENCES

Bayoumi, Tamim; Eichengreen, Barry, (1992), *Shocking Aspects of European Monetary Unification*, NBER Working Paper No. 3949, Cambridge MA.

BIS, (1992), Bank for International Settlements: *Annual Report 1992*, Basles.

Böttger, Gert, et al, (1981), Finanzierungspotentiale kompensatorischer Staatsbudgets, *Konjunkturpolitik*, pp. 207-221.

Commission of the European Communities, (1991) *One Market, One Money*, European Economy 44, Brussels.

Eichengreen, Barry, (1990), One Money for Europe? Lessons from the US Currency and Customs Union, *Economic Policy 10*, pp. 118-187.

Fratianni, Michele; v. Hagen, Jürgen, (1992), *European Monetary System and European Monetary Union*, Boulder, Westview.

Frenkel, Jacob A.; Goldstein, Morris, (1991), Monetary Policy in an Emerging European Economic and Monetary Union, *IMF-Staff Papers* Vol. 38, pp. 356-373.

Gretschmann, Klaus, (1991), Economic and Monetary Union – Alice in Wonderland or Malice in Blunderland, *Futures*, Vol. 23, pp. 695-708.

Healy, Nigel M.; Levine, Paul, (1992), Unpleasant Monetarist Arithmetic Revisited: Central Bank Independence, Fiscal Policy and EMU, *National Westminster Bank Quarterly Review*, August 1992, pp. 23-37.

Katseli, Luca, (1987) *Macroeconomic Policy Coordination and the Domestic Base of National Economic Policy-Making*, mimeo: Andover, MA.

MacDougall, Donald, (1977), *The Role of Public Finance in European Integration*, Brussels.

MacDougall, Donald, (1992), Economic and Monetary Union and the European Community Budget, *National Institute Economic Review*, May 1992, pp. 64-68.

Mankiw, Gregory, (1987), The optimal collection of seigniorage: Theory and Evidence, *Journal of Monetary Economics* Vol. 20 pp. 327-341.

Nicolaides, Phedon (ed.), (1992), *Industrial Policy in the EC*, Dordrecht: Nijhoff.

Ploeg van der, Frederick, (1990), *Macroeconomic Policy Coordination During the Various Phases of Economic and Monetary Integration in Europe*, mimeo: Tilburg.

Ranki, Sinimaaria, (1992), *The EMS After German Monetary Union: Exchange Rate Developments*, Working Paper No 26 – Geld, Währung, Kapitalmarkt, University of Frankfurt.

Vanheukelen, Marc et al, (1992), *Stable Money – Sound Finances: Community Public Finance in the Perspective of EMU*, Report to the EC, mimeo: Brussels.

Recent EIPA Publications

The Trade Policy of the European Community: Legal Basis, Instruments, Commercial Relations
Phedon Nicolaides (ed.)
EIPA 1993, 80 pages
(Only available in English)
ECU 11

Tendances actuelles et évolution de la jurisprudence de la Cour de justice des Communautés européennes: suivi annuel, Volume 1
Sous la direction de Spyros A. Pappas
IEAP 1993, 242 pages
(An English version will be available in summer 1993)
ECU 19

Les accords de Schengen: abolition des frontières intérieures ou menace pour les libertés publiques?
Alexis Pauly (éd.)
IEAP 1993, 269 pages
(Texts in original language – French, English and German)
ECU 15

Industrial Policy in the European Community: A Necessary Response to Economic Integration?
Phedon Nicolaides (ed.)
EIPA 1993, 134 pages
(Only available in English)
Paperback   (available from EIPA) ECU 22
Hardcover   (available from Martinus Nijhoff Publishers) approx. ECU 65

Les socialistes à l'épreuve du pouvoir
Costas Botopoulos
Editions Bruylant, Brussels 1993, approx. 700 pages
(Only available in French)
Price as yet to be fixed

General Recognition of Diplomas and Free Movement of Professionals
Jacques Pertek (ed.)
EIPA 1992, 158 pages
(Also available in French)
ECU 11

The Intergovernmental Conference on Political Union: Institutional Reforms, New Policies and International Identity of the European Community
Finn Laursen and Sophie Vanhoonacker (eds)
EIPA, 1992, 505 pages
(Only available in English)
Paperback   (available from EIPA) ECU 22
Hardcover   (available from Martinus Nijhoff Publishers) approx. ECU 85

Pension Schemes in the European Public Sector
Pierre Neyens and Edmond Koob
EIPA, 1992, 180 pages
(Also available in French)
ECU 11

EC Competences and Programmes within the Field of Education / Compétences et programmes communautaires en matière d'éducation
Jacques Pertek and Marie Soveroski (eds)
EIPA, 1992, 102 pages
(Mixed texts in both English and French)

Subsidiarity: The Challenge of Change
(Proceedings of the Jacques Delors Colloquium 1991)
EIPA, 1991, 161 pages
(Also available in French)
ECU 9

'The Effective Presidency' (An Information Video-Film on the Presidency)
Producer: *Marian Creely*
Director: *Justin McCarthy*
Special Adviser: *Declan Kearney*
This video-film explains the decision-making process of the Community with an emphasis on the role of the Presidency
ECU 152